KIERKEGAARD

ON

WOMAN, GENDER, AND LOVE

Books by Sylvia Walsh

Editor, *Truth Is Subjectivity: Kierkegaard and Political Theology: Essays in Honor of Robert L. Perkins*. Mercer University Press, 2019.

Kierkegaard and Religion: Personality, Character, and Virtue. Cambridge University Press, 2018.

Translator and Editor, *Discourses at the Communion on Fridays by Soren Kierkegaard*. Indiana University Press, 2011.

Kierkegaard: Thinking Christianly in an Existential Mode. Oxford University Press, 2009.

Translator and Co-editor (with C. Stephen Evans), *Fear and Trembling* by Soren Kierkegaard. Cambridge University Press, 2006.

Living Christianly: Kierkegaard's Dialectic of Christian Existence. Pennsylvania State University Press, 2005.

Editor (with Céline Léon) *Feminist Interpretations of Soren Kierkegaard*. Pennsylvania State University Press, 1997.

Living Poetically: Kierkegaard's Existential Aesthetics. Pennsylvania State University Press, 1994.

KIERKEGAARD

ON

WOMAN, GENDER, AND LOVE

Sylvia Walsh

MERCER UNIVERSITY PRESS
Macon, Georgia

MUP/ P652

Published by Mercer University Press
1501 Mercer University Drive
Macon, Georgia 31207

26 25 24 23 22   5 4 3 2 1

Books published by Mercer University Press are printed on acid-free paper that meets the requirements of the American National Standard for Information Sciences—Permanence of Paper for Printed Library Materials.

Printed and bound in the UNITED STATES.

This book is set in ADOBE CASLON PRO.

Cover/jacket design by BURT&BURT.

ISBN 978-0-88146-861-8
Cataloging-in-Publication Data is available from the Library of Congress

CONTENTS

SIGLA

AN "Armed Neutrality." See *Point of View* (PV)

BA *The Book on Adler,* ed. and trans. Howard V. Hong and Edna H. Hong. Princeton NJ: Princeton University Press, 1995.

C *The Crisis and a Crisis in the Life of an Actress.* See CD.

CA *The Concept of Anxiety*, ed. and trans. Reidar Thomte in collaboration with Albert B. Anderson. Princeton, NJ: Princeton University Press, 1980.

CD *Christian Discourses* and *The Crisis and a Crisis in the Life of an Actress*, ed. and trans. Howard V. Hong and Edna H. Hong. Princeton, NJ: Princeton University Press, 1997.

CI *The Concept of Irony* together with "Notes on Schelling's Berlin Lectures," ed. and trans. Howard V. Hong and Edna H. Hong. Princeton, NJ: Princeton University Press, 1989.

COR *The Corsair Affair*, ed. and trans. Howard V. Hong and Edna H. Hong. Princeton, NJ: Princeton University Press, 1982.

CUP *Concluding Unscientific Postscript to Philosophical Fragments,* 2 vols. ed. and trans. Howard V. Hong and Edna H. Hong. Princeton, NJ: Princeton University Press, 1992.

EO I *Either/Or,* two vols. ed. and trans. Howard V. Hong and Edna H. Hong.EO II Princeton, NJ: Princeton University Press, 1987.

EPW *Early Polemical Writings*, ed. and trans. Julia Watkin. Princeton, NJ: Princeton University Press, 1990.

EUD *Eighteen Upbuilding Discourses*, ed. and trans. Howard V. Hong and Edna H. Hong. Princeton, NJ: Princeton University Press, 1990.

FPOSL *From the Papers of One Still Living.* See *Early Polemical Writings.*

FSE *For Self-Examination* and *Judge for Yourself!*, ed. and trans. Howard V. Hong and Edna H. Hong. Princeton, NJ: Princeton University Press, 1990.

FT *Fear and Trembling* and *Repetition*, ed. and trans. Howard V. Hong and Edna H. Hong. Princeton, NJ: Princeton University Press, 1983.

JC *Johannes Climacus* or "De omnibus dubitandum est." See *Philosophical Fragments.*

JFY *Judge for Yourself!* See *For Self-Examination.*

JP *Søren Kierkegaard's Journals and Papers*, ed. and trans. Howard V. Hong and Edna H. Hong, assisted by Gregor Malantschuk. Bloomington and London: Indiana University Press, 1, 1967; 2, 1970; 3–4, 1975; 5–7, 1978.

KAC *Kierkegaard's Attack upon 'Christendom,' 1854–55,* trans. Walter Lowrie, Princeton, NJ: Princeton University Press, 1944.

LD *Letters and Documents*, ed. and trans. Hendrik Rosenmeier. Princeton, NJ: Princeton University Press, 1978.

NA Newspaper Articles, 1854–1855. See *The Moment and Late Writings.*

NSBL "Notes on Schelling's Berlin Lectures. See *The Concept of Irony.*

OMWA "On My Work as an Author." See *The Point of View* (PV).

P *Prefaces* and "Writing Sampler," ed. and trans. Todd W. Nichol. Princeton, NJ: Princeton University Press, 1998.

PC *Practice in Christianity*, ed. and trans. Howard V. Hong and Edna H. Hong. Princeton, NJ: Princeton University Press, 1991.

PF *Philosophical Fragments* and "Johannes Climacus," ed. and trans. Howard V. Hong, and Edna H. Hong. Princeton, NJ: Princeton University Press, 1985.

PV *The Point of View:* 'On My Work as an Author;' 'The Point of View for My Work as an Author;' "Armed Neutrality," ed. and trans. Howard V. Hong and Edna H. Hong. Princeton, NJ: Princeton University Press, 1998.

R *Repetition.* See *Fear and Trembling* (FT).

SLW *Stages on Life's Way*, ed. and trans. Howard V. Hong and Edna H. Hong. Princeton, NJ: Princeton University Press, 1988.

SUD *The Sickness unto Death*, ed. and trans. Howard V. Hong and Edna H. Hong. Princeton, NJ: Princeton University Press, 1980.

TA *Two Ages: The Age of Revolution and the Present Age. A Literary Review,* ed. and trans. Howard V. Hong and Edna H. Hong. Princeton, NJ: Princeton University Press, 1978.

TDIO *Three Discourses on Imagined Occasions*, ed. and trans. Howard V. Hong and Edna H. Hong. Princeton, NJ: Princeton University Press, 1993.

TM *'The Moment' and Late Writings,* ed. and trans. Howard V. Hong and Edna H. Hong, 1998.

UDVS *Upbuilding Discourses in Various Spirits*, ed. and trans. Howard V. Hong and Edna H. Hong. Princeton, NJ: Princeton University Press, 1993.

WA *Without Authority*, ed. and trans. Howard V. Hong and Edna H. Hong. Princeton, NJ: Princeton University Press, 1997.

WL *Works of Love*, ed. and trans. Howard V. Hong and Edna H. Hong. Princeton, NJ: Princeton University Press, 1995.

WS "Writing Sampler." See *Prefaces.*

Danish Editions

SKP *Søren Kierkegsaards Papirer,* 2nd enl. ed. by Niels Thulstrup, bd. I-XVI (25 vols.) with index vols. by Niels Jørgen Cappelørn. Copenhagen: Gyldendal, 1968–78.

SKS *Søren Kierkegaards Skrifter,* ed. Niels Jørgen Cappelørn, Joakim Garff, Jette Knudsen, Johnny Kondrup, and Alastair McKinnon. Published by Søren Kierkegaard Forskningscenteret. Copenhagen: Gads Forlag, 1997ff.

KSKS *Kommentar til Søren Kierkegaards Skrifter,* published by Søren Kierkegaard Forskningscenteret, Copenhagen: Gads Forlag, 1997ff.

SV3 *Samlede Værker,* 3rd ed. by P. P. Rohde, bd. 1–20. Copenhagen: Gyldendal, 1968–78.

PREFACE

In looking over my *curriculum vitae* recently I was struck by how many essays I have written over the years relating to the topics of woman, gender, and love in Kierkegaard's thought, none of which was included in the several books I have written and published on him. Some of these essays were published in the *International Kierkegaard Commentary*, edited by my late husband and fellow Kierkegaard scholar, Robert L. Perkins. Others appeared in various journals and collections of articles on Kierkegaard, and one was delivered at a Kierkegaard conference but never published. It has seemed appropriate, therefore, to gather them into a single volume and offer them as a related body of work for the consideration of both present and future Kierkegaard scholars as well as other individuals who are or might be interested in Kierkegaard's views on these topics and their relevance to the task of becoming a self or fully developed human being as a woman or man in the present age. For the most part, these essays are reprinted as they originally appeared in print, although a few corrections and emendations have been made in some of them. Rather than impose a single style upon all the essays, I have left references to the works of Kierkegaard and others in their original formats, which vary from article to article, some appearing in the text in parentheses while others are given in footnotes or at the end of the essay in a bibliography of works cited. It is my fervent hope that this collection of essays will serve to encourage a continued interest in and academic exploration of the topics of woman, gender, and love in Kierkegaard's thought.

—Sylvia Walsh

MERCER UNIVERSITY

MERCER UNIVERSITY PRESS

Endowed by

TOM WATSON BROWN

and

THE WATSON-BROWN FOUNDATION, INC.

1

ISSUES THAT DIVIDE: INTERPRETING KIERKEGAARD ON WOMAN AND GENDER*

When Kierkegaard writes in his journals that woman is "personified egotism" (JP, 4: 5000) and a "born virtuoso in lying" (JP, 4: 4998); that she is "the lust for life" in contrast to man, who is essentially structured to be spirit (JP, 4: 4999); that "no woman can endure the dialectical redoubling" characteristic of the essentially Christian, whose task "requires a man" (JP, 4: 5007); that everything revolving around woman is "chatter, trivialities, and...sexual relations" (JP, 4: 4998); that "she corrupts all men who get married by finitizing and mediocritizing them" (JP, 4: 5003); and that the emancipation of women is "the invention of the devil" (JP, 4: 4992), to mention only a few passages that might be cited, what is the interpreter, especially a feminist interpreter, to make of such blatantly misogynist remarks?[1] Should they be discounted as the embittered musings of a disappointed, unhappy lover who, now approaching the end of his life, has lost not only his youthful passion but also the dialectical clarity characteristic of his thought and sex? Should they be taken at face value as particularly virulent examples of a negative, stereotyped attitude toward woman and the feminine that is pervasive in Kierkegaard's authorship? Should they be regarded merely as relative remarks, expressing the accidental, historical character of woman rather than her essential nature and destiny? Could Kierkegaard be writing here—consonant with a practice believed by some to constitute his mode of

---

*Reprinted by permission from *Kierkegaard Revisited*, ed. Niels Jørgen Cappelørn and Jon Stewart (Berlin and New York: Walter de Gruyter, 1997), 191–205.

[1] For a range of feminist interpretations of Kierkegaard's writings, see *Feminist Interpretations of Søren Kierkegaard*, ed. Céline Léon and Sylvia Walsh (University Park: The Pennsylvania State University Press, 1997) and the select bibliography contained therein.

writing throughout the authorship—as the consummate "master of irony" whose words mean the opposite or negation of what they seem to be saying? Or to state the question more broadly, what does Kierkegaard mean when he makes such remarks about woman, and does he really mean them?

Indeed, all the problems that plague the interpretation of Kierkegaard generally are heightened and intensified when his writings are scrutinized on the related topics of woman and gender, for on no other topics does the reader encounter more ambiguity and ambivalence, agreement and disagreement, consistency and contradiction in the authorship. For the feminist interpreter of Kierkegaard, consideration of these topics is accompanied by a whole subset of issues that present similar problems of interpretation: questions concerning the nature of woman and the use of gender and sexual stereotyping in defining that nature; the role of culture or social environment in determining or shaping the life and meaning of woman; sexual differences and/or sameness between the sexes; the emancipation of woman and the question of her social and/or spiritual equality with man; relations between the sexes; and the possibility of selfhood for woman. These are critical issues that serve to divide as well as to unite, through common concerns, feminist interpretations of Kierkegaard.

Given the vastness and complexity of Kierkegaard's writings, I cannot, of course, address all of these issues, nor any of them fully, within the confines of the present essay. But I do want to touch on several of them in the process of examining, first of all, the fundamental feminist issue of whether social environment (nurture) or some given essence of woman (nature), defined in terms of the feminine gender, is seen as being determinative in shaping the life, meaning, and character of woman in Kierkegaard's writings; and second, two gender characteristics that are particularly associated with woman in the texts, namely devotedness and a lack of reflection. In exploring these topics, I intend to range widely over the authorship rather than concentrate on a single text in the hope of providing a broader perspective of them than is frequently found in the secondary literature. Such a procedure, I realize, is hazardous, since exceptions to almost any general claim that can be made about woman and gender may be found somewhere in Kierkegaard's vast authorship. Still, taking these exceptions into account and allowing for a multiplicity of voices and viewpoints in his writings, I hope to show that there is a remarkable consistency as well as some disturbing ambivalences and contradictions that cut across the stages of life as delineated and/or represented by the various "authors" and spokespersons in the authorship. This seemingly paradoxical state of affairs suggests that—on the topics of woman and gender at least—Kierkegaard's writings need to be read and interpreted dialectically, not one-sidedly or monolithically, and that from a feminist standpoint there remains much that is sexist and misogynist in his writings even as they offer, in many instances, astute analyses of woman's existential situation and open up possibilities for the clarification and fulfillment of woman's selfhood, as well as man's, in the present age.

Let us begin, then, with the fundamental question of whether woman's character is "man-made," a product of social environment and cultural conditioning, or whether she has a given nature or essence. Ever since Simone de Beauvoir's classic formulation of this issue in *The Second Sex,* it has dominated feminist discussions in both Europe and America, with the prevailing opinion being in agreement with Beauvoir's anti-essentialist thesis that "one is not born, but rather becomes a woman" through a process of social construction.[2] As the so-called father of existentialism—and now presumably of postmodernism as well—Kierkegaard would be expected to concur with that thesis.[3]

But on this issue, like so many others in his authorship, one finds a combination of perspectives which stand in tension with, if not outright contradiction to, one another.

---

[2] Simone de Beauvoir, *The Second Sex*, tr. and ed. H.M. Parshley (New York: Vintage Books, 1989), 267.

[3] For a feminist interpretation of Kierkegaard that emphasizes his existentialism and views essentialist elements in the authorship as a contradiction and "lapse" from his "own existential truth criterion as well as his view of human existence," see Wanda Warren Berry, "Judge William Judging Woman: Existentialism and Essentialism in Kierkegaard's *Either/Or*, Part II" in *International Kierkegaard Commentary: Either/Or, Part II*, Vol. 4, ed. Robert L. Perkins (Macon: Mercer University Press, 1995), 33–57. For another interpretation that sees Kierkegaard as attacking the social institutions and social situation of women, rather than women themselves, in his polemic against women, see Birgit Bertung, *Om Kierkegaard Kvinder og Kærlighed—en studie i Søren Kierkegaards kvindesyn* (Copenhagen: C. A. Reitzel, 1987).

That the social environment into which a woman is born plays an important role in the formation of her character is a viewpoint clearly voiced by Kierkegaard himself in *Two Ages*, a literary review of a novel by that name penned anonymously by Thomasine Gyllembourg, an accomplished female writer of the time whose works were greatly admired by Kierkegaard.[4] Although ordinarily read for the light it sheds on Kierkegaard's social philosophy and critique of the present age, this review focuses primarily on the influence of social conditions upon the lives of individuals.[5] Taking his cue from Madame Gyllembourg's preface, in which she notes that the power of external conditions is more pronounced in the present age than in the previous century (TA, 154f), in this review Kierkegaard explores the way different ages produce different consequences in the lives of the characters of the novel, particularly in its two female heroines, Claudine in the age of revolution and Mariane in the present age. In his character study of Claudine, Kierkegaard notes how she was "almost oppressively brought up by her aunt" and matured in inwardness through the maintenance of a "singular infatuation" for her lover, to whom she remained constant in love and faithfulness in spite of the isolation, despair, and hardships she experienced as a result of bearing his child out of wedlock (TA, 26f, 42). The main motif of the first part of the novel, as Kierkegaard interprets it, is that in maintaining this romantic constancy to her lover Claudine has fallen victim to "the idea of her age," with the result that her domestic life is a reflection of the distinctive character of the age itself (TA, 26, 41).

Taking as the principle of his aesthetic critique the question of whether a girl like Claudine could appear as *typical* of, not merely possible in, the present age (since "the most extreme variant can appear in any and every age"), Kierkegaard compares her with the principal female

[4] For a brief introduction to this writer, see Grethe Kjær, "Thomasine Gyllembourg, Author of 'A Story of Everyday Life,'" in *International Kierkegaard Commentary: Early Polemical Writings*, Vol. 1, tr. Julia Watkin and ed. Robert L. Perkins (Macon: Mercer University Press, 1998), 87–108. See also Katalin Nun, "Thomasine Gyllembourg's *Two Ages* and her Portrayal of Everyday Life" in *Kierkegaard and His Contemporaries: The Culture of Golden Age Denmark*, ed. Jon Stewart (Berlin and New York: Walter de Gruyter, 2003), 272–97.

[5] For a collection of essays focusing primarily on social aspects in this work, see *International Kierkegaard Commentary: Two Ages*, Vol. 14, ed. Robert L. Perkins (Macon: Mercer University Press, 1984).

character representative of the present age, Mariane, whose life bears certain similarities to Claudine's (TA, 32f). Like her romantic counterpart, Mariane has also been adversely affected by the social environment into which she was born. "Left out in the cold" by the second marriage of her father, "insulted and ignored" by her stepmother, and treated as a "housemaid in her parents' home," she has been "stunted" by the externalities—the triviality, formlessness, superficiality, and obsequiousness—that characterize the present age, so that "her whole environment is damaging in its meaninglessness" and serves to exacerbate "the daily harms and hurts" of her life, Kierkegaard maintains (TA, 29, 48, 50). Moreover, both women are abandoned (initially at least) by their lovers, although for different reasons, and both are forced into the cultivation of a quiet inwardness by their situations. But whereas "Mariane wanted to be true to herself with the same inwardness as Claudine," Kierkegaard concludes that "her love affair would forever be essentially different from Claudine's" because of the differing psychological predispositions and conditions of the ages in which they live (TA, 49). Whereas the age of revolution is characterized, above all, by passion, and thus by form, culture, a sense of propriety, and decisive action, the present age is formless, egoistic, prudential, apathetic, reflective, superficial, talkative, philandering, envious, and subject to a process of social leveling (TA, 61–68, 77f, 81–84, 96f, 100, 102). Although having "no automatic consequences" in the lives of individuals, the distinctive character of an age determines how their internal conflicts will be expressed and "the particular direction" their psychological development will take, Kierkegaard claims (TA, 41f).

Not only is the life and destiny of a woman shaped by the age in which she lives, she is also subject to the influence of, and sometimes even control and exploitation by, male agents within her social environment. Nowhere in the literature is this more evident than in "The Diary of the Seducer" in *Either/Or,* Part I, where Johannes the Seducer undertakes, in a highly calculated fashion, the psychological development of a young girl, Cordelia Wahl, in order to evoke, first of all, a naïve erotic passion in her, and then a "deeper womanliness" in which she is enabled to make a "feminine leap" into the infinite that transcends the boundaries of the universal by breaking off her engagement to Johannes and freely choosing to give herself to him outside of marriage (EO, I: 345, 359f, 363, 365, 386, 391, 411f, 425). Although Cordelia is led to believe that this "higher" freedom is discovered through her own agency, woman first becomes free in this deeper sense, Johannes claims, only through man: "man proposes...woman chooses" (EO, I: 397, 400, 411–412, 431). In this moment woman is born, fully grown, as a woman, but at the same time she becomes a weak and relative being whose worth is instantly deflated in value (EO, I: 331, 339, 431f, 445).

While Cordelia's psychological development is thoroughly under the influence and control of Johannes, it is evident that she is molded by him in conformity with an ideal conception of "womanliness" and the "feminine" that constitutes the essence of woman for him, which suggests that the social construction of woman is not incompatible with the notion that there is a female essence or given nature according to which woman's being is defined and modeled in the authorship (although that notion itself may be a product of social construction). In associating woman's being with such an essence, Johannes reflects a viewpoint commonly held in the authorship, although woman is also construed by several of Kierkegaard's aesthetic spokesmen, including Johannes, in a postmodernist fashion as an indeterminate being whose nature is indefinable, indescribable, and incomprehensible under any criterion, formula, or concept of woman. In *Repetition,* for example, Constantine Constantius claims to have no opinion of the other sex at all since he "has rarely seen a girl whose life could be comprehended in a category" due to her lack of consistency and self-deception (R, 218). Likewise, Victor Eremita begins his oration in "In Vino Veritas" in *Stages on Life's Way* thanking God that he was not born a woman, since "to be a woman is something so special, so mixed, so compounded that there are no predicates to describe it, and the many predicates, if they were used, contradict one another in a manner only a woman can tolerate" (SLW, 56). For him, woman is an "undefinable quantity" whose life is meaningless, having no significance in itself and only a negative meaning and function in relation to man, for whom she serves as an inspiration to become productive in the realm of ideality by his *not* getting her (SLW, 59–61). In like manner, Johannes the Seducer also claims in this text that "woman cannot be exhausted in any formula but is an infinitude of finitudes" and that "[t]rying to conceive the idea of woman is like gazing into a sea of misty shapes continually forming and reforming" (SLW, 76). He thus characterizes woman as "an inexhaustible heterogeneity" yet conceives her abstractly in terms of the "whole kingdom of womanhood," that is, as a totality of feminine beings blended together, as "a collective noun" or "generality that is not exhausted by any woman" but in which each has her own little share, complete in itself (SLW, 76, 80; EO, I: 331, 428).

On the whole, however, woman is widely viewed in the authorship under the category of gender as the instantiation of the idea of femininity, which embraces all phases of a woman's life but first comes into existence in the transformation of a young girl into a wife and mother (EO, I: 88, 100; C, 91; SLW, 131n; SUD, 50n). Unlike the sex of a person, which is biologically fixed, gender is a psycho-sociological category that is typically, although not exclusively, associated with a particular sex in each of its two forms—masculinity with the male sex and femininity with the female. In Kierkegaard's writings, these categories are understood in a traditionally Western stereotyped fashion, the feminine being associated with passivity, weakness, sympathy, sacrificial love, self-giving, devotedness, modesty, and substantiality, while the masculine is considered to be active, strong, auto-pathetic, self-assertive, independent, prideful, willful and reflective in nature (EO, I: 339, 388, 395, 429; EO, 2: 326; R, 143, 147f, 183; CA, 15, 47, 61, 144; SLW, 112, 142, 270; SUD, 50n, 67; WL, 341; TA, 16, 46). Of the various gender characteristics associated with the feminine and woman in Kierkegaard's writings, I shall limit my discussion here to a brief consideration of two that are particularly important in defining woman's nature and self-identity in the literature, namely devotedness and a lack of reflection.

Devotedness is widely recognized in the authorship as constituting the very essence of woman and the feminine, but with varying meaning and consequences attached to it by spokesmen at different stages of existence. At the aesthetic level, for example, Johannes the Seducer identifies woman's essence as a devotedness that paradoxically takes the form of an unreflected subjective resistance overcome in submission to man and suggests that she may be viewed categorically as "being-for-other," a qualification shared with all of nature, which has its for-otherness in relation to spirit (EO, I: 388, 429f). As a consequence woman may be said to have being, but not existence, since she does not subsist out of herself but rather has her fundamental qualification in being company for the man (EO, I: 340, 431).

That woman is to be regarded fundamentally as a companion to man is reiterated in the ethical sphere by Judge William, who likewise associates womanliness with devotedness, but in the context of woman being a wife and mother rather than aesthetically devoted to man outside of marriage. Consequently, the judge defines not only woman's life but man's also as being essentially relational in character: "What I am through her she is through me, and neither of us is anything by oneself, but we are what we are in union. Through her I am man, for only a married man is an authentic man" (SLW, 93; cf. also EO, II: 92, 125, 326). From the religious perspective of Anti-Climacus in *The Sickness unto Death,* however, only woman's nature is essentially defined in terms of devotedness, which in his view "is the one unique quality that woman has" (SUD, 50n). Although man also gives himself, his self is not defined as devotion as is woman's, nor does he gain his self by devotion as she does, since he possesses and retains a consciousness of himself as a self apart from any self-giving to others (SUD, 50n). Only in relation to God is the self defined as devotion for both man and woman, which suggests that ultimately the self is defined in terms of the feminine for Anti-Climacus and that a distinction must be made between the penultimate selfhood or self-identity of man and woman in terms of their sexual identities, wherein they are different, and their ultimate selfhood as human beings in relation to God, wherein they are the same and equal.[6]

While devotedness constitutes woman's self-identity as a woman as well as a religious personality, it may also serve as a mode of despair in her inasmuch as, according to Anti-Climacus, woman has a tendency to abandon or lose herself in the object of her devotion, with the result that she possesses a sense of self-identity only in and through that object (SUD, 50n). If the object of her devotion is taken away, she then loses her self altogether in "feminine despair" or the despair of weakness in not

---

[6] Cf. *The Concept of Anxiety,* where the formula for this viewpoint is stated very early as a "dissimilarity…within the essential likeness" (CA, 66). From the standpoint of Vigilius Haufniensis, the pseudonymous author of this text, both woman and man are essentially qualified as spirit, and in that they are essentially alike, but man is *more qualified* as spirit than woman, which introduces a *quantitative* difference between them at the spiritual level (CA, 66f, 70, 189). Although Vigilius is not entirely explicit or clear in explaining why this is so, it would appear that the reason lies in the fact that woman, being more sensuous and thus more anxious than man, moves beyond herself to another human being, to man, with the result that her life culminates ethically in procreation, while his does not (CA, 47, 64, 66, 71).

willing to be a self independently of the other.[7] This perspective is complemented by Kierkegaard's claim in *Works of Love* that devotion to the other in erotic love is really an expression of self-love, since in this form of love one identifies with the other, and that a girl who sacrifices herself for erotic love does not sacrifice for the highest, which is God (WL, 53f, 89f, 310f).[8] The devotion with which a woman naturally attaches herself to another human being, generally to a man, and establishes her self-identity as a woman thus is quite different from the kind of devotion appropriate to God, which requires a separate or independent sense of self-identity and sacrifice of oneself in love for all, not just one other person. Potentially, then, woman's penultimate self-identity as a woman is at odds with her ultimate identity as a self before God.

A second characteristic widely attributed to woman across the literature is a lack of reflection (EO, I: 391, 431; EO, II: 310f; SLW, 46, 52, 90f, 270f, 274, 303, 306; C, 86). Woman's existence, we are told by aesthetes, ethicists, and religious personalities alike, resides in immediacy and imagination, while man's being is characterized by reflection. This is not to say, of course, that woman lacks a capacity for reflection altogether. Indeed, in his very first publication, "Another Defense of Woman's Great Abilities," Kierkegaard himself ironically lauds woman's "talent for speculation" and "craving for deeper knowledge" as well as her "feminine eloquence," "deep insight . . . into the secrets of nature," superior dialectical capacity, and superiority in intellectual matters generally, extending to "all the branches of the mental faculties" (EPW, 3f). Noting that reason itself was represented by a woman in the French Revolution and that women were placed on equal footing with men in the Saint-Simonist movement of that era, Kierkegaard cites a long list of women's accomplishments in his own time, including theatrical works, novels, treatises, esthetic reviews and works of art, and suggests that they keep abreast of current events by studying the "spirit of the age" in fashion magazines – a

---

[7] For a more extended discussion of despair in *The Sickness unto Death*, see my article, "On 'Feminine' and 'Masculine' Forms of Despair" in the present collection.

[8] For more extensive discussions of *Works of Love* see "Kierkegaard's Philosophy of Love" and "Forming the Heart: The Role of Love in Kierkegaard's Thought" in the present collection.

sure tip-off that he means to satirize rather than truly praise women's reflective capacity in this early work (EPW, 4).[9]

Woman's reflective capacity is later recognized in a more serious and positive manner by Kierkegaard in *The Crisis and a Crisis in the Life of an Actress* (1848), where he compares and praises the artistic genius of two actresses of his day (Madame Heiberg and Madame Nielsen) who are able, each in a different way, to bring dialectic or reflection to bear in their theatrical interpretations of the idea of femininity (C, 85–90; cf. SLW, 131n). While the first incorporates dialectic within herself in the cultivation of an inwardness that enables her to portray the idea of feminine youthfulness better at a more mature age than when she was seventeen, the second covers the whole range of roles included in the idea of femininity through a steady process of change and maturation as an artist. It should be noted, however, that both women are regarded as exceptions by Kierkegaard (C, 91).

In the pseudonymous literature as well we may note that in *Either/Or*, Part I, A's modern Antigone, in "The Tragic in Ancient Drama Reflected in the Tragic in Modern Drama," is distinguished from her classical counterpart primarily on the basis that she possesses a *reflective* consciousness in relation to her situation that is lacking in the Greek heroine (EO, I: 147f, 153–55, 158). The reflective sorrow secretly harbored in her is also indirectly evident in the female victims of seduction in "Silhouettes," although for different reasons (EO, I: 170–73, 178, 188, 199, 205). The best example of women's capacity for subjective reflection at the aesthetic level, however, may be seen in Cordelia Wahl, in whom Johannes the Seducer claims to have awakened a "multiple-tongued reflection" that later enables her to recall him "with a *clairvoyance* that only shows how highly developed she is" (EO, I: 309). Johannes undertakes the psychological development of Cordelia in order to elevate her to a level of reflective passion that will enable her to make the "feminine leap" into the infinite mentioned above. But he does not develop or educate her in the usual manner by taking her to the theatre, concerts, dances, and the like, as in his opinion girls developed in this fashion lack the originality necessary for the unspoiled awakening he has in mind (EO, I:

[9] In like manner the Fashion Designer in "In Vino Veritas" ironically credits woman with being reflective "to an incomprehensibly high degree" in that she knows how to relate everything to adornment or fashion (SLW, 67).

328, 331). Rather, he proceeds in the opposite manner by first isolating Cordelia from social contact with other young girls (EO, I: 399f), then neutralizing her immediate womanliness with prosaic common sense, ridicule, and intellect to a point where she "almost loses the feeling of being a woman," is unable to stand alone, and consequently throws herself into his arms—whereupon her womanliness is aroused and subsequently raised to supernatural heights (EO, I: 345f, 353, 363, 365f, 386). Johannes brings about Cordelia's simultaneous *birth/downfall* as a woman in this *higher/deeper* sense by evoking an erotic passion in her that eventually will permit him to do anything he pleases with her, after which that passion is destroyed and replaced with irony (EO, I: 339f, 345f, 353, 363, 365f, 386). In the process of her development Cordelia moves from the level of a naïve, immediate passion for Johannes, prompting her to become engaged to him, to a reflected passion that uses the erotic as a weapon to hold and conquer him when he begins to pull back from her, and finally to a still higher form of the erotic that is *dialectical* in nature, a "mental erotic" state in which she breaks off the engagement herself and gives herself to him in a devoted yet free love that no longer recognizes the forms and boundaries of the universal (EO, I: 411f, 425).

In spite of the fact that Johannes is successful in developing a high level of reflectivity in Cordelia, his feat is not as impressive as it seems, for two reasons. First of all, Cordelia recognizes, in one of her retrospective letters to A, that "every thought I think is only through him" (EO, I: 309). While the discoveries she makes seem to her, at the time, as if they are the result of her own thought and impulses, this is really an illusion on her part, purposely cultivated in her by Johannes (EO, I: 397, 400, 411). Thus she cannot be said to have attained a state of true independence in reflectivity. Second, even though Cordelia has advanced to a high state of reflectivity, Johannes claims that her leap into the infinite occurs by way of imagination, "the natural cosmetic of the fair sex," rather than by thought (EO, I: 391, 395). There is a difference, he points out, between a "feminine leap" and a "masculine leap" into the infinite. Whereas man's leaping is dialectical in nature, requiring many advance preparations and calculations, several practice tries, and a running start, for woman the leap is no more than a hop in which she glides effortlessly to the other side, arriving there "more beautiful, more soulful than ever" (EO, I: 391f).

Similar viewpoints concerning woman's lack of and/or capacity for reflection may be noted in the writings of two other pseudonymous spokesmen in the literature: the ethicist, Judge William, in *Either/Or*, Part II, and *Stages on Life's Way*, and the demonic religious personality, Quidam, in *Stages on Life's Way*. As Judge William sees it, woman is not supposed to engage in critical evaluation, as "that kind of reflection is not suitable for her," and the ideas she does have come "secondhand" from man (SLW, 91; EO, II: 311). Nevertheless, he admits that a good deal of what he has to say is owed to his wife, desires her approval of what he writes, and allows her an absolute veto over it (SLW, 96). Happily, however, the judge claims to express "what obscurely moves within her" in such a way as to say "exactly what she wanted to say," while he, in turn, acquires "an inspiration, an inwardness, a charm" from her that enables him to claim, justifiably he thinks, that they are not his thoughts but her own (SLW, 96). Thus he regards her as being, to a certain extent, a *coauthor* of his texts who sanctions the use of what he owes to her in his writings on marriage (SLW, 96). But while the judge credits his wife with playing a larger and more positive role in his reflective and artistic life than the male aesthetes of *Either/Or* and *Stages on Life's Way* grant to woman in general, he still speaks for her and claims to articulate her thoughts better than she is able to do herself.

Woman is also credited by Judge William with having more faith than man, since she believes that for God all things are possible (EO, II: 315), but the resolution by which she is propelled into the religious sphere, like that which motivates Cordelia's feminine leap into the infinite, is viewed by him as being immediate rather than reflective in nature (SLW, 166f). Since the feminine soul does not, and should not, have reflection the way a man does, she does not come to a religious resolution through reflection and ethical development like man, the judge claims, but rather moves from aesthetic immediacy to a religious immediacy in a romantic fashion by *swooning*, that is, by fainting at the first intimation of the religious idea, which occupies man's reflection completely (SLW, 167). Clearly, therefore, the religious immediacy of woman does not correspond to the "second immediacy" or immediacy after reflection that characterizes faith and the religious sphere in the strictest sense for Judge William (and Kierkegaard as well) (SLW, 157, 160–64; JP, 1: 9, 49, 84f, 214, 235, 972, 1032; JP, 2: 1101, 1123, 1335, 1942; JP, 3: 3560, 3561; JP, 5: 6135).

The judge's deprecation of woman's reflective ability also has the effect of compromising his claim of an essential equality between man and woman at the ethical-religious level. For while he envisions a new prototype for marriage in the figures of Romeo and Juliet, with her standing upright by Romeo's side rather than kneeling before him as she is usually portrayed, the judge nevertheless thinks that a wife will love her husband so much that she will always want him to be dominant (SLW, 144,168). Moreover, of all spokesmen in the literature, Judge William is most outspoken in opposition to the emancipation of women, an event which, were it to happen—although he is certain it will not, must not, and cannot happen—and spread to his wife, would cause him to weep in the "marketplace! (EO, II: 22, 311f)."

When one moves on to consider the views of the quasi- or would-be religious personality, Quidam, in *Stages on Life's Way*, one finds him to be in close agreement with both Johannes and the Judge on these matters. In Quidam's opinion, woman is not by nature reflective and rarely possesses much dialectical capacity; infinite reflection is not essential for her, nor is she capable of double reflection (SLW, 270, 274, 303, 306). As he sees it, "For a feminine psyche, reflection is like candy for the child. A little of it is tempting but *en masse* the candy loses its seduction" (SLW, 270, 274). Too much reflection could bring on insanity in a woman, he thinks, and certainly the dialectical dilemma Quidam finds himself in with respect to his fiancée—torn as he is between loving her and wanting to break off with her—introduces more than enough reflection possibilities "sufficient to disturb a feminine head" (SLW, 269f). But these possibilities are not invented or produced by the girl herself; rather they are introduced by Quidam, who so overwhelms her with his superior reflective ability that any attempt at reflection on her part is made to seem *futile* and *disgusting* to her (SLW, 271). Indeed, Quidam's explicit aim is "to absorb all reflection out of her" so that she can make a resolution that will set her free from him (and him free from her). Like Johannes the Seducer, he desires that *she*, rather than *he*, be the one to make the break between them. But whereas Johannes uses his reflective superiority in order to succeed in seducing a girl, thereby achieving a masculine victory over her, Quidam relates to his beloved in a feminine mode rather than in a masculine one; that is, he combines within himself both passion and reflection, feeling and irony, in such a way as to take her part by suffering sympathetically, adopting the strategy of making himself seem to be a depraved person in her eyes in order that she might suffer autopathetically, or free of sympathy for him and without any dialectical self-reproach on her part (SLW, 265, 269, 654f).[10]

While Quidam's motive in *eliminating* woman's reflective capacity, like that of Johannes Seducer's in *developing* it, may be suspected of being self-serving rather than self-sacrificing, enabling him to get out of a love relation that cannot be consummated in marriage, a further question is raised concerning the consequences of his view, as in the case of Judge William, for the concomitant claim of a spiritual—not to speak of social—equality between man and woman. Although Quidam fervently desires such equality and considers it to be "the vital force" of his spiritual existence, he himself is led to question whether there really is equality in the religious, since it is apparent to him that his fiancée, whom he describes as almost totally lacking in reflection, does not share his level of spirituality (SLW, 239, 270, 315). Indeed, it seems to Quidam that she has no need of, and cares nothing for, the religious (SLW, 315). Yet it is absolutely essential to him that she does need and care for it, as he cannot exist intellectually in communion with her unless she is able to exist in the same spiritual state as he. Thus, he desires a woman who is as strong if not stronger than he is, since the more she surrenders herself, the more responsibility is placed on him, involving him in self-conflict and suffering (SLW, 315). How incongruous, then, that Quidam undertakes to eliminate, rather than to develop, his fiancée's reflective capacity in order to establish spiritual parity between them!

---

[10] A similar example of gender reversal may be seen in the figure of the young man in *Repetition* and *Stages on Life's Way*. In the first text, the young man, who prides himself for never having fallen in love with a woman, is described by Constantine Constantius as possessing an unusual degree of imagination, which serves as a substitute for erotic love in him and makes him immune to "all feminine intriques" by a girl out to get him (R, 184). Constantine accounts for the young man's feminine nature by assuming that he must have been a woman in a previous existence, which he now recollects as a man, enabling him to go over to her side and "to take on her *partes* [role]" so eagerly that he is able to see her excellent points and to set them forth "even better than she does herself" (R, 184). Similarly, the figure of the young man in "In Vino Veritas" is described as possessing an "almost femininely luxuriant softness and transparency" and a "sympathetic" demeanor (SLW, 21).

Indeed, it would appear that woman does not so much lack reflection due to a gender difference between man and woman, as Kierkegaard and his pseudonymous spokesmen assume, but rather that her capacity for reflection is co-opted, controlled, and destroyed by man for his own purposes. Moreover, the assumption of such differences at the aesthetic and ethical levels creates a discrepancy or imbalance at the religious level, for it would seem that both reflection and devotion are essential to the religious as Kierkegaard understands it. Yet woman is conceived as lacking in reflection while man is unequipped to give himself in devotion as woman, by nature, is capable of doing (although devotion may serve as a mode of despair in her, preventing her from forming an independent sense of self-identity as a woman and from becoming a devoted self in a religious sense). If both woman and man are structured to become spirit, as Kierkegaard and his pseudonyms, with great ambivalence, want to claim, then both must possess and be encouraged to develop the capacities essential to such an existence. This suggests that, rather than emphasizing gender and sexual differences between man and woman, as Kierkegaard and his pseudonyms, in conformity with the trend of the time, frequently did, the present age needs to recognize and promote their common humanity, a goal that Kierkegaard himself, in his clearest and finest moments of insight, also embraced. In this way it may be hoped that woman will at last come into her own as a woman and true self before God.

2

VENI, VIDI, VICI: IMMEDIACY AND REFLECTION AS GENDERED CATEGORIES IN KIERKEGAARD'S THOUGHT*

In general, immediacy and reflection function as non-gendered categories that are characteristic, in one form or another, of all three stages of life in Kierkegaard's writings, but they are also often construed as gendered categories in his thought.[1] Immediacy is associated stereotypically

---

* Reprinted by permission from *Immediacy and Reflection in Kierkegaard's Thought*, ed. Paul Cruysberghs, Johan Taels, and Karl Verstrynge (Leuven, Belgium: Leuven University Press, 2003), 25–39.

[1] The fundamental distinction between immediacy and reflection is first set forth in the unfinished, posthumously published work, *Johannes Climacus*, which Kierkegaard was writing at more or less the same time as *Either/Or.* Already in this early, ironic narrative on how philosophical thinking begins traditional gender associations with respect to the categories of immediacy and reflection are evident inasmuch as Johannes Climacus is described as a young man whose "whole life was thinking" in contrast to that of a woman, whose "whole life is love" (JC, 123 / SKP, IV B 1, 109; see also JC, 118 / SKP, IV B 1, 104). More importantly, however, Kierkegaard defines immediacy as indeterminateness or the lack of consciousness in the sense of not being able to make distinctions between truth and untruth (JC, 167 / SKP, IV B 1: 145–46). As soon as the question of truth is raised, immediacy is cancelled by mediacy or reflection, which presupposes it. Immediacy thus corresponds to reality and actuality, while mediacy or reflection is associated with ideality and possibility (JC, 167–68 / SKP, IV B 1: 146–47). Not until these correspondences are brought into relation to one another, however, does consciousness come into existence, since in themselves neither reality nor ideality, actuality nor possibility, constitutes consciousness. Thus consciousness is not the same as reflection, which constitutes only the possibility of a relation to reality, not the actual relation itself. As the possibility of a relation to reality reflection is essentially disinterested, whereas consciousness, being the relation itself, is "interested" in the sense of constituting the *interesse* or "being between" ideality and reality, or possibility and actuality, as a contradiction or collision of opposites (JC, 170–71 / SKP, IV B 1:148–49). Along with

with woman as the instantiation of the idea of femininity, reflection with man as the embodiment of the masculine.[2] Among the various qualities associated with woman and femininity (such as devotedness, passivity, weakness, sympathy, love, self-giving, and imagination) in the literature, immediacy or a lack of reflection is viewed by aesthetes, ethicists, and religious personalities alike as being particularly characteristic of woman's nature and self-identity, while man enjoys the advantage of reflection and self-consciousness that are prerequisite for becoming a self and acquiring faith. Initially, however, one may observe an interesting and ironic reversal with respect to these gender associations, as immediacy in the form of the sensuous erotic is represented in *Either/Or*, Part I in its various stages of development not by female but rather by male figures whose immediate desire is directed toward the seduction of women. This immediate male orientation toward the seduction of women is later taken up into masculine aesthetic consciousness or reflection and honed into an art partly as a way of retrieving man's lost immediacy but also to establish male control and superiority over women.[3] The initial reversal and use of gender associations with respect to the categories of immediacy and reflection thus entail some potentially problematic consequences for both men and women which I wish to bring out in the present essay through an examination of the pathology of desire in four demonic male figures in Kierkegaard's pseudonymous writings: Don Juan (prefigured by two other male figures, Cherubino and Papageno), Faust, Johannes the Seducer, and Quidam. For men, these figures point to a disturbing tenden-

---

immediacy and reflection, therefore, Kierkegaard regards consciousness, mind, or spirit [*Aand*] as a third category that presupposes not only immediacy but also reflection (JC, 169 / SKP, IV B 1:148). Moreover, only when there is consciousness can there be a repetition or continuity of relation, since reality exists only in the moment, while ideality is static or always the same and thus not subject to repetition (JC, 171 / SKP, IV B 1:149–50).

[2] For a fuller discussion of these gender associations in Kierkegaard's writings, see my essay "Issues That Divide."

[3] For a comparable analysis of male seduction in *Either/Or* Part I, see also Céline Léon, "The No Woman's Land of Kierkegaardian Seduction," in *International Kierkegaard Commentary: Either/Or,* Part I, Vol. 3, ed. Robert L. Perkins (Macon: Mercer University Press, 1995), 229–50. Léon, however, further concludes that it is "the feminine within" man himself that he fears and seeks to repress through control of "the feminine without."

cy in the male psyche toward sexual domination of women that must be overcome in order for true selfhood to be realized. For women, whose presumed incapacity for reflection would seemingly prevent them from developing fully as selves or religious personalities, the ironic consequence of (at least seeming) seduction is that they emerge with a higher state of consciousness or the very reflection assumed to be lacking in their sex. But the capacity for reflection is either corrupted and stalemated in them as well as in men or else it is deceptively eliminated by the male in order to free himself from a relationship with a woman. Either way, women are denied the possibility of cultivating both immediacy and reflection in such a way as to achieve authentic selfhood, while men forfeit the possibility of entering into genuine human relations with women as their social and spiritual equals.

1. The Stages of Immediacy in the Aesthetic Sphere: Cherubino, Papageno, and Don Juan

In the essay on "The Immediate Erotic Stages or the Musical-Erotic" in *Either/Or*, Part I, the aesthetic author "A" explores the concept of immediacy in the form of the sensuous erotic, which he associates with the indeterminate or abstract in contrast to reflection, which is given expression in the concrete medium of language (EO, I: 55–56, 70 / SKS, 2: 62–63, 75). "The most abstract idea conceivable," says A, "is the sensuous in its elemental originality" (EO, I: 56 / SKS, 2: 64). As such, it can be presented only through music, which in his view is the only medium capable of expressing the immediate in its immediacy (EO, I: 70 / SKS, 2: 76). "Since reflection is implicitly in language, language cannot express the immediate," A observes; concomitantly, because the immediate is indeterminate, it cannot be grasped by language, which is the proper medium for the expression of consciousness or spirit (EO, I: 70 / SKS 2: 76). Consequently, sensuousness in its elemental originality constitutes the absolute theme of music (EO, I: 71 / SKS, 2: 77). However, A identifies two types of immediacy in this essay, one that is qualified by spirit in such a way as to stand *outside* the realm of spirit and another that stands *inside* the realm of spirit (EO, I: 70 / SKS, 2: 77). Only the former, or sensuous immediacy, is excluded by spirit and has its absolute expression in music (EO, I: 70–71 / SKS, 2: 77).[4] Being the absolute medium for the expression of that which is excluded by spirit, music is demonic in nature, as is the type of immediacy to which it gives expression. A states: "When sensuousness manifests itself as that which must be excluded, as that with which the spirit does not wish to be involved, but when spirit has not as yet convicted it or condemned it, sensuousness takes this form, is the demonic in aesthetic indifference" (EO, I: 90 / SKS, 2: 95).

To arrive at its full-blown constitution and expression as the demonic, however, sensuous immediacy must undergo several stages of development or metamorphosis. In using the term "stages" to characterize this development, A explains that "[t]he different stages collectively make up the immediate stage, and from this it will be seen that the specific stages are more a disclosure of a predicate in such a way that all the predicates plunge down in the richness of the last stage, since this is the stage proper" (EO, I: 74 / SKS, 2: 80). Although the previous stages lack any independent existence, they nevertheless receive separate expression, as does the final stage, in the form of representative figures in several operas by Mozart. The first stage is represented by the page Cherubino in *The Marriage of Figaro.* Here sensuous immediacy manifests itself prior to consciousness as the immediate erotic or desire in the form of a quiet, substantial longing. At this stage, however, desire is not yet qualified as desire, but exists only in a state of dreaming, not yet awake and present only as a quiet intimation or still presentiment of itself (EO, I: 6 / SKS, 2: 82). A points out that it is "very significant" that the music representing this stage is written for a woman's voice, for although the page is masculine, the object of desire, which is femininity, rests "androgynously in the desire" so that both genders are present and united as one neuter gender without any separation or distinction between them or between desire and the object of desire (EO, I: 7 / SKS, 2: 83). In this androgynous, dreaming state of immediacy, the object of desire is vague and un-

[4] The latter form of immediacy may also be expressed in music but essentially has the task of becoming spirit and thus has its proper expression through language (EO, I: 1 / SKS 2: 77). In a certain sense, however, A regards music as a higher, more spiritual art than language inasmuch as it exists only in the moment of performance and thus continually gives expression to the negation or exclusion of sensuousness (EO, I: 68–69 / SKS, 2: 75–76).

defined and thus not present as an object of desire as such; rather, it is continually present in the desire as that which is possessed without having been desired, and thus as that which desire does not possess (EO, I: 5–76 / SKS, 2: 81–82). This ambiguous, contradictory state of immediacy causes a certain melancholy or sadness to resonate throughout this stage and in the music expressing it, inasmuch as in its unawakened state desire becomes depressed and almost anxious in its inability to begin actively desiring (EO, I: 76, 78 / SKS, 2: 81, 83–84). Being substantially contained in desire itself, the object of desire fascinates and captivates desire but at the same time threatens to suffocate it, creating the need for desire to escape and be free (EO, I: 76 / SKS, 2: 81–82). This finally happens when the object of desire, like a bashful woman, "shyly flees," causing a separation between them and thus the emergence of the next stage in the development of the sensuous erotic or desire.

Before moving on to an examination of the second stage, however, let us briefly pause to consider what A is suggesting concerning the nature of immediacy and desire in the first stage. Although both genders are regarded as being present in an androgynous, substantial unity, one can already detect a gender distinction being made between desire, which is conceived here as masculine, and the object of desire, which is feminine. This has the effect of identifying sensuous immediacy as being fundamentally heterosexual in nature, but more importantly, it sets the stage for understanding the relation between the sexes in terms of a male desire to conquer and possess the female. We shall return to this problem and its implications later in the essay. For now, I only want to call attention to the way in which, for A, if not for Kierkegaard as well, this understanding of the sexual relation is rooted in the very structure of sensuous immediacy or erotic desire itself.[5] It is obvious, too, that A's depiction of the first stage of immediacy is modeled on Plato's Myth of the Androgyne in the *Symposium*, where Aristophanes describes human nature in the beginning as containing both male and female elements.[6] But where-

5.·That Kierkegaard essentially agrees with A's analysis of the stages of immediacy is indicated in a journal entry form 1837 in which he briefly outlines the three stages presented in *Either/Or*, Part I, and states that "I am of the opinion that in these three stages Mozart has perfected and perfectly presented a development of love on the level of immediacy" (SKP, I C: 125 / SKS, 17, BB: 24).

6 Cf. *Symposium*, 189e" and below.

as A restricts his account of desire to two elements, one male and the other female, Aristophanes introduces three kinds of beings (male, female, and androgynous), making room for unisexual or homosexual and lesbian pairs and forms of desire as well as the androgynous or heterosexual kind.[7] Given this important difference, it is apparent that the heterosexual context within which A's account is constructed is a calculated one and that his association of sensuous immediacy in its most elemental form with male desire for the feminine is clearly based on, even as it significantly modifies, the Platonic account.

Now let us move on to the second stage in A's account of the development of sensuous immediacy or desire. If the first stage is characterized by dreaming and an indeterminate, substantial longing, in the second stage desire awakens and begins to see the object of desire from which it has been separated, although it still is not qualified as desire *per se* since it merely seeks for that which it can desire without ever finding or actually desiring the proper object of its exploration (EO, I: 81 / SKS, 2: 86). This stage is epitomized by the figure of Papageno in *The Magic Flute*, although it is the mythical Papageno, that is, the ideal embodiment of the essential elements of the stage, that A identifies as its representative, not the actual character in the play, who in his opinion "has become embroiled in all sorts of dubious nonsense" or accidental aspects of the opera (EO, I: 78–79 / SKS, 2: 84). In this stage there occurs a co-instantaneous birth of both desire and the object of desire, for "only when there is an object is there desire," and "only when there is desire is there an object" (EO, I: 80 / SKS, 2: 85). Thus they come into existence as fraternal twins, separated and torn out of their substantial unity in the womb of the first stage, with the further result that the object of desire emerges in its particularity not as a single object to be pursued but split up into a multiplicity of particulars which desire, in its endless wandering about in search of the object of desire from which it has been substantially parted, continually discovers and enjoys in a momentary fashion.

Sensuous immediacy finally comes into its own in the third stage as an immediate synthesis of the two previous stages in desire qualified for the first time as desire in the form of "desiring desire" (EO, I: 81, 84–85 / SKS, 2: 86, 90). According to A, this stage is epitomized not simply by a single character as in the previous stages but by the entire opera *Don*

[7] Cf. *Symposium*, 190B, 191D-192A (see above).

Giovanni, which in his opinion gives classic expression to "the idea of the elemental originality of the sensuous" in desire presented as a demonic principle (EO, I: 85 / SKS, 2: 90). The central character in the opera who expresses this idea and around which the whole opera is oriented is the figure of Don Giovanni or Don Juan, who according to A is a product of the Middle Ages' penchant for representing the totality of a particular aspect of an idea in a single individual (EO, I: 87 / SKS, 2: 92). As the representative of the demonic principle of desire, however, Don Juan is "both more than and less than an individual" (EO, I: 87 / SKS, 2: 92). As A puts it: "Don Juan continually hovers between being and idea—that is, power, life—and being an individual" (EO, I: 92 / SKS, 2: 97). Moreover, when conceived in music, he is not a particular individual at all but rather represents desire or the sensuous erotic qualified as a demonic power or force of nature asserting itself in aesthetic indifference to spirit (EO, I: 90, 92 / SKS, 2: 95. 97).

A goes on to claim that "[t]he sensuous as it is conceived in Don Juan, as a principle, has never before been so conceived in the world; for this reason the erotic is qualified by another predicate: here the erotic is *seduction*" (EO, I: 93 / SKS, 2: 98). Greek culture, A contends, lacked the idea of seduction, emphasizing instead the individual and the psychical or mental element in harmony with the sensuous. Moreover, Greek love, being psychical rather than sensuous in nature, was essentially faithful to one person, whereas "according to its concept sensuous love is not faithful but totally faithless: it loves not one but all—that is, it seduces all" (EO, I: 94 / SKS, 2: 98). As in its previous stages of development, the object of desire in this stage remains abstract femininity, of which Greek culture also had no intimation since in it everyone constituted "the beautiful personality" (EO, I: 62 / SKS, 2: 93). But whereas desire in its earlier stages focused one-sidedly on either the one (the universal or woman as the eternal feminine) or the many (a multiplicity of particular females, none of whom embodies the object of desire adequately or completely), Don Juan desires the "particular absolutely" or "the universal expressed in the concretion of immediacy," in other words, all women without distinction. Young or old, beautiful or ugly, ordinary or extraordinary—they are all the same to him, since each embodies the total femininity he desires in every woman. A imagines Don Juan as saying: "every girl has what makes me happy, and therefore I take them all" (EO, I: 97 / SKS, 2: 101). All finite differences vanish over against the main point, which is to be a woman, with the result that "everything that is woman is his prey" (EO, I: 100 / SKS, 2: 104).

Moreover, Don Juan is always victorious in his seductions. In describing the third stage, A points out that in it "desire is absolutely genuine, victorious, triumphant, irresistible, and demonic" (EO, I: 81 / SKS, 2: 86). Like Julius Caesar, Don Juan is "a knight who is out for victories": *veni, vidi, vici* [I came, I saw, I conquered] is his motto (EO, I: 81 / SKS, 2: 86). Not only is he a great success at seducing girls (1003 in Spain alone!), in A's estimation "he makes the girls happy—and unhappy—yet strangely enough in such a way that that is what they want, and it would be a poor girl who would not wish to become unhappy in order to have been happy once with Don Giovanni" (EO, I: 101 / SKS, 2: 104). But there is another, ironic side to this picture that A is honest enough to also point out with respect to the female victims of Don Juan. Having once been seduced they become dangerous enemies whom he fears. In the opera this is especially true of Elvira, but it applies to Zerlina as well. According to A, these women become dangerous because they are raised by seduction to a higher consciousness than that of Don Juan, who as the representative of sensuous immediacy lacks reflection and is magnetically, not consciously, drawn toward the gratification of desire in the seduction of women (EO, I: 97–98 / SKS, 2: 101–102 / SKP, XI 1 A 34). For this reason too, A is compelled to modify his original claim that Don Juan is a seducer. Since he lacks reflection and consciousness, Don Juan is not a genuine seducer, for that requires the exercise of "craftiness and machinations and subtle wiles" that are altogether lacking in the Don (EO, I: 98 / SKS, 2: 102). Strictly speaking, then, Don Juan does not seduce but simply desires and in his desire acts seductively. Consequently, A prefers to call him a deceiver, not a seducer, but he is a deceiver whose deceptions are not planned in advance; rather, "it is the power of the sensuous itself that deceives the seduced," A claims (EO, I: 99 / SKS, 2: 103).

For a representative of genuine seduction, therefore, we must look elsewhere, in the realm of reflection, but before turning to that, let us pause once again to reflect on the depiction of desire in its various stages of development proffered by A and his Danish creator. First of all, we have seen that desire or sensuous immediacy is consistently conceived and represented as being masculine in gender in all three stages of development, although the feminine is also present within and apart from masculine desire as the potential or actual object of desire. Second, there is no reciprocity in this assignment of gender roles, inasmuch as desire is not equally imagined as being feminine in nature, nor the masculine as being the object of feminine desire. Likewise, as noted earlier, there is no accommodation for homosexual and lesbian desire and objects of desire. Clearly then, the picture of desire presented here is wholly and solely the product of the male heterosexual, if not also heterosexist, psyche seeking to identify itself with sensuous immediacy and the desire to conquer and possess woman—all women—as the embodiment of abstract femininity.[18] Third, we may note that the further qualification of sensuous immediacy as seduction in A's account reverses the traditional association of seduction with the female (Eve) and identifies it with the male instead, although that is a dubious gain for women inasmuch as they move from an active role in seduction to a passive one as the victims of male seduction. With regard to this reversal, it may be instructive to take note of a passage from *The Concept of Anxiety*, in which the pseudonymous author Vigilius Haufniensis makes the following interesting observation: "So when the Genesis story, contrary to all analogy, represents the woman as seducing the man, this is on further reflection quite correct, for this seduction is precisely feminine seduction, because only through Eve could Adam be seduced by the serpent. In every other place where there is a question of seduction, linguistic usage (delude, persuade, etc.) always attributes superiority to man" (CA, 66 / SKS, 4: 370–71). In an earlier draft of this passage Vigilius makes it even clearer that Eve's "feminine seduction" of Adam is an exception to the rule and that seduction is commonly attributed to the man rather than the woman:

---

[18] On the heterosexual orientation of "The Immediate Erotic Stages" and the difference between a heterosexual and heterosexist imagination, see Wanda W. Berry, "The Heterosexual Imagination and Aesthetic Existence in Kierkegaard's *Either/Or*, Part One," *International Kierkegaard Commentary: Either/Or, Part I,* Vol. 3, ed. Robert L. Perkins (Macon: Mercer University Press, 1995), 201–28. As Berry defines them, "the heterosexual imagination is the conscious or unconscious tendency to express dualities, polarities, or dialectics found in human existence in terms of imagery of the two sexes," while "[a] heterosexual imagination that tends to rule out the possibility that authentically human existence also might be imagined through relations between members of the same sex could be called heterosexist" (201–02).

> In a way it has always seemed remarkable to me that the story of Eve has been completely opposed to all later analogy, for the expression 'to seduce' used for her generally refers in ordinary language to the man, and the other related expressions all point to the woman as weaker (easier to infatuate, lure to bed, etc.). This, however, is easy to explain, for in Genesis it is a third power that seduced the woman, whereas in ordinary language the reference is always only to the relationship between man and woman and thus it must be the man who seduces the woman (SKP, 5: 5730).

Thus, seduction is clearly regarded as a male phenomenon by both pseudonyms, even though, in Vigilius' view at least, it originated in a feminine seduction of man as a ploy of the serpent.[9] Fourth, it should also be noted that A's account perpetuates the male myth that women want to be seduced and are happy to sleep with Don Juan even if it is for only a one night stand. It matters not, or so A wants to believe, that the Don is faithless and deceptive; they love him and want to be loved by him anyway. But this momentary happiness comes at a high price, for not only are they deceived and abandoned, they are viewed as objects of an immediate masculine desire to conquer and possess the other sex that is later taken up into reflection and refined into an art for establishing male superiority, victory, and control over women. Finally, although they are raised to a higher consciousness by seduction, this again is a dubious gain for women inasmuch as it implies that the only way they can move out of the state of immediacy into reflection is through seduction, which is reprehensible to the female psyche.

---

[9] See also "In Vino Veritas" in *Stages on Life's Way* where Johannes appeals to Greek mythology to account for the seduction of man by woman as a "stratagem on the part of the gods" (SLW, 74–75 / SKS, 6: 74). Although Johannes admits that this stratagem was largely successful, he points out that it did not always succeed inasmuch as some men, whom he calls "devotees of erotic love" and other men call "seducers," "became aware of the deception." As a result, they "always eat only the bait" and are never trapped.

2. The Masculine Superiority of Faust

According to A, the reflective counterpart of Don Juan is Faust, who is also a product of the Middle Ages. But whereas Don Juan "is the expression for the demonic qualified as the sensuous," Faust constitutes "the expression for the demonic qualified as the spiritual that the Christian spirit excludes" (EO, I: 90 / SKS, 2: 95). And whereas the Don represents the idea of sensuous immediacy as a power or force asserting itself in aesthetic indifference to spirit, Faust is the embodiment of the spiritual-demonic as an individual in conscious opposition to spirit and thus falls essentially under ethical categories (EO, I: 92 / SKS, 2: 96–97). Like Don Juan, Faust is a seducer, but he does not merely act seductively, as does the Don; rather, he is a genuine seducer by virtue of the fact that he possesses reflection and consciousness. But whereas Don Juan seduces many girls, Faust seduces only one, and that through the power of words or language, which we may recall presupposes reflection and is the proper medium for the expression of spirit (EO, I: 99 / SKS, 2: 103). As the representative of the spiritual-demonic, however, Faust seduces through the misuse of language or spirit, that is, by lying. From an aesthetic point of view, therefore, he falls under the category of the interesting, in which the emphasis falls on the "how" or the method of seduction rather than the sensuous enjoyment of seduction itself. Consequently, "the object of his desire is also something more than the merely sensuous" (EO, I: 100 / SKS, 2: 103).

What this something more might be, however, is not identified in the essay on the musical-erotic, since it is primarily concerned with the idea of sensuous immediacy as represented by the figure of Don Juan. But in a later essay titled "Silhouettes" A returns to the figure of Faust and discusses him in relation to Margarete, the young maiden whom Faust seduces. In this essay A claims that Faust is a "reproduction of Don Juan" in the sense that "all the elements of the preceding stage" are preserved in him, but he is also different from the Don in that, although he desires the same thing, which is abstract femininity, he desires it "in a different way" (EO, I: 205–06 / SKS, 2: 201–02). Having lost his immediacy through doubt or reflection, what Faust seeks in seduction is "not only the pleasure of the sensuous but the immediacy of the spirit" or a rejuvenation of his soul through the momentary enjoyment of the "innocence and childlikeness" of a young girl (EO, I: 206–07 / SKS, 2: 201–02). As A expresses it, "What he desires is the pure, undisturbed, rich, immediate joy of a feminine soul, but he desires it sensually, not spiritually" (EO, I: 207 / SKS, 2: 202). For this reason Faust does not desire an intellectually developed and refined woman who matches his own intelligence but rather an innocent young girl who is "nothing" compared to his intellect, yet in another sense enormously much "since she is immediacy," and "only in this immediacy is she a goal for his desire" (EO, I: 207 / SKS, 2: 203). Consequently, "[t]hat whereby Faust…captivates Margarete is not Don Juan's seductive talent but his prodigious superiority" (EO, I: 210 / SKS, 2: 205). "Her first impression of him…is completely overwhelming," with the result that, in childlike faith "and without the slightest reflection," she becomes attached to him as a god and he becomes everything to her (EO, I: 209–10 / SKS, 2: 205). "The more she is convinced of his divine superiority," the less she becomes in herself until finally she "completely disappears" in him and exists only through him (EO, I: 210 / SKS, 2: 205). When at last she is abandoned by Faust, she "collapses completely and is not even able to think about her loss" (EO, I: 211 / SKS, 2: 206). Gradually, however, reflective sorrow sets in, and she is left continually to sigh under the sway of a basic, total, and unmitigated mood or sense of her own insignificance and nothingness without him (EO, I: 212–14 / SKS, 2: 206–09).

3. Mental Concupiscence: Johannes the Seducer

If Faust constitutes a genuine seducer by virtue of a superior intellect that enables him to completely overwhelm and annihilate his female victim, Johannes the Seducer represents the reflective seducer *par excellence*. But he is no ordinary seducer, nor even, in his own eyes, a seducer at all; rather he is an "eroticist" and aesthete who knows not only how to poetize himself into a girl but also how to poetize himself out of her (EO, I: 306–07 / SKS, 2: 296, 356–57). For Johannes, therefore, seduction is not merely a means of sexual gratification or just a way of recovering a lost immediacy but rises to the status of an art by which a man is able to establish his masculine superiority, victory, and control over woman at the reflective as well as immediate level. His method is subtle and highly deceptive, for he wants to appear to be the one who is seduced, while all along it is really he who is seducing the girl. According to Johannes' principles of aesthetics, either the girl deceives the man or the man deceives the girl (EO, I: 380 / SKS, 2: 368). In order to assure that he is the victor in this life-or-death battle of deception and seduction between the sexes, he picks his victims very carefully. Like his immediate and reflective counterparts, Johannes desires woman in her totality or abstract femininity (EO, I: 331 / SKS, 2: 320, 416), but for him to love all is superficial, to love only one is too little (EO, I: 331, 361, 428 / SKS, 2: 320, 350, 416). Rather, "the art is to be as receptive as possible to impressions, to know what impression one is making and what impression one has of each girl. In that way, one can be in love with many girls at the same time, because one is in love in a different way with each one...while the consciousness nevertheless embraces the whole" (EO, I: 361 / SKS, 2: 350). Johannes nevertheless prefers young girls over young women, because in his view the latter are less natural, more coquettish, while the former possess the purely immediate femininity or womanliness that he wishes, like Faust, to manipulate and enjoy for the entertainment and rejuvenation of his being (EO, I: 324 / SKS, 2: 314). It is important, too, that the young girl, like Margarete, be innocent and childlike, for he intends to vanquish her, not by all at once overwhelming and annihilating her with his prodigious superiority as Faust does Margarete, but rather more subtly and gradually by becoming her schoolmaster, developing her inwardly and aesthetically in such a way as to awaken a "multiple-tongued reflection" in her (EO, I: 309, 360 / SKS, 2: 299, 349).[20] His diary plots the history of the development of the psyche of one such girl, Cordelia Wahl, who in his opinion possesses all the essentials—imagination, spirit, and passion—of femininity but which are not yet subjectively reflected within her (EO, I: 343, 359 / SKS, 2: 332, 349). Unlike vulgar seducers, Johannes does not find his enjoyment in crudely forcing himself on a girl in a manner tantamount to rape but rather in developing her inwardly to the point where she is willing to give and devote herself to him freely. This total self-giving and devotion in freedom constitutes the "deeper womanliness" he wishes to develop in Cordelia (EO, I: 307, 342, 386 / SKS, 2: 296–97, 331, 374). To this end he enters

[20] On the young girl as the seducer's protégé, see also my book, *Living Poetically: Kierkegaard's Existential Aesthetics* (University Park: The Pennsylvania State University Press, 1994), 91–96.

into an intellectual rather than a physical relationship with her and proceeds by way of repulsion rather than attraction, initially making her hate and fear him because of his superior intellect (EO, I: 351, 362 / SKS, 2: 340, 351). As Johannes sees it, a girl fears intellect because it "constitutes the negation of her entire womanly existence," which is a life in immediacy (EO, I: 362 / SKS, 2: 351). "Woman is substance, man is reflection," Johannes contends (EO, I: 431/ SKS, 2: 419).

If a man is going to war with a girl, therefore, he must not do battle in her sphere of power (beauty, for example), where she is "always the stronger" and he can "never win a complete victory;" rather, he must bring her into his sphere and match wits with her in a battle that he is sure to win (EO, I: 362–63 / SKS, 2: 351). For this, a "double-movement" involving two steps or two kinds of conflict is required (EO, I: 363, 384–86 / SKS, 2: 352, 372–374). First, he tempts her into battle through a display of his pride, defiance, cold ridicule, callous irony, and fierce independence, which has the effect of making her want to compete with him at the intellectual level (EO, I: 363 / SKS, 2: 352). He lends her books—all carefully chosen by him of course—and engages in intellectual conversations with her (EO, I: 364, 412 / SKS, 2: 353, 400). When she has been duped in this manner long enough, the first conflict begins in earnest as he begins to pull back from her, thereby evoking a naïve erotic passion in her that eventually results in an engagement being formed between them. Then, in response to his continued coldness, a more bold and reflected passion is evoked within her as she seeks to capture him completely by breaking off the engagement in order to give herself to him freely (EO, I: 363, 384, 411–12 / SKS, 2: 352, 372, 399). The first conflict, therefore, is a "war of liberation" that Cordelia has the illusion of winning; in it she becomes "the temptress" who seemingly seduces Johannes "into going beyond the boundary of the universal" (EO, I: 384–85, 425 / SKS, 2: 372–373, 412). The second conflict constitutes the "war of conquest" which Johannes wins the minute she gives herself to him, after which he is done with her and ready to move on to another victim (EO, I: 385, 445 / SKS, 2: 373, 432). In this conflict woman, in accordance with her concept, is "the vanquished" one, while man, in accordance with his, is "the victor," but the profound irony of masculine seduction as Johannes practices it is that "the vanquished" has the appearance of being the dominant one while "the victor" seemingly submits to "the defeated one" (EO, I: 431 / SKS, 2: 418).

At the end of "The Seducer's Diary" Johannes contemplates an epilogue in which he muses that "it would really be worth knowing whether or not one could poetize oneself out of a girl in such a way as to make her so proud that she imagined it was she who was bored with the relationship" (EO, I: 445 / SKS, 2: 432). In the diary Johannes educates Cordelia to the point where she willingly breaks their engagement in order to give herself freely to him, but when the second conflict is over, she finds herself in the same state of reflective sorrow, doubt, and restlessness that other female victims of seduction experience. She is unsure within herself whether she is innocent or guilty in the affair, whether she still loves or hates him, and even whether he was a deceiver and seducer or not, although she strongly suspects that the former is the case (EO, I: 309–13 / SKS, 2: 298–303).[11] Would it be possible, Johannes asks himself, to poetize himself out of a girl in such a way that she also imagines it is she, not he, who is responsible for breaking off the relation between them?

4. Suffering Superiority: Quidam

The question with which "The Seducer's Diary" ends is the one with which the thought experiment "Guilty/Not Guilty?" in *Stages on Life's Way* begins. In a journal entry dated 1846 Kierkegaard makes the following observation:

> Viewed categorically, the experiment relates to "The Seducer's Diary" in such a way that it begins right there where the seducer ends, with the task he himself suggests: 'to poetize himself out of a girl'....The seducer is egotism; in *Repetition* feeling and irony are kept separate, each in its representative: the young man and Constantin. These two elements are put to-

---

[11] For a more positive assessment of the effects of Johannes's seduction of Cordelia, see G. Lacoste, "The Dialectic of the Real Erotic and of Eroticism in Kierkegaard's *Seducer's Diary*," *Kierkegaardiana*, Vol. 22 (Copenhagen: C. A. Reitzels Forlag), 125–38. Lacoste envisages Cordelia "as having undergone an initial self-transformation" through seduction that will enable her "to realize herself authentically as a human being." On the victimization of Cordelia and the other female figures in *Either/Or*, Part I, see also Wanda W. Berry, "The Heterosexual Imagination and Aesthetic Existence in Kierkegaard's *Either/Or*, Part One," *International Kierkegaard Commentary: Either/Or, Part I*, Vol. 3, ed. Robert L. Perkins (Macon: Mercer University Press, 1995), 201–228.

> gether in the one person, Quidam, of the experiment, and he is sympathy. To seduce a girl expresses masculine superiority; to poetize oneself out of a girl is also a superiority but must become a *suffering* superiority if one considers the relationship between masculinity and femininity and not a particular silly girl. Masculinity's victory is supposed to reside in succeeding; but the reality...of femininity is supposed to reside in its becoming a story of suffering for the man. Just as it is morally impossible for Quidam to seduce a girl, so it is metaphysically-aesthetically impossible for a seducer to poetize himself out of a girl when it is a matter of the relationship between masculinity and femininity, each in its own strength, and not of a particular girl. The seducer's egotism culminates in the lines to himself: 'She is mine, I do not confide this to the stars...not even to Cordelia, but say it very softly to myself,' while Quidam culminates passionately in the outburst: 'The whole thing looks like a tale of seduction.' What is a triumph to one is an ethical horror to the other (JP, 5: 5865 / SKP, VII 1 B 83).

Like the reflective seducers in *Either/Or*, Part I, Quidam is trained in deception and cunning, but unlike his aesthetic counterparts, he has some ethical qualms about breaking off a relationship with a girl to whom he is engaged but cannot, for personal and religious reasons, see his way through to actually marry her (SLW, 195–96, 355 / SKS, 6: 183–84, 330). Thus he looks like a rogue but is just the opposite; that is, his actions are calculated to make himself look like a depraved person and a scoundrel while in fact he is doing everything he can to free her from the relation by making her loath the whole affair and feel no sympathy for him (SLW, 220, 224, 246–47, 268–69, 305, 321, 359, 394 / SKS, 6: 230, 250–51, 283, 299, 334, 366). Unlike Johannes the Seducer, who has no sympathy for his victims, Quidam suffers sympathetically for the girl and thinks that deceiving her in this way will actually be a benefit to her, enabling her either to gain a new love through an illusory resignation of their relation or, preferably, to undergo a religious metamorphosis that would empower her magnanimously to set him free (SLW, 423 / SKS, 6: 392). While Quidam fervently wishes for the latter solution, the former, in his view, is a more realistic possibility, since the girl, typical of her sex, is not reflective by nature and does not care for religion or have any need for it (SLW, 270–71, 315, 357 / SKS, 6: 252, 292, 320. Consequently, the approach he takes is exactly the opposite from that of Johannes the Seducer; that is, rather than developing reflection in her as a way of securing feminine freedom, he seeks to do away with what little reflective capacity she does possess by overwhelming her with his own superior intellect, as Faust does to Margarete, and absorbing all reflection out of her (SLW, 270–71, 274 / SKS, 6: 252, 255). The goal of this deceptive operation is to lead her to an immediate resolution that not only will set her free from the relation but also is an expression of her own will, not one Quidam has instilled in her (SLW, 271, 305 / SKS, 6: 252, 284). Ironically, however, such a deception constitutes a defeat, not an advantage for Quidam himself, for while in an external sense he succeeds in it, he becomes guilty of misleading the girl and is thereafter led into a dialectical suspension concerning the justification of his actions that he cannot resolve (SLW, 448, 450 / SKS, 6: 414, 416). Thus, from a religious point of view, Quidam constitutes a demonic, not a religious, personality, and the self-torment which he heaps upon himself must be regarded as reprehensible and sinful since religious healing can only be gained through repentance (SLW, 257, 447, 468, 484 / SKS, 6: 240, 413, 431–32, 446).

But the girl, Quaedam, for all her immediacy and innocence, is not without some guilt as well, at least as Frater Taciturnus, the author of this thought experiment, sees it (SLW, 434 / SKS, 6: 402). One of the reasons Quidam pursues a deceptive course to liberate Quaedam is because she bestows an excessive devotion upon him which he cannot understand or reciprocate, given the inclosing reserve of his personality. Moreover, he thinks it is inappropriate for marriage, for her total dependence upon him would place him in a position of complete power over her, which he does not want, since the more she surrenders herself to him, the more responsibility he must assume in the relation (SLW, 311, 315 / SKS, 6: 289, 293). Quaedam also uses all the familiar ploys of femininity to bind him, claiming that she cannot live without him and that he will be a murderer if he leaves her (SLW, 330 / SKS 6: 307). But were she to win through these tactics, Quidam would be lost, since he would not be able to work through his inclosed reserve, and his whole spiritual life would then be on her conscience (SLW, 429 / SKS, 6: 397). Consequently, he is forced to adopt an extreme tactic himself in order to battle his way free from her. Ironically and sadly, Quidam's tactic violates his own principle of equality, according to which he is "unable to exist intellectually unless she must be able to exist in the same thing" (SLW, 305, 331 / SKS, 6: 283, 308). By denying Quaedam the possibility of developing the capacity for reflection, he closes out the possibility of a truly religious resolution of the situation for her as well as himself. And while he desires a strong woman who is his intellectual equal and who is not psychologically dependent upon him, he ironically ends up assuming all the responsibility in relation to Quaedam anyway.

The upshot of this sad tale of suffering, therefore, is that while Quidam undoubtedly constitutes an ethical advance over his reflective and immediate aesthetic counterparts by virtue of his capacity to combine feeling and irony in sympathy for the feminine, the methods and outcome of his actions are exactly the same as theirs. To wit: he poetizes himself out of the girl through the use of deception and the assertion of a suffering superiority that nevertheless maintains full control of the girl and the relationship itself. It is precisely the manipulative, destructive, demonic consequences of masculine seduction and its suffering look-alike at the levels of both immediacy and reflection that Kierkegaard, the master artist, sought to portray through these representative figures in his pseudonymous writings in order to illuminate the pathology of desire in the male psyche. To the extent that Kierkegaard himself manifested this pathology in relation to Regine Olsen, he is personally implicated, along with legions of men, by his own analysis. But unlike many men, he was able to see beyond the pathology to the possibility of a different sort of relationship between man and woman that is based on love, commitment, and faith and that combines immediacy and reflection in upbuilding rather than demonic ways. While that vision, from a feminist standpoint at least, is admittedly limited and flawed, it nevertheless urges us forward to a re-examination and reconstruction not only of male-female relations but of human relations in general.[12]

[12] For a range of feminist critiques of Kierkegaard, see *Feminist Interpretations of Søren Kierkegaard*, ed. C. Léon and S. Walsh (University Park: The Pennsylvania State University Press, 1997).

3

DESIRE AND LOVE IN KIERKEGAARD'S *EITHER/OR**

Love is a major theme in Kierkegaard's writings, forming a central concern of *Either/Or, Repetition, Stages on Life's Way, Two Ages,* and *Works of Love.* These works establish Kierkegaard as a major thinker and perhaps the most penetrating and profound modern Christian philosopher of love. In the present essay, however, I shall limit my examination to *Either/Or* (1843), and within this work I shall focus on three sections from Part I ("The Immediate Erotic Stages or the Musical Erotic," "The First Love," and the infamous "The Seducer's Diary"), and on the first essay in Part II entitled "The Esthetic Validity of Marriage."[1]

The first thing that should be noted about *Either/Or* is that it is made up of a collection of writings by an anonymous esthete referred to as "A" (Part I) and by a civil judge named William who is designated as "B" (Part II). These writings were supposedly discovered and published by a pseudonymous "editor" named Victor Eremita. The work is thus deliberately twice removed from Søren Kierkegaard as its author and should not be interpreted as setting forth his own viewpoints on love, which are spelled out more directly in writings published under his own name, for example, *Works of Love.* Rather, *Either/Or* should be understood as presenting only the viewpoints of the esthete and the judge, whose writings are intended as representations of an esthetic-romantic and a bourgeois-ethical life view, respectively. By allowing the representative authors to speak for themselves and to criticize one another,

* Reprinted by permission from *Sex, Love, and Friendship,* ed. Alan Soble (Amsterdam and Atlanta: Rodopi, 1997), 609–22.

[1] All references to this work in the present essay are from Søren Kierkegaard, *Either/Or,* 2 vols. ed. and trans. Howard V. Hong and Edna H. Hong (Princeton: Princeton University Press, 1987). References will be placed in the text, using the siglum EO followed by volume and page number. See the list of sigla for references to other works by Kierkegaard cited in this essay.

Kierkegaard himself stands in the background as an indirect critic of both. This is not to say, however, that Kierkegaard is entirely opposed to everything written by the esthete and the judge in *Either/Or*. The knowledgeable reader can find many points of agreement with both authors, although Kierkegaard's own standpoint is much closer to the ethical perspective of Judge William than to the hedonistic viewpoint of the romantic esthete.

That a characterization and critique of romanticism are intended in Part I of *Either/Or* is not self-evident but is suggested by the *form* of the work, which takes the shape of a romantic novel in the form of an arabesque or mixture of genres, and also by the *content* of A's thought, which reflects an ironic and esthetic standpoint typical of the German romantic movement as understood and criticized by Kierkegaard in his academic dissertation, *The Concept of Irony* (1841). In this work, the estheticism of the German romantics is identified with irony understood not merely as a rhetorical device but as a negative standpoint toward existence, which they find to be meaningless, inadequate, and boring. Thus they seek to transcend actuality by way of the imagination and a recovery of esthetic or sensuous immediacy in their lives and art in an effort to create themselves and their environment via experimentation with an infinity of possibilities. It is this romantic-ironic mentality and its fascination with the erotic as an expression of sensuous immediacy, on the one hand, and as a reflective, seductive, manipulative sensuality, on the other, that we find reflected in the writings of A in Part I of *Either/Or*. Kierkegaard seeks to expose and counteract this negative standpoint in a twofold fashion, first by depicting the irony, despair, illusion, fragmentation, and moral bankruptcy of the romantic-esthetic lifestyle in and through an artistic portrayal of its erotic moods, attitudes, viewpoints and actions, and second through a direct critique of the romantic esthete from an ethical standpoint by the pseudonym Judge William.

1. Desire and Love as Seduction: "The Immediate Erotic Stages or The Musical Erotic"

Turning now to an examination of selected sections from the romantic esthete's collage of writings, let us look first at his interpretation of desire and love as represented by the figure of Don Juan, a perennial character in Western drama, music, and literature since the Middle Ages. According to A, Don Juan is a product of the Middle Ages' unconscious penchant for representing single aspects of life in figurative form. The aspect or idea Don Juan represents is that of the sensuous-erotic in its abstract or elemental originality qualified as desire. As A understands it, the sensuous-erotic constitutes the elementary passion or primitive life-force in humanity manifested as an insatiable desire for enjoyment through an immediate gratification of the senses, especially in the form of sexual desire. As such, the sensuous-erotic or desire characterizes the esthetic stage of human life at its most immediate level, or that stage in which we live primarily on the basis of our natural drives and inclinations.

A views the expression of desire or the sensuous-erotic as developing in three stages, which he finds artistically represented in several of Mozart's operas. The first stage is portrayed by the Page in *The Marriage of Figaro*; the second by Papageno in *The Magic Flute;* and the third is epitomized by the opera *Don Giovanni*, the whole of which "is essentially the expression of the idea" of desire, although that idea is represented more specifically in the opera by the figure of Don Juan (EO, I: 84). According to A, the first stage consists in a state of dreaming or intoxication in erotic love, in which there is still a substantial unity between desire and the desired and only a presentiment of a deeper desire separated from its object. The second stage is one in which desire actively seeks to discover its object in the multiplicity of particularity, but without actually having an object or desiring it. The third stage is characterized by desire of the particular absolutely in a unity of the two previous stages, the one and multiplicity or the particular and the universal (EO, I: 75–85). This last stage is the only one that concerns us here. A claims that desire is manifested in Don Juan as a *principle*, not as an element in a particular individual, although it is personified in the opera in a figure who appears to be an individual, or more accurately, who is "continually being formed but is never finished" as an individual, so that he hovers between being an individual and an idea, that is, a power or life force (EO, I: 92).

As a power or life force, Don Juan is the embodiment of the sensuous-erotic determined as a *demonic* principle in opposition to spirit. Being an aspect of our given nature, sensuousness is not intrinsically immoral or sinful, but A claims that with the coming of Christianity into the world sensuousness was excluded in favor of a spiritual form of existence. The sensuous-erotic then began to assert itself in its raw, pristine form as an independent power or force in esthetic indifference to the spiritual, whereas previously in the Greek psyche it had been harmoniously integrated as an element in the beautiful personality. Being the representative of sensuousness in this demonic form, Don Juan thus represents, on a spiritless level, the rebel in us, the desire to gratify our natural inclinations without constraints, without regard for others, in total freedom and total enjoyment of the senses. In his kingdom, where "everything is only one giddy round of pleasure," we hear "only the elemental voice of passion, the play of desires, the wild noise of intoxication" (EO, I: 90).

It is the romantic esthete's contention that the sensuous-erotic in its immediacy, and especially in all its demonic force as represented in the figure of Don Juan, can be artistically represented only in music, for music is the only medium that is capable of expressing the immediate *in its immediacy* (EO, I: 70). Other media either destroy immediacy by bringing it under the power of reflection in language or else give the sensuous static expression, as in painting and sculpture (EO, I: 67, 70). Music is essentially a sensuous medium and has the sensuous as its absolute subject. Moreover, like the principle of sensuousness, it is also abstract and demonic, being essentially a medium for the expression of that which is general or indeterminate and which lies outside the realm of spirit (EO, I: 65, 73).

As a representative of the immediate or sensuous-erotic in demonic form, Don Juan was given classic expression, A claims, in Mozart's opera *Don Giovanni*, for in this work there is achieved a perfect unity of form and content or medium and idea (EO, I: 57). Being the embodiment of sensuous desire, Don Juan deceives and seduces women, but in the romantic esthete's opinion he is not, strictly speaking, a seducer, since that requires a level of consciousness and cunning that is lacking in the Don, who always acts with a passion, energy, and exuberance that is completely spontaneous and unreflective. Rather, he desires and therein acts seductively to obtain the satisfaction of his desire. As soon as he has enjoyed it, however, he seeks a new object in a repetitive process that goes on indefinitely (EO, I: 99). His love for a woman, therefore, is always momentary and faithless. As soon as he has had one woman, he desires another, for it is not a particular woman but all women or more precisely the ideal of total femininity in every woman that he desires indiscriminately in all (EO, I: 95, 100). Thus it is not the extraordinary woman but the ordinary woman who constitutes the object of his desire, since every woman is ordinary by virtue of the fact that she is a woman (EO, I: 97).

The fact that Don Juan is a male figure and the preceding stages of the immediate-erotic are also represented by male figures raises an interesting question as to whether the immediate-erotic qualified as desire is gender specific, and more specifically whether the seductiveness of demonic desire is limited to males. In his analysis of the stages of desire the romantic esthete identifies desire with the male and the desired with the female, and in all three stages the object of desire is femininity (EO, I: 77–8, 100). But if the sensuous-erotic is to be understood as an aspect of human existence in its esthetic condition or "elemental originality," then desire and the seductive character of desire would have to be a feature of woman as well as men. Either the romantic esthete has committed the male chauvinist sin of identifying humanity solely with males or else he clearly intends to identify demonic desire and seduction as a male tendency. This is a point of view that runs contrary to the traditional stereotyped view of woman as a seductress derived from the biblical story of Adam and Eve but which is consistent with A's philosophy of male dominance elsewhere in the text.

That the second alternative is intended is supported by a passage from another book, *The Concept of Anxiety*, published under the pseudonym Vigilius Haufniensis, in which Haufniensis says:

> So when the Genesis story, contrary to all analogy, represents the woman as seducing the man, this is on further reflection quite correct, for this seduction is precisely a feminine seduction, because only through Eve could Adam be seduced by the serpent. In every other place where there is a question of seduction, linguistic usage (delude, persuade, etc.) always attributes superiority to man. (CA, 66)

And in an earlier draft of this passage, Haufniensis writes:

> In a way it has always seemed remarkable to me that the story of Eve has been completely opposed to all later analogy, for the expression "to seduce" used for her generally refers in ordinary language to the man, and the other related expressions all point to woman as weaker (easier to infatuate, lure to bed, etc.). This, however, is easy to explain, for in Genesis it is a third power

> that seduces the woman, whereas in ordinary language the reference is always only to the relationship between man and woman and thus it must be the man who seduces the woman. (JP, 5: 5730)

Although this passage is by another pseudonym, one who stands much closer to Kierkegaard's own thought than does the romantic esthete, it reflects a point of view that is compatible with the esthete's practice of associating desire and seduction with the male and in fact provides a rationale for understanding the biblical story and feminine seduction as atypical, since in this instance the seduction of both the man and the woman is carried out by a third power, namely the serpent, and woman is simply the intermediary or instrument by which the male is seduced by the serpent. In ordinary situations, however, Haufniensis seems to be saying that seduction is generally perpetrated by man, since woman is the weaker sex. The possibility of woman being a seducer is not ruled out, but the phenomenon is primarily associated with males, or in the case of the figure of Don Juan, with male fantasy life.

This leads to a consideration of why the romantic esthete is so infatuated with Mozart's opera and the figure of Don Juan in the first place. Being highly reflective by nature or training, A seeks to lose himself in fantasy and to expand his own erotic moods by rediscovering them artistically in the music of Mozart. Finding Mozart's music tempting and irresistible as a stimulus and medium for fantasizing in this manner, A asks:

> where is the young man who has not had a moment in his life when he would have given half his kingdom to be a Don Juan, or perhaps all of it, when he would have given half his lifetime for one year of being Don Juan, or perhaps his whole life? But that was as far as it went. The more profound natures, who were moved by the idea, found everything, even the softest breeze, expressed in Mozart's music; in its grandiose passion, they found a full-toned expression for what stirred in their own inner beings, they perceived how every mood strained toward that music just as the brook hurries on in order to lose itself in the infinitude of the sea. (EO, I: 104)

The point A is making here is not that men should be inspired by the Mozartian Don Juan to act out their male fantasy life and become Don Juans themselves. This is made clear as he goes on to say:

> The bunglers, who think themselves a Don Juan because they have pinched a peasant girl's cheek, put their arms around a waitress, or made a young girl blush, of course understand neither the idea nor Mozart, or how to produce a Don Juan themselves, except as a ludicrous freak, a family idol, who perhaps to the misty, sentimental eyes of some cousins would seem to be a true Don Juan, the epitome of all charm. (EO, I: 104)

It is not the indulgence in *actual sensuousness* in comic imitation of Don Juan (who, being a mythic figure larger than life and the symbol of a power or force rather than an individual, is not a role model for virile males), but rather a *poetic sensuousness* that A and all the "more profound natures" moved by the idea seek to enjoy. As a romantic ironist, A has essentially rejected actuality and taken flight into the realm of fantasy as a way of recovering a lost immediacy or eroticism that can never be regained in actuality but might be momentarily, that is, *illusively* recaptured and enjoyed in an infinity of erotic moods stimulated by music and the imagination. Thus, while A claims that the essay on Don Juan "is written only for those who have fallen in love" (EO, I: 58), he does not really believe in love, not even the sensuous love of Don Juan in any real sense. That love is an illusion nourished by the wrong sort of fantasy life, that is, by the conception of love portrayed in romantic novels, is the subject of another esthetic essay by A, "The First Love," to which we shall now turn.

2. Love as an Illusion: "The First Love"

"The First Love" is a review of a play by that title written by a nineteenth-century French dramatist, Augustin Eugène Scribe, a playwright little remembered today but one who enjoyed immense popularity in his own time, especially in the tiny country of Denmark, where his works were performed more than 900 times (almost twice as often as Shakespeare) during Kierkegaard's lifetime (1813–55).[2] *Les Premières Amours* or

[2] Ronald Grimsley, *Søren Kierkegaard and French Literature* (Cardiff, Wales: University of Wales Press, 1966) 112–14.

The First Love, a modern situation comedy in one act, was the most popular of Scribe's plays in Denmark. Just as A praises Mozart's *Don Giovanni* as an unparalleled masterpiece of music, in agreement with popular opinion he lauds *The First Love* as "a flawless play, so consummate that it alone is bound to make Scribe immortal" (EO, I: 248).

The First Love centers around two characters, Emmeline and Charles, who according to A's interpretation illustrate respectively the results of having been nurtured on romantic novels: either a sinking into a state of illusion in which one is hidden from oneself, as in the case of Emmeline, or a gaining of a talent for mystification by which one can hide oneself from others, as in the case of Charles. Emmeline espouses the romantic dictum that "the first love is the true love, and one loves only once" (EO, I: 254). She is convinced that she loves her cousin Charles, whom she has not seen since she was eight years old, and she holds fast to this illusion during the course of a comic mix-up in which Charles courts her under another name and is roundly rejected. When it is at last revealed to her who he is and that he is already married, she agrees to marry another man who had pretended to be Charles. She will marry him, however, not out of love (for an "ideal" Charles remains her first and only love), but to be obedient to her father's wish and to get even with the real Charles for having been untrue to her. For his part, Charles, who has squandered all his money and become dissolute, thinks he can hide his identity and ingratiate himself to his uncle in the disguise of a respectable man. The man whose identity he assumes is the man who is passing himself off as Charles in order to court Emmeline. In the end both Charles and Emmeline effect the opposite of what they sought, so that the play ends in irony. Emmeline's illusion, however, remains intact, as she looks to the future still in love with the ideal Charles who was her first and only love. Thus it is not a real man but an ideal one created in her own imagination whom she thinks she loves.

A uses the occasion of a performance of Scribe's play as an occasion for poetically recollecting and reliving his own first love, or what he thought was his first and only love. Although he seeks in this manner to renew his first love, confident that "the poetic power of this play will prompt the love in my breast to spring forth," he does not actually want to renew his relation to his first love but prefers instead to feel the beauty of loving her at a distance (EO, I: 241–2). Even when he was experiencing love for the first time, he admits, they saw each other infrequently and felt more comfortable and closer when they were apart (EO, I: 240). In this he sees a similarity between his situation and that of heroes in novels and comedies and thus thinks of himself as a poetic character and as leading a poetic life (EO, I: 241). What he really hopes to recover and re-experience poetically is his youth and the spontaneous passion of love, which he expects to burst forth forcefully like the snap of a passion flower or the popping of the cork on a bottle of champagne (EO, I: 241).

But while A seeks to recapture and enjoy the illusion of first love, he is under no illusion about the illusory nature of romantic love (EO, I: 244). Although A admits that as a young man he went through a period of illusion in which he believed in first love, he later lost faith in it so as to "believe no more in the first" (EO, I: 244). This disillusionment is further confirmed by the fact that his former first love informed him upon a later chance meeting at a performance of the play that she had never loved him and that her present love was her first love. This prompts him to undertake a review of the play in order to determine what first love really means. The thesis adhered to by Emmeline and his own "first love" (and other women as well, since in A's opinion "[a] girl is more likely to become immersed in illusion" than is a man) A finds sophistical in that it confuses what is supposed to be a qualitative category, "the first," which is thought to be essentially different from later loves, with a numerical category inasmuch as it is possible to love more than once (EO, I: 250, 254). The typical way of conflating these categories, illustrated by A's former first love, is to maintain that although we might love several times, each time is really the first time, thus negating the validity of the previous times. Emmeline is not guilty of this sort of confusion, since her first love is Charles and she has loved only him since she was eight years old. Her confusion consists in the fact that "[s]he understands the thesis numerically and so conscientiously that she believes that an impression in her eighth year is decisive for her whole life" (EO, I: 254).

A finds such a sentimental view of love ridiculous though representative of "a large class of people" (EO, I: 254). Contending that Scribe presents "an infinitely witty mockery of Emmeline's sentimentality" in almost every situation in the play, he concludes that the drama should be interpreted ironically, that is, as a parody that negates romantic love rather than affirms it (EO, I: 261, 273, 277). Having contended that A is himself a representative of romanticism, we are thus required to make a distinction between two forms of romanticism, a sentimental kind that naively believes in romantic love, and a pessimistic brand characterized by romantic irony that regards love as an illusion. This second form of romanticism, reflecting A's own view of love, is developed to its logical conclusion in "The Seducer's Diary," the final section from *Either/Or* Part I to be considered here.

3. The Irony of Erotic Love: "The Seducer's Diary"

In "The Seducer's Diary," A brings before us another esthete by the name of Johannes, who specializes in the seduction of young girls. A character of A's own creation and perhaps a reflection of his own darker nature (although he claims to be only the editor of the seducer's diary, which he supposedly found in a secretary drawer), the seducer figure portrayed here is designed as an analogue to the immediate Don Juan at the reflective level; that is, he is a conscious seducer and thus constitutes a genuine seducer, whereas the immediate Don Juan merely acts seductively in the process of desiring. Unlike the musical Don Juan, this seducer is much more interested in the art of seduction, the method of conquering, than in the act of seduction or the sensuous experience itself. The mode of treatment in this instance, therefore, centers on a portrayal of the craftiness with which the seducer wins over his victim and carries out the seduction. We might find an analogy, and possibly even a model, for the seducer figure and his diary in several works of the eighteenth century: Samuel Richardson's epistolary novel *Clarissa. Or, The History of a Young Lady* (1747–8), recently cast for television on Masterpiece Theatre; Choderlos de Laclos's epistolary novel *Les Liaisons dangereuses* (1782), brilliantly made into a film starring Glenn Close and John Malkovich; the Marquis de Sade's *La philosophie dans le boudoir* (1795), a tale of seduction in dialogue form; and Friedrich Schlegel's *Lucinde* (1799), a romantic novel considered to be "obscene" by Kierkegaard and widely regarded as pornographic in the early nineteenth century.[3] There is no evidence

[3] For Kierkegaard's critique of Schlegel's novel, see *The Concept of Irony*, 286–301. On the hostile reception of Schlegel's novel, see the "Introduction" to *Friedrich Schlegel's "Lucinde" and the "Fragments,"* trans. Peter Firchow (Minneapolis: University of Minnesota Press, 1971), 3–8. On Kierkegaard and the Marquis de Sade, see Henning Fenger, *Kierkegaard, the Myths and Their Origins:*

that Kierkegaard was familiar with Richardson, de Sade, or Laclos, but a Danish translation of Laclos' novel was published in Copenhagen in 1832, making it at least possible that Kierkegaard had read it.[4]

Unlike the figures in these writers' works, however, Kierkegaard's Johannes is more than a master seduction artist; indeed, he claims not to be a seducer at all but rather an *eroticist*, that is, a person who, according to his definition, "has grasped the nature and point of love, who believes in love and knows it from the ground up," and who also knows that "the highest enjoyment imaginable is to be loved, loved more than anything else in the world" (EO, I: 368). For an eroticist, love is the absolute, but in Johannes' view it is a short-lived experience that must be carefully cultivated and controlled for maximum enjoyment. In his opinion, "no love affair should last more than half a year at most and...any relationship is over as soon as one has enjoyed the ultimate" (EO, I: 368). Unlike "vulgar seducers" who deceptively entice girls with false promises of marriage, the eroticist makes no promises but receives everything as a gift of freedom (EO, I: 367–68). "Only in freedom is there love; only in freedom are there diversion and everlasting amusement," he proclaims, for otherwise the girl will fall "like a heavy body" as a burden and obligation upon him (EO, I: 360–1). To bring about this freedom requires a special kind of artfulness, a "discerning touch" that knows how to evoke devotedness along with freedom (EO, I: 342). "The majority enjoys a young girl as they enjoy a glass of champagne, at one effervescent moment" that, in Johannes' view, corresponds to rape (EO, I: 341–2). By contrast, the eroticist is able to enjoy more and to make the experience more interesting for himself by artfully developing a young girl within herself. As techniques in this educative process, he employs deception, dissimulation, psychological conflict, irony, erotic stimulation, anything that will aid her development. Essentially, however, his method is passive in nature, relying on and being alert to making the right impression on her. Johannes writes:

> The art is to be as receptive as possible to impressions, to know what impression one is making and what impression one has of

---

Studies in the Kierkegaardian Papers and Letters, trans. George C. Schoolfield (New Haven: Yale University Press, 1980), 204–12.

[4] Grimsley, *Søren Kierkegaard and French Literature*, 27.

> each girl. In that way, one can be in love with many girls at the same time, because one is in love in a different way with each one. To love one girl is too little, to love all is superficiality; to know oneself and to love as many as possible, to let one's soul conceal all the powers of love inside itself so that each receives its specific nourishment while the consciousness nevertheless embraces the whole—that is enjoyment, that is living. (EO, I: 361)

To this end Johannes undertakes, and recollects in his diary, the education of a young girl of seventeen, named Cordelia Wahl, in the art of erotic love. Unlike other young girls he has loved in the past, Johannes senses something special about this one. She is lovely, lively, passionate, innocent, imaginative, proud, full of confidence, ripe for an awakening of love. Much to his surprise, she also stirs up in him the passion and rapture of erotic love, which he had not expected to experience again and which necessitates all the more breaking the relationship to her once he has accomplished his objective with her. That consists, first of all, in implanting himself into her life and becoming engaged to her even though she does not yet love him. Then her education begins in earnest as she learns to love him with all the powerful force of erotic love, and in learning to love comes to love him doubly so because she has learned to love from him (EO, I: 377). Patiently, cautiously, Johannes cultivates love in her through a series of letters, which he uses to develop the power of imagination in her by which she can discover and make a leap into the infinite. Johannes writes: "What she must learn is to make all the motions of infinity, to swing herself, to rock herself in moods, to confuse poetry and actuality, truth and fiction, to frolic in infinity. Then when she is familiar with this tumult, I shall add the erotic: then she will be what I want and desire" (EO, I: 392). To evoke the erotic in her, he switches from letters to notes and with these arouses her to the level of a naïve erotic passion.

But the eroticist has a higher form of the erotic than this in mind for his pupil. What he wants to develop in her is a reflected passion that is bold and free as well as "definite, energetic, determined, dialectical" in character (EO, I: 412). Having cultivated her passion within the bounds of the universal through an engagement, he now seeks to break the engagement in order to go beyond the universal in the expression of a devoted yet free love that recognizes no earthly bounds. As Johannes puts it:

> The point now is to guide her in such a way that in her bold flight she entirely loses sight of marriage and the continent of actuality, so that her soul, as much in pride as in her anxiety about losing me, will destroy an imperfect human form in order to hurry on to something that is superior to the ordinarily human. (EO, I: 428)

Here we have a clear statement of the ironic standpoint toward actuality that the romantic esthete and his alter ego Johannes espouse in the pitting of free love against marriage, the unconventional against convention, the exception against the universal. With ironic detachment, Johannes transcends and cuts himself off from actuality, its only significance for him being to serve as a temporary stimulus to sensual experimentation and reproduction of the same in poetic form. But Johannes' irony extends beyond this to love itself. The moment Cordelia gives herself to him in freedom and total devotion everything is over. He is rejuvenated and ready to move on to another young girl in waiting; she is relativized and made weak and insignificant by her deflowering. For as the eroticist interprets woman's existence, she is a "being-for-others" whose value is instantly deflated in the moment of her birth and baptism as a woman (EO, I: 429). From Johannes Cordelia has learned to love, but through him she has also learned the irony of erotic love, which is what he ultimately sought to teach her.

As an eroticist, then, Johannes is the consummate esthete and diabolical seducer, a prospect so terrifying in its ultimate implications that even A is frightened by the shadowy, dreamlike relation of this character to his own being. We find him repulsive, too, whether we identify with the victims of his psychological manipulation and subliminal control or with the perpetrator of these actions who has gone so far astray in his inner being that there is little or no chance of exit from the self-entrapment in irony and moral bankruptcy concealed there. Yet the flight into boundless freedom that Johannes and Cordelia take is an alluring one that constitutes the essence of the romantic-esthetic view of life and love as Kierkegaard sees it. In a letter to A that likens him to a "matchless instrument" of music (an appropriate medium for expressing "the demonic," we may recall), Cordelia describes her reaction to Johannes:

"With an indescribable but cryptic, blissful, unnameable anxiety, I listened to this music I myself had evoked and yet did not evoke; always there was harmony, always I was enraptured by him" (EO, I: 310).

In emphasizing the sensuous, illusory, and temporary character of romantic love, Kierkegaard's portrayal of it in Part I of *Either/Or* is consonant with the usual understanding of this form of love. But his figurative analysis of the romantic esthete's philosophy of love goes further in revealing it to be *anti-sensuous* in its desire for a poetic rather than actual recovery and indulgence in the sensuous-erotic; *anti-woman* in its characterization of woman as the object and victim of male seduction, on the one hand, and as a silly, sentimental believer in the illusion of love, on the other; and finally, *anti-love* in its ironic negation of any real and lasting erotic relationship between a man and a woman. At the end of Part I we are left wondering, then, whether erotic love can be given expression in actuality in such a way as to preserve and enhance its sensuous nature without negating the existence of woman and ultimately of love itself. For a possible answer to that question, let us turn finally to Judge William's view of love in *Either/Or*, Part II.

4. The Ennoblement of Erotic Love in Marriage: "The Esthetic Validity of Marriage"

Part II of *Either/Or* consists of two long epistles (only the first of which will be considered here) written by Judge William to A, whom the Judge claims to love as a son, brother, and friend. The Judge seeks to help A secure an ethical-religious center for his life by confronting him with a well-meaning critique of his esthetic-ironic lifestyle and countering it in the first letter with a strong defense of love and marriage (EO, II: 6–7).

Judge William believes in first love just as adamantly as does Emmeline, claiming that his wife is "the only one I have ever loved, the first," a sentiment that, according to him, is mutually shared by his wife (EO, II: 9; see also 37, 41, 60). But for Judge William love "is not a venture in the imaginary erotic," as it is for Emmeline, A, and Johannes the Seducer; rather, it is "the earnestness of life," which in his view does not make it "cold, unbeautiful, unerotic, unpoetic" but more beautiful, more deeply erotic, and truly poetic (EO, II: 10). As his marriage has gained stability over the years, first love, the judge claims, has been continually rejuvenated in it in such a way as to acquire religious as well as esthetic meaning. For him, however, rejuvenation is not a "sad looking back" or a "poetic recollecting of past experience" as it is for A but rather an action that is situated in striving (EO, II: 10).

Although the judge does not presume to set forth his own marriage as normative, he finds esthetic treatments of love and marriage in literature to be generally untrue and unsatisfactory. On the one hand, he claims, novels about love tend to glorify marriage by having the story end in a happy marriage, as if all the struggles and difficulties of life were now over. On the other hand, in his view modern literature no longer really believes in love; thus love is ridiculed and shown to be an illusion, as in the works of Scribe (EO, II: 18–19). Working against the literary stream, therefore, Judge William seeks to establish not only the esthetic validity of marriage, that is, the possibility of preserving erotic love in marriage, but also the validity of love itself.

Beginning with an analysis of the nature of erotic or romantic love, the judge emphasizes first of all its immediate, sensuous quality but goes on to point out that erotic love is not merely sensuous, since it contains a consciousness of the eternal, which gives it nobility and distinguishes it from lust (EO, II: 21). Whereas the merely sensuous is momentary and in its more refined expression makes the moment of enjoyment into a "little eternity" or a "sensuous eternity" in "the eternal moment of the embrace," the true eternal factor in romantic love "rescues it first out of the sensuous," he claims (EO, II: 22). Thus, while the judge admits that "romantic love is rather overworked these days," he has "a certain faith in the truth of it" and "a certain respect for it" (EO, II: 20). However, in partial agreement with the modern literary viewpoint, the judge regards the eternal factor in romantic love as illusory and presumptive, since in his view it is based on nothing more than the conviction of the lovers that their love will last forever (EO, II: 21). This is the weakness, the fatal flaw in romantic love against which modern literature has unleashed its devastating and sometimes amusing ironic polemic. But in the judge's considered opinion modern literature has nothing to put in its place, or rather, it goes off reflectively in two directions, neither of which is acceptable to him because the first is immoral and the second "misses out on what is more profound in love" (EO, II: 22). The first path is one of indulging in a transitory sensuality that is antithetical to marriage or else enters into marriage as a temporary civil arrangement until someone more attractive comes along (EO, II: 23). The other path moves in the opposite direction toward a neutralization of the sensuous in a marriage of convenience based on calculation and involving only the "prose of love," that is, social and economic considerations (EO, II: 23, 27). In contrast to these paths, both of which effectively annihilate love, Judge William holds that romantic love can be delivered from its "illusory eternal" or transient nature and given a deeper erotic or sensuous expression by being assumed, transfigured, and ennobled in a marriage that has its center and authority in the divine (EO, II: 29–30, 43).

The notion of a "higher concentricity" in which love and marriage are oriented in a religious perspective is central to Judge William's doctrine of love (see EO, II: 43, 47, 55, 57, 89, 94). It is not marriage *per se* that secures and ennobles romantic love, as he has already shown in his critique of secular forms and motives for marriage. Only those marriages that take their point of departure in the saying of vows before God, in the recognition of the authority and power of the divine in their lives, have the possibility of doing so. In the higher concentricity of the religious, marital love becomes a unity of contrasting elements: sensuous yet spiritual, necessary (bound) yet free, momentarily present yet eternal (EO, II: 30, 60).

In Judge William's view, then, there a close bond between the erotic and the religious and between marriage and the religious. In this regard he is particularly concerned to point out the essential relation between Christianity, marriage, and the erotic. In an apparent reference to A's claim in his essay on the musical erotic that the sensuous is "excluded" by Christianity (EO, I: 61–62), Judge William denies that sensuousness is negated or annihilated in Christianity (EO, II: 48–9). While admitting that the Christian God is spirit and that spirit and the flesh stand in discord with one another in this religion, he stresses that the flesh is not identical to the sensuous but rather is to be understood as selfishness (EO, II: 36, 49). Thus Judge William avers: "the joy and fullness that are in the sensuous in its innocence can very well be caught up in Christianity" (EO, II: 49). In another passage he notes that "it would indeed be beautiful if the Christian dared to call his God the God of love in such a way he thereby thought of that inexpressibly blissful feeling, that never-ending force in the world: earthly love" (EO, II: 30). And he concludes that "if marital love has no place within itself for the eroticism of first love, then Christianity is not the highest development in the human race" (EO, II: 31). In Judge William's opinion, however, marriage provides the connecting link between the erotic and the religious inasmuch as it contains, or should contain, both of these elements. Furthermore, in his view "marriage belongs essentially to Christianity," more so than in paganism and Judaism, because sex differences are more deeply reflected in Christianity than in these other religions, enabling woman to attain her full right as a separate and independent being (EO, II: 29). Although, somewhat contradictorily, the judge declares himself against female emancipation, regarding it as a male plot to corrupt and exploit woman, marriage oriented in the religious is viewed as emancipating both man and woman from a patriarchal mentality (EO, II: 22, 52, 61). By referring marriage to God, man is freed from a false pride that leads him to conquer and assert superiority over woman and woman is freed from a false humility that causes her to surrender and submit herself to him as if she were nothing.

Marriage oriented in the religious also has a historical character lacking in immediate love that enables it to gain continuity and the eternal in time. Marital love is historical in the sense that it is a process of inward blossoming in which such qualities as humility, patience, constancy and faithfulness are acquired and possessed through daily repetition and a steady acquisition over the years. The ideal husband or wife, therefore, is not one who is that once in his or her life but who is that every day (EO, II: 135). This form of repetition is not identical with habit, which Judge William regards as evil and thus something that ought to be changed (EO, II: 127). The way to counteract boredom and habit in marriage, he claims, is not by changing partners or distancing oneself from the beloved so as to maintain interest, mystery, and secretiveness, but by developing a shared history and a shared consciousness or mutual understanding characterized by sincerity, self-giving, and openness. For Judge William, understanding is "the life principle of marriage" and "the absolute condition for preserving the esthetic [or love] in marriage" (EO, II: 116–7). Without it marriage is neither beautiful nor moral. With it repetition in the ethical sphere becomes a forward movement in which one constantly repeats what one already possesses in the form of love, faithfulness, patience, and so forth, and thereby gains content and continuity in the midst of the ongoing flux of life. In this way marital love preserves eternity in time and time in eternity, for the qualities acquired through daily repetition constitute the eternal in the individual and have within them the qualification of time, that is, the condition that their veracity consists in being continually realized in time rather than once and for all (EO, II: 139).

From Judge William's standpoint, therefore, every individual has a duty to marry. Capitalizing on the possibility of a play on words in Danish to make this point with respect to men, Judge William claims that it is only as a married man (*Ægtemand*) that one proves oneself to be a "genuine man" (*ægte mand*) in the trials of life (EO, II: 125).

Although, in his opinion, it is not sinful for a person to remain single unless that individual is responsible for it, he regards marriage as advantageous and superior to the single life and to any erotic relationship outside of marriage, for several reasons. First of all, from an ethical standpoint, marriage must be understood as an expression of the universal rather than the accidental; that is, it puts an emphasis on the ordinary, what might be said of or experienced by every couple, rather than the extraordinary, the differences that set an individual or couple apart from others. Although differences are not canceled in marriage, they become transfigured in the relationship so that one is able to see the universal in the differences and to appreciate differences as differences without making them determinative for the relation. A second advantage of marriage, therefore, is that it makes the universal, that is, the marital relationship itself, not differences, the absolute. Whether or not a person is uncommonly beautiful or handsome is thus inconsequential in marriage, as there is essentially no difference from others at the fundamental level. On the matter of beauty, however, a third advantage shows itself in that marriage reveals the true beauty of love, which consists not in the accidental beauty of the lover's or loved one's good looks but in an "historical beauty" of freedom, whose task is to fashion something great and beautiful out of the ordinary, not merely to develop the differences or out-of-the-ordinary features that distinguish a marriage or the parties in a marriage (EO, II: 304–5).

Although *Either/Or* ends without validating either the judge's or the romantic esthete's view of love and marriage, requiring us to reflect upon and make a fundamental choice between them, we know from a journal entry of Kierkegaard that he regarded the judge as "unconditionally the winner" of the contest between their contrasting life views (JP, 5: 5804). But this does not mean that he viewed Judge William's perspective as final or without shortcomings. Indeed, the parson's sermon on the theme that "in relation to God we are always in the wrong" at the conclusion of the book is intended to suggest just the opposite. In particular, one can detect in Judge William vestiges of the patriarchal mentality that a religious orientation of marriage is supposed to overcome, and he assumes a natural compatibility between the erotic and the religious that will later by questioned and reformulated in *Works of Love* in a more strictly Christian perspective. It is to this later work, therefore, that one must turn for a full account of Kierkegaard's philosophy of love.[5]

[5] On *Works of Love* see my articles, "Kierkegaard's Philosophy of Love" and "Forming the Heart: The Role of Love in Kierkegaard's Thought," in the present collection.

4

WHEN "THAT SINGLE INDIVIDUAL" IS A WOMAN*

Kierkegaard's *Eighteen Upbuilding Discourses* is a collection of his religious discourses from 1843 and 1844. Nine discourses were published each of these two years, grouped into three series of two, three, and four discourses respectively and issued separately at various times during the year. Each series is accompanied by a preface that is repeated, with minor variations, throughout the collection. The preface always begins with a statement attesting that the speaker is neither a preacher nor a teacher but rather an author without authority who sends these upbuilding discourses—in themselves only a "trifle" or "superfluity"—on a journey in search of "that single individual" (*hiin Enkelte*) who will be "favorably disposed" to receive them and become his reader (EUD, 5, 53, 107, 179, 231, 295). This designation for the intended reader of these discourses poses an interesting puzzle as to the identity of this figure, but it also prompts a reconsideration of the relation between the particular and the universal, difference and sameness, with respect to the audience and meaning of the discourses. In his journals Kierkegaard remarks that "the point of departure of the pseudonymous writers is continually in the differences—the point of departure in the upbuilding discourses is in the universally human" (EUD Supplement, 476 / SKP, VIII 2 B 192). The upbuilding discourses thus may be understood as being addressed to every individual and are upbuilding for precisely that reason; that is, they apply equally to all individuals regardless of differences in sex, class, age, education, and religious sophistication (EUD, 240).[1]

---

* Reprinted by permission from *Kierkegaard Studies Yearbook 2000*, ed. Niels Jørgen Cappelørn, Hermann Deuser, and Jon Stewart together with Christian Fink Tolstrup (Berlin and New York: Walter de Gruyter, 2000), 1–18, and *International Kierkegaard Commentary: Eighteen Upbuilding Discourses*, Vol. 5, ed. Robert L. Perkins (Macon, GA: Mercer University Press, 2003), 31–50.

This emphasis on sameness or our common humanity rather than on differences or particularity as the point of departure for the upbuilding discourses is immediately apparent in the opening discourse from 1843, where Kierkegaard states that faith

> is not only the highest good, but it is a good in which all are able to share, and the person who rejoices in the possession of it also rejoices in the countless human race, 'because what I possess,' he says, 'every human being has or can possess.' The person who wishes it for another person wishes it for himself; the person who wishes it for himself wishes it for every human being, because that by which another person has faith is not that by which he is different from him but is that by which he is like him; that by which he possesses it is not that by which he is different from others but that by which he is altogether like all. (EUD, 10)

---

[1] For example, concerning the difference between the simple or uneducated person and the cultured or educated person, Kierkegaard says: "In my opinion, culture by no means makes upbuilding superfluous: it just makes it more and more necessary...because the *cultured person*, if he understands himself,...will become aware that what we call culture leaves a whole side of the soul unsatisfied, without nourishment and care...and he will make it his concern to see to it that this need for upbuilding will increase equally with his increasing culture....With regard to upbuilding, the explicit task is precisely to *develop* deeper and deeper the need that everyone *ought to have*.—For the *simpler people*, however, who also have the advantage neither of the time nor of the circumstances for the cultivation of the spirit, the upbuilding becomes that which cultivates, that which genuinely and nobly cultivates one who nevertheless remains uninitiated into that which cultivates intellectually and aesthetically.—Genuine education never makes one grow away from the upbuilding as something one needs less and less, but makes one grow up to the upbuilding as something one needs more and more....The upbuilding does not want to consolidate differences between people any more than the ocean wants to separate. Just like love, the upbuilding wants to unite, if possible, the most different in essential truth" (EUD, Supplement, 474 / SKP, VIII 2 B 188). See also EUD Supplement, 470 (SKP, VIII B 220) where Kierkegaard writes: "Something that is supposed to serve for upbuilding must never contain a split, as if there were one kind of upbuilding for the simple and another for the wise."

Consequently, Kierkegaard goes on to affirm in this same discourse that, with respect to sexual differences, "whether he is the mighty male who defies the storm or the defenseless female who only seeks shelter from the gale—this has nothing to do with the matter, my listener, absolutely nothing" (EUD, 13).

Although differences are downplayed in favor of unity and sameness in the universal human reference of the upbuilding, they nevertheless play an essential role in the identity and experience of that single individual who is the intended recipient of the discourses. In Kierkegaard's journals the category of the single individual is defined dialectically and ironically on the one hand as "the most unique of all" and on the other as "what every human being is" (EUD Supplement, 475 / SKP, VIII 2 B 192; see also JP 5: 5975 / SKP, VIII 1 A 15). This double meaning of the category, Kierkegaard claims, is operative in the distinction between the pseudonymous works, which employ the first meaning, and the upbuilding discourses, which understand it in the second sense. But this duplexity of meaning, I shall contend, is also operative within the upbuilding discourses themselves.

To see how this is so, let us return to the opening discourse of 1843 on faith, where Kierkegaard uses the example of a "perplexed man" who wishes, in a paternalistic fashion, to do everything for someone he loves in order to procure faith for that individual (EUD, 10–16). What the perplexed man comes to realize is that this is the wrong way to love and that no human being can give faith to another. Thus he is constrained to let go of the other, leaving that person alone to will or grasp faith for him- or herself (EUD, 10–14). This release or withdrawal on the part of the perplexed man precipitates a change in both parties and in their relation to one another. They become like strangers to one another in the installation of the perplexed man "in his limits" and the other "in his rights" (EUD, 14). But the perplexed man also comes to perceive that this separation constitutes "the true meaning" of their relationship, for if he were able to bestow the highest good upon the other, this would mean that he would also have the power to deprive the other of it (EUD, 15). Thus, he thanks God that the other owes him nothing in this regard.

This example is used by Kierkegaard to emphasize not only the singularity of each individual with respect to acquiring faith, which is at the same time a possibility for everyone, but also the need for a proper separation between individuals in personal relations that protects them from abuse of power by one over the other. Given the fact that the first party in the example is referred to as a perplexed man (*Mand*) rather than a perplexed person (*Menneske*), one is tempted to interpret the text as alluding specifically to heterosexual relations (although it need not be limited to them) and thus to the need for establishing and maintaining non-paternalistic (if not non-patriarchal) and non-abusive treatment of women by men in religious matters.[2] If that is its meaning, then the discourse contains a promising message of edification for women in particular—a possibility we shall return to consider more closely later in this essay.

Kierkegaard goes on in this same discourse to further underscore the importance of particularity and difference in individuals by noting that "[w]hen two people learn different things from life, it can be because they themselves are different" (EUD, 22). He illustrates the point this time with an example of two children who are brought up together and always share the same things but "still learn altogether different things" (EUD, 22). Several discourses from 1844 make the same or a similar point. In discussing the necessity for patience in expectancy, Kierkegaard points out the diversity of expectancy in human life, suggesting that persons expect "very different things according to different times and occasions and in different frames of mind" (EUD, 206). In another discourse he notes that what separates individuals from God is "very different for different people" (EUD, 246). And in distinguishing between indifferent and concerned truths—an important epistemological observation that anticipates the distinction between objective and subjective truth in *Concluding Unscientific Postscript*—Kierkegaard characterizes concerned or subjective truths as "not applying universally to all occasions but only specifically to particular occasions" (EUD, 233).[3] In contrast to indifferent or objective truth, which is "equally valid [*lige gyldig*] whether anyone accepts it or not" and "indifferent to the individual's particular condition," concerned truths "are not indifferent to how the individual re-

[2] One is reminded here of the notorious passage in *The Sickness unto Death* in which Anti-Climacus states that "in most cases the woman actually relates to God only through the man" (SUD, 50n).

[3] On the contextual nature of feminist epistemology and its compatibility with Kierkegaard's epistemology in *Concluding Unscientific Postscript*, see my article, "Subjectivity versus Objectivity: Kierkegaard's *Postscript* and Feminist Epistemology" in the present collection.

ceives" the truth, that is, "whether he wholeheartedly appropriates it or it becomes mere words to him" (EUD, 233). In making a similar distinction between self-knowledge and general truths, Kierkegaard points out in another discourse:

> General discussion of general truths can certainly give a person much to remember and can develop his understanding, but it is of only very little benefit to him....Above all, generality is not for upbuilding, because one is never built up [*opbygges*] in general, any more than a house is erected [*opføres*] in general. *Only when the words are said by the right person in the right situation in the right way, only then has the saying done everything it can to guide the single individual to do honestly what one otherwise is quick enough to do—to refer everything to oneself.* (EUD, 276, emphasis added).

These passages amply demonstrate the particular, contextual nature of the upbuilding discourses within a universal frame of reference. They indicate that context matters; indeed, it is what gives content to, or puts flesh on, the bare bones of the universal, without which the discourses would become general or abstract and consequently not upbuilding for anyone.

Another way Kierkegaard tries to emphasize the importance of context in these discourses is by making a "pilgrimage...with the text into differences," that is, by multiplying the number of possible situations addressed in the text, as in the discourse on "Every Good Gift and Every Perfect Gift Is From Above" from 1843 (EUD, 145). Almost half of the paragraphs in this discourse begin with an "Or" that introduces another variation on the conditions under which a person might be willing to give to others (EUD, 147–56). Of course, it is impossible to mention every possible situation in a text, and Kierkegaard addresses just this impossibility and its possible consequences in a discourse from 1844. Here he has the single individual protest that "my experience was very different from what you are talking about," implying that the discourse does not apply to him or her (EUD, 193). To this Kierkegaard replies that when "this emphasis on the different" becomes "a staring at heterogeneity" it is not conducive to preserving one's soul and that "if unity does not lie at the base of diversity, similarity at the base of dissimilarity, then everything has disintegrated" (EUD, 193). Even if one's particular situation is not specifically mentioned in a text, then, there is still a common core of human experience to identify with in it.

A second qualification with respect to specificity is set forth in a discourse from 1844. Reflecting on the passage in Ecclesiastes 12:1 which admonishes the reader to "think about your creator in the days of your youth," Kierkegaard suggests that even though the admonition "can be repeated again and again and applies to countless numbers of people, it speaks every time to the single individual…as if it spoke to him alone, as if it came into existence solely for his sake, as if it were unconcerned about all the rest of the world" (EUD, 238). Yet, while "it is indeed the case that the admonition's concerned truth addresses itself specifically to the single individual in a particular circumstance of life…the discourse about it nevertheless must take good care lest it make the upbuilding conditional upon the accidental," thus becoming untrue (EUD, 239). This would be the result "if one wanted to be built up by the thought of old age, but in a special way so that youth could not be built up by the same thought," or vice versa (EUD, 139–40). Even though a discourse may specifically address itself to a particular condition or time of life, then, it must be applicable to other circumstances or ages as well.

Taking these two qualifications into account, we may nevertheless conclude that both the discourses and "that single individual" who is their intended recipient must be understood specifically as well as universally, in terms of the particular situation and differences that characterize each reader, yet without excluding anyone on the basis of those factors. Since the particular situation and distinguishing characteristics of individuals vary from reader to reader, we may also conclude that the understanding of the discourses will vary according to the particular circumstances of each reader. While each discourse has a general message that applies universally to everyone, it will not be interpreted and appropriated by all readers in the same way, as if their circumstances in life were all the same. Rather, the message is interpreted within the context of the particular circumstances of each person's own life, so that, on the basis of these differences, what each person gleans from them is context-specific, understood and appropriated in terms of the particular conditions of that person's life rather than as a generality.

On the basis of these conclusions, let us now pose a test case of the specificity or contextuality of reference and meaning in this particular collection of discourses. Let us suppose that, on occasion, "that single individual," or the "favorably disposed" intended reader of these discourses, is a woman. As a matter of fact, there is textual evidence that Kierkegaard had one particular woman in mind—Regine Olsen—as the designated reader of these discourses, especially the first series of discourses from 1843, for he indicates as much in his journals (JP, 5: 6388, 6472 / SKP, X 1 A 266; X 5 A 149). Moreover, Regine confirms in her memoirs (as told to Hanne Mourier and Raphael Meyer) that the religious discourses were dedicated to her, that a copy of the first ones was sent to her by Kierkegaard through F. C. Sibbern, and that she read them with her fiancé and later husband, Fritz Schlegel.[4] If a third party thus reads the first two discourses with Regine Olsen specifically in mind as their intended recipient, it is obvious that Kierkegaard is quite explicitly addressing her recent experience of loss, sorrow, disappointment, and unhappiness over the breakup of their engagement to one another. In the first discourse he encourages her to face the future in the victorious expectancy of faith, which is based on the eternal and thus is never disappointed, rather than approach it with "multifarious expectancy" or "expectancy of something particular," which may or may not be substantiated in time or eternity (EUD, 27–28, 36). Kierkegaard entertains the possibility that her continued faith in him "when the inexplicable happened" may have been wrong (even though commendable in comparison with others who turned away from him) because it is inappropriate to have faith in a human being "in this way," possibly leading one to forget that there is a higher truth in God. However, he rejects this scenario and credits her instead with having, or at least successfully regaining, the expectancy of faith that will see her through this crisis and others (EUD, 24–26). Read in this context, it becomes apparent too that "the perplexed man" mentioned earlier in the discourse is Kierkegaard himself, who records here his own realization that faith, like love, must be presupposed in others and in any case is not something that can be wished into existence for Regine by him or anyone else (EUD, 13,15; WL, 216–24). In view of the non-paternalistic, non-abusive character of the relationship that evolves between the perplexed man and his beloved

---

[4] *Encounters with Kierkegaard: A Life as Seen by His Comtemporaries*, collected, edited, and annotated by Bruce H. Kirmmse and translated by Bruce H. Kirmmse and Virginia R. Laursen (Princeton: Princeton University Press, 1996), 36–37, 40.

in the discourse, it reveals considerable maturity in Kierkegaard's understanding of the proper attitude and behavior he should maintain toward Regine Olsen in religious matters. Not only does she not owe him anything, he credits her with perseverance in faith at a time when it might have been lacking, precipitating her downfall in doubt and despair.[5]

The second discourse encourages Regine to thank God for the many good and perfect gifts bestowed upon her rather than tempting God to make the divine idea of what is best for her coincide with her own wishes or trying to persuade and implore her beloved (Kierkegaard) to do something he did not consider to be right (EUD, 19–21, 35, 37). In a journal entry from 1849 Kierkegaard alludes to the latter possibility, suggesting that "in the book itself there is a slight hint about giving up, that one loses the beloved only if one gets him to act against his conviction" (JP, 6: 6472 / SKP, X 5 A 149:18). Entertaining the possibility that, for a time at least, she may have succumbed to anger, hardness of heart, despair, and complaints against God because of her suffering and grief, Kierkegaard goes on to remind Regine that when she finally humbled herself before God, "your countenance was renewed, and God's compassionate grace had loved forth [*fremelsket*] in your barren mind the meekness that is receptive to the words" of scripture referred to in the text (EUD, 37–38). In using the phrase "loved forth"—a beautiful expression that is employed again in *Works of Love* in variant forms (*opelsker* and *at elske frem*) to convey the need "to love forth love" in others—Kierkegaard alludes to an earlier communication to Regine (JP, 5: 5526 / SKP, III A

[5] In response to a diary entry in which Kierkegaard presumably states that "she [Regine] was not religiously inclined," Regine suggests in her memoirs that this statement "must have been based on a passing impression" since "the fact that he dedicated the whole of his religious works to [me] . . . indicates that he must have regarded [me] as religious" (Bruce H.Kirmmse, ed. and tr., *Encounters with Kierkegaard: A Life as Seen by His Contemporaries* (Princeton: Princeton University Press, 1996), 35–36; see also 40. As Kirmmse points out, the statement attributed to Kierkegaard cannot be found in the journals, but he does say in one entry that "she has no intimation of the specifically religious" (JP, 6: 6304 / SKP, XI A 15) and in another that she "has had no religious upbringing" (JP, 5: 5689 / SKP, IV A 142). Against the latter charge Regine counters in her memoirs that she "had had a profoundly religious upbringing" (Kirmmse, 40). Of course, what Kierkegaard meant by "religious upbringing" may have been very different from what Regine understood it to mean.

171; WL, 217; see also EUD, 508, note 100). In it he credits her with having loved forth a flowering plant by her "ardent gaze" and the "warmth of her love," reminding her that "there were also times when you despaired of my love or had fearful intimations that our happiness would not last, and a gentle dew of tears refreshed it, and look, it doubled its growth, became twice as beautiful; in this way, too, it was loved forth." Thus, like the first discourse from 1843, the second one in the series is filled with very specific personal allusions and meaning for Regine Olsen in particular, and both are meant to be upbuilding for her specifically in her time of trouble.

But surely these discourses and others in the collection were not written for her alone. We have seen that as upbuilding discourses they have a universal significance which makes them personally applicable to other "favorably disposed" readers as well, including other women. Indeed, we know from the recent research of Bruce Kirmmse and Habib Malik that Kierkegaard had a sizable coterie of female readers in his own time—not altogether to his liking.[6] The celebrated Finnish-Swedish writer, Fredrika (or "Frederikke") Bremer (1801–65), reports in her book, *Life in the North* (*Liv I Norden*), published in 1849, that Kierkegaard "has gained a not inconsiderable audience in happy, pleasant Copenhagen, particularly among ladies," who were attracted to his "philosophy of the heart."[7] As the following passage from Kierkegaard's journals of that year indicates, he thought her statement absurd: "Frederikke has made me into nothing but a psychologist and has supplied me with a considerable audience of women [*Dame-Publikum*]. That is really ridiculous, how in all the world I can be seen as a ladies' author [*Dame-Forfatter*]" (SKP, X 1 A 658).

Nevertheless, it is true that women as well as men at that time in Denmark and abroad were attracted to Kierkegaard's writings, especially his religious discourses. Regine reports in her memoirs that she loved the religious discourses "more than all the rest," and Petronella Ross, a friend

[6] See Kirmmse, *Encounters with Kierkegaard*, 94, 95, 101–103, 106, 110, 124, 297, and Habib Malik, *Receiving Søren Kierkegaard: The Early Impact and Transmission of His Thought* (Washington: Catholic University of America Press, 1997), 54–77.

[7] Kirmmse, *Encounters with Kierkegaard*, 94. See also Malik, *Receiving Søren Kierkegaard*, 57.

of F. C. Sibbern, comments in a letter to him that Kierkegaard's "writings are my favorite reading—among the religious sort," although she admits that she has read only "a little of him."[8] Moreover, H. C. Rosted, an assistant school inspector and local historian of the town of Hørsholm, reports in his memoir that Kierkegaard regularly sent copies of his writings to Regine ("Tagine") Reinhard, proprietress of the inn at Hørsholm where he frequently stayed, and that he often had long talks with her about religious questions.[9]

These citations, of course, provide only anecdotal evidence of interest in Kierkegaard's authorship among women of his time, but they do establish that the contemporary audience included female as well as male readers. Of particular interest to us here, however, is whether this group of female readers may have included any *feminists* among them, and if so, whether it is possible for "that single individual" to be a female feminist (assuming that men can be feminists too) who may find something upbuilding in these discourses for her specifically as a feminist. With regard to the first question, recent scholarship indicates that at least two of Kierkegaard's early female admirers were leading feminists of the time. One was Fredrika Bremer, who in addition to writing travel books started the Swedish suffragette movement and wrote a novel, *Hertha* (1856), on the condition of women in Sweden. The other was Camilla Collett (1813–1895), a Norwegian novelist and advocate of women's rights who published an anonymous novel, *The Governor's Daughters* (*Amtmandens Døtre*), in 1855 on the condition of women in Norwegian society.[10] In

[8] Kirmmse, *Encounters with Kierkegaard*, 40, 101. Kirmmse notes that in an earlier letter to Ross, Sibbern especially recommended to her the discourse on Job's words in the series of four upbuilding discourses from 1843, and on one occasion Ross wrote to Kierkegaard requesting a copy of his *Christian Discourses*, which he apparently sent to her.

[9] Kirmmse, *Encounters with Kierkegaard*, 110. See also Malik, *Receiving Søren Kierkegaard*, who reports that the diary of Linda Keyser Preus (1829–1880), wife of a Norwegian immigrant pastor in Wisconsin, indicates that she also read several of Kierkegaard's religious works (72–75).

[10] Kirmmse, *Encounters with Kierkegaard*, 95; Malik, *Receiving Søren Kierkegaard*, 62–68 on Bremer, including references to secondary works on her, and 68–71 on Collett, with corresponding references to secondary literature on her. See also Julia Watkin, "Serious Jest? Kierkegaard as Young Polemicist in Defense of Women," in *International Kierkegaard Commentary: Early Polemical*

spite of the fact that Kierkegaard personally offended both women by refusing to meet with them when they came to Copenhagen, Bremer contemplated, but finally decided against, including long excerpts from *The Moment* in the English translation of her novel because she thought Kierkegaard would be "almost incomprehensible to foreigners," and Collett may have crafted the heroine of her novel with several female characters from *Either/Or* in mind.[11] Although Malik credits Kierkegaard with being a "negative stimulus" for these women inasmuch as their novels represent a protest of conventional views of woman reflected in his authorship, neither of them seems to have been positively affected by Kierkegaard on the subject of woman, especially on the burning issue of female emancipation, which he consistently opposed in both his pseudonymous and non-pseudonymous writings.[12] It would appear, therefore, that Kierkegaard had little or nothing upbuilding to say to them or other feminists on this score.

If that were the case, however, it would serve to undermine the universal reference and character of the upbuilding discourses, making the

---

Writings, Vol. 1, ed. Robert L. Perkins (Macon: Mercer University Press, 1999), 7–25. Watkin also refers to Mathilde Fibiger (1830–1872), a teacher and social theorist who wrote a sensational book, *Clara Raphael, Twelve Letters* (1850), challenging the social and ecclesiastical narrow-mindedness of the time, but it is not known whether she was acquainted with Kierkegaard's writings. However, her sister, Ilia Marie Fibiger, was Kierkegaard's nurse at Frederiks Hospital when he was dying, and Kierkegaard's close friend, Emil Boesen, reports that she sent him flowers, which made him happy (Watkin, "Serious Jest," 14 and n. 29; Kirmmse, *Encounters with Kierkegaard*, 124, 126).

[11] Malik, *Receiving Søren Kierkegaard*, 64–65 and 69–70. See also Fredrika Bremer, *Hertha*, trans. Mary Howitt (New York: G. P. Putnam & Co., 1856). The English translation does retain some specific references to Kierkegaard, including a brief quotation from a short tract from 1855, "This Must Be Said: So Let It Now Be Said," which the heroine initially responds to quite favorably, according to the narrator, who reports that "she felt that a combating and suffering heart throbbed here in unison with her own, embittered, bleeding, loving, and still, though as in the midst of the flames, seeking to lay hold upon God; and she felt less solitary in the world" (242–43). Later, however, her despair at presumably having been deceived by her lover became so great the "[t]he words of Kierkegaard no longer consoled her," and she threw the tract into the waters of the falls where she had stopped on her journey to confront him (245).

[12] Malik, *Receiving Søren Kierkegaard*, 67, 71.

female feminist an exception to the universal and presenting a situation to which the discourses do not apply. To consider this possibility, let us return, "once more with feeling," to the upbuilding discourses of 1843 and 1844 and read them empathetically through the eyes of a modern feminist who, if she has any prior acquaintance with Kierkegaard's writings, may not be as kindly disposed toward them as Regine and other conventional female readers of his time were inclined to be.[13]

Beginning with the first discourse from 1843 and interpreting it in terms of her own expectancy about the future, our feminist reader may at first be encouraged by the gender inclusiveness or universality of the possibility of faith affirmed in it and by the non-paternalistic, non-abusive character of male-female relationships advocated by the author with respect to the acquisition of faith. But her expectancy or wish, like that of Regine, is for something particular in the world. For her, however, it is not marriage to the beloved for which she yearns, as in the case of Regine, but rather for social equality. As she reads on in the text, however, she learns, as did Regine, that her wish may not be granted. Indeed, in a subsequent discourse from 1843, Kierkegaard suggests that while equality before God obtains for both man and woman and is the basis of every upbuilding view of life, it constitutes the divine law and has validity "only when the single individual fights for himself with himself within himself and does not unseasonably presume to help the whole world to obtain external equality, which is of very little benefit, all the less so because it never existed" (EUD, 143). Thus our feminist reader is seemingly being advised not only to give up her wish for social equality but also her fight for it in the world, since such external activity "produces nothing but confusion and self-contradiction, as if true equality could be expressed in any externality as such, although it can be victorious and be preserved in any externality whatever" (EUD, 143).

Here we encounter very early in Kierkegaard's writings a point of view that remains constant throughout his authorship and which pre-

[13] The quoted phrase is from Louis Mackey, "Once More With Feeling: Kierkegaard's *Repetition*," in *Points of View: Readings of Kierkegaard* (Tallahassee: Florida State University Press, 1986), 68–101. For a range of feminist critiques of Kierkegaard's views on women, see the essays in *Feminist Interpretations of Søren Kierkegaard*, ed. Céline Léon and Sylvia Walsh (University Park: The Pennsylvania State University Press, 1997).

sents a problem not only for feminist readers but for other modern social theorists as well. For while a spiritual equality between man and woman, rich and poor, high and low before God is unqualifiedly endorsed in his writings, he does not envision a corresponding social equality that would give concrete expression to this spiritual ideal in external forms. Anticipating the claim in *Works of Love* that Christian equality is not the same as worldly similarity, in these discourses Kierkegaard clearly is not willing to equate genuine equality with a particular external condition or state of affairs in the world (WL, 72).[14]

In the final clause of the statement quoted above, however, he does leave the door open for the victory and preservation of true equality within any and every external order. But this concession is also problematic inasmuch as it would seem to be exceedingly difficult if not impossible to establish and preserve true equality for women under certain social conditions—as in the current situation of Afghanistan women under Taliban rule, or the wholesale marketing of girls and women for sex slavery in Asia and Africa, or the objectification and denigration of women both locally and globally in pornography over the internet and in literature and films readily available at media outlets everywhere—to mention only a few of the ways in which women continue to be subjugated, abused, and exploited in patriarchal cultures of the present age. Surely some social climates are more conducive than others to securing a measure if not the full realization of social equality for women as well as other disenfranchised groups in the temporal realm. But that insight, true as it undoubtedly is, is somewhat beside the point being made here by Kierkegaard, since for him the issue is not quantitative, that is, a matter of particular societies being more or less receptive to the rights of women, but qualitative, inasmuch as in his view true equality is not equivalent to social equality, however much the latter may be realized in any particular society.

Given the inherent imperfection of the temporal realm, which in Kierkegaard's view is wedded to the preservation of differences rather

[14] On the social ethic of *Works of Love*, see my article, "Forming the Heart: The Role of Love in Kierkegaard's Thought," in the present collection. See also Jamie Ferreira, "Other-Worldliness in Kierkegaard's *Works of Love*" in *Philosophical Investigations* 22/1 (1999): 65–79, and my response to her article in the same issue, "Other-Worldliness in Kierkegaard's *Works of Love*—A Response," 80–85.

than sameness or equality of persons in likeness to God, how then can true equality be victorious and preserved in the world? The answer put forth in these discourses is that it is only in and through "the hallowed place," that outer and/or inner sanctuary where "every externality is discarded as imperfect, and equality is true for all" and where the single individual is "educated to preserve increasingly this equality in the clamor of the world and with it to penetrate the confusion" (EUD, 141–42, 267). It is clear from the last passage quoted that our feminist reader is not being admonished to give up her fight for equality in the world. On the contrary, she is encouraged

> to fight the good fight with flesh and blood, with principalities and powers, and in the fight to free [her]self for equality before God, whether this battle is more a war of aggression against the differences that want to encumber [her] with worldly favoritism or a defensive war against the differences that want to make [her] anxious in worldly perdition.[15] (EUD, 143)

She must continue to contend with the differences, then, but not for the sake of establishing social equality for herself and others in the world. Rather, she must contend with them in order to free herself inwardly for an inner appropriation of the spiritual equality before God which she already has. The goal of this spiritual struggle, as Kierkegaard sees it, is not to do away with the differences as such but rather to blind one's eyes to them, allowing the divine equality to burn, like a fire, "ever more intensely in the difference without…consuming it" (EUD, 143).

According to Kierkegaard, what is needed to sustain our feminist reader in this fight with differences is, first of all, an eternal goal (*Maal*) and criterion (*Maalestok*) that will always be valid and which can serve as a measure for understanding herself in temporality in such a way that neither good fortune and prosperity nor sorrow and affliction can rob her of hope (EUD, 260–61). In Kierkegaard's estimation the goal and criterion of experience in temporal life are too low and too limited since "events can still come along that are beyond the scope of experience,"

---

[15] In order to indicate the context-specific character of the text in relation to the female feminist reader, I have substituted and placed in brackets female pronouns for the male ones used by Kierkegaard in the passage here and in passages quoted below.

making one prey to despair (EUD, 260). "[E]ven if [she] manages to slip through life without having any such misfortunes challenge [her] calculations, then, if [she] has learned nothing higher in life, [she] is still a child of temporality for whom the eternal does not exist" (EUD, 260).

For Kierkegaard, the goal and criterion of the eternal, as opposed to those of temporality, are to be found in the expectation of eternal salvation, which in his view has a meaning and consequences for the present life as well as in heaven in that it provides "comfort beyond all measure" and "is a refuge in distress, a fortress that life cannot take by storm, an assignment that distress and sufferings cannot cancel" (EUD, 263). Kierkegaard goes on to aver that "life together with this conception is more nourishing for a person than mother's milk to the nursing child, and [she] returns from this conception strengthened, strengthened most of all precisely when [her] striving is not to wean [her]self from this nourishing but to make it [her] wont" (EUD, 263, 264).

It is perhaps here that one finds the greatest relevancy of the upbuilding discourses to the lives of women, especially those who continue to suffer greatly from maltreatment in patriarchal societies around the world. For even if it is impossible, humanly speaking, to free themselves from such temporal conditions, the expectation of eternal salvation provides a consolation and hope that can help them to endure their awful situations and be saved from despair (EUD, 267).[16] But even the modern feminist who has gained a measure of freedom and social equality in the temporal realm and looks forward to a full realization of these in the future may benefit from an expectancy of an eternal goal and criterion against which the relative gains and losses of temporal equality may be measured. In that way, she too may be saved from despair when her fondest earthly wish does not fully materialize or is lost after having once been gained.

---

[16] Anticipating *The Sickness unto Death*, Kierkegaard speaks here of the expectancy of eternal salvation as "the eternal remedy that heals all sickness, even the sickness unto death," and the two forms of despair—despair in weakness and despair in defiance—are prefigured as well in the distinction between "the soft person" and "the defiant person" in an earlier discourse (EUD, 111). For an analysis of the two forms of despair in terms of their association with gender categories, see my essay "On 'Feminine' and 'Masculine' Forms of Despair" in the present collection.

Another internal requirement for fighting the good fight for female equality in the temporal realm is patience. Kierkegaard devotes no less than three discourses in this collection to the need for patience in the battles of life, although he concedes that "it cannot be endorsed with full certainty as the one thing needful in the external: perhaps at times impatience would be more profitable and would hasten the gain of what is coveted" (EUD, 169). Even in the spiritual realm he credits "apostolic speech," which in his view is essentially different from all human speech, with being "as impatient as that of a woman in labor" (EUD, 69). Extending the analogy to feminist speech, one may liken the impatience of apostolic speech to it as well, inasmuch as apostolic speech, like much feminist discourse, is

> concerned, ardent, burning, inflamed, everywhere and always stirred by the forces of the new life, calling, shouting, beckoning, explosive in its outbursts, brief, disjointed, harrowing, itself violently shaken as much by fear and trembling as by longing and blessed expectancy, everywhere witnessing to the powerful unrest of the spirit and the profound impatience of the heart. (EUD, 69)

Kierkegaard distinguishes this "very different apostolic impatience," which maintains calm and order in anticipation of the end of all things, from "the rashness of an excited person" who acts impatiently in such a way as to throw everything into disorder in times of crisis (EUD, 71). Although he would undoubtedly label feminist impatience as an example of such rashness, I would argue that it bears a closer resemblance to apostolic impatience in its ardor for human equality and that, given the unequal social status of most women in the world today, feminist impatience is not only needed but also justified in the fight for social equality.

But patience is also needed, especially since "the most crucial issues are decided slowly, little by little, not in haste and all at once" (EUD, 199). While almost every endeavor in life requires a measure of patience, Kierkegaard points out that it is even more imperative in the spiritual realm, where patience is needed to gain and preserve that inner being or soul by which one relates oneself to God or the eternal and possesses oneself in one's eternal validity independently of the external realm. Contrary to what one might expect, the model for patience set forth in these discourses is not Job, although he does serve as a prototype for humanity in other respects elsewhere in the collection (see EUD, 109–24). Rather, it is the New Testament prophetess Anna, who is lauded not only for her decision to remain faithful to the memory of her deceased husband and to herself in freely continuing to bind herself to him in love, but also for setting her expectancy in the future on the coming of the eternal in time (EUD, 209). Unlike the foolish and impatient virgins in the gospel story from Matthew 25:1–13 with whom she is contrasted in the discourse, Anna patiently sustained an expectancy for the eternal regardless of its fulfillment or non-fulfillment in time and thus was never disappointed (EUD, 213–23).

Finally, Kierkegaard suggests that "the armor of love" and forgiveness will also be needed for a victorious fight for true equality in the world, especially on the battleground of one's inner being where that single individual who is a woman must fight "for [her]self with [her]self within [her]self" (EUD, 77, 143, 378).[17] Reminding us "that every human being, if he [or she] is honest, only all too often catches himself [or herself] in being able, protractedly, penetratingly, and expertly, to interpret the sad truth that revenge is sweet" in such a way as to justify it, Kierkegaard indirectly entreats his feminist reader to forego revenge against those who have wronged her, forgiving them in such a way as to abolish the partition wall of differences between them (WL, 57–58). Concerned not to admonish or judge others on this score, however, he emphasizes instead the power of Christian love "to love forth...the good in the impure" by hiding a multitude of sins in oneself and others (EUD, 57, 61). Once again, the human paradigm used to exemplify the point being made here is a woman—the woman in Luke 7: 36–50 who is forgiven much and who forgives much because she loved much (EUD, 75–78).[18]

---

[17] On the need for forgiveness in contemporary feminist liberation movements, see Wanda Warren Berry, "Finally Forgiveness: Kierkegaard as a 'Springboard' for a Feminist Theology of Reform," *Foundations of Kierkegaard's Vision of Community: Religion, Ethics, and Politics in Kierkegaard*, ed. George B. Connell and C. Stephen Evans (Atlantic Highlands: Humanities Press, 1992), 196–217.

[18] Kierkegaard returns to this biblical figure numerous times in his later religious writings, where she is extolled as a prototype of piety. See especially "An Upbuilding Discourse" in *WA,* 149–60. For a list of scripture references to her, see the appendix in L. Joseph Rosas III, *Scripture in the Thought of Søren Kierke-*

In the discourse that focuses most explicitly on equality, however, Kierkegaard suggests that it is in the giving of love and receiving it in return as a gift that true equality between human beings is effected and preserved in the temporal realm (EUD, 157–58). Since the gift of love is "from above" and thus more significant than either the giver or the receiver, it establishes an equality in love between them, which is the only thing that is temporally lasting (EUD, 158).

In conclusion, our empathetic reading of the early upbuilding discourses from the standpoint of that single individual who is a woman and modern feminist suggests that while they do not endorse female liberation in the temporal realm, a feminist reader may still find much in them that is upbuilding and supportive of her fight for true equality in the world. First and foremost, her fundamental and complete spiritual equality as a human being before God is affirmed and recognized as the qualitative criterion against which any and every expression of social equality or inequality in the temporal realm must be measured. Second, while no particular form of temporal equality is endorsed, the victory and preservation of true equality in the world remains a possibility for every woman, especially in the inner battleground of the soul where she must fight for self-preservation and freedom against temporal influences and gain the inner strength and resources to persevere in life no matter what her external circumstances, gains and losses, victories and failures. Third, spiritual consolation for herself and her sisters is offered in temporal situations of subjugation and abuse that seemingly are intractable and show little or no possibility of change. Fourth, the discourses are supportive of gender inclusiveness and non-paternalistic, non-abusive treatment of women by men in religious matters and, by extension, in other areas of sociality as well as through the establishment of temporal equality in love. Fifth, guidance for women in particular is provided through the use of female models who exemplify essential qualities needed in the fight for true equality.

Far from finding the *Eighteen Upbuilding Discourses* irrelevant to her particular situation, therefore, that single individual who is a woman and a feminist may turn to them for the inner support, perspective, and guid-

---

gaard (Nashville: Broadman & Holman Publishers, 1994). See also my essay, "Prototypes of Piety: The Woman Who Was A Sinner and Mary Magdalene," in the present collection.

ance needed to be victorious in her fight for true equality in the world. What a pity, though, that Kierkegaard could not, or did not, embrace and support that cause in external forms which seek to establish female social equality as well—or at least to make a substantial difference in woman's earthly lot and situation. For that his favorably disposed feminist readers may forgive him, but only those who love much in spite of what must be regarded as a major shortcoming in these otherwise truly upbuilding discourses for "that single individual" who is a woman.

5

ON "FEMININE" AND "MASCULINE" FORMS OF DESPAIR*

Of the two forms of conscious despair, despair in weakness (not willing to be oneself) and despair in defiance (willing to be the self one wishes to be rather than the self one essentially is), the first is characterized by Kierkegaard as "feminine" despair, the second as "masculine" despair (SUD, 49). This distinction between the forms of despair in terms of sexual categories figures importantly in Kierkegaard's analysis of selfhood and despair in woman and man, but it has received little or no attention in studies of his thought.[1]

---

*Reprinted by permission from the *International Kierkegaard Commentary: The Sickness unto Death*, Vol. 19, ed. Robert L. Perkins (Macon, GA: Mercer University Press, 1987), 121–34, and *Feminist Interpretations of Søren Kierkegaard*, ed. Céline Léon and Sylvia Walsh (University Park: The Pennsylvania State University Press, 1997), 203–15.

[1] Recent studies of selfhood and despair in Kierkegaard's thought that do not treat the distinction between feminine and masculine despair include Mark Taylor, *Kierkegaard's Pseudonymous Authorship: A Study of Time and the Self* (Princeton: Princeton University Press, 1975) as well as his *Journeys to Selfhood: Hegel & Kierkegaard* (Berkeley: University of California Press, 1980); J. Preston Cole, *The Problematic Self in Kierkegaard and Freud* (New Haven: Yale University Press, 1971); *Kierkegaard's Truth: The Disclosure of the Self*, ed. Joseph H. Smith (New Haven: Yale University Press, 1981); Kresten Nordentoft, *Kierkegaard's Psychology*, tr. Bruce H. Kirmmse (Pittsburgh: Duquesne University Press, 1978); Jann Holl, *Kierkegaards Konzeption des Selbst: Eine Untersuchung über die Voraussetzungen und Formen seines Denkens* (Meisenheim am Glan: Anton Hain, 1972); Vincent A. McCarthy, *The Phenomenology of Moods in Kierkegaard* (The Hague/Boston: Martinus Nijhoff, 1978); John Elrod, *Being and Existence in Kierkegaard's Pseudonymous Works* (Princeton: Princeton University Press, 1975); Alastair Hannay, *Kierkegaard* (London: Routledge & Kegan Paul, 1982). Libuse Lukas Miller, *In Search of the Self: The Individual in the Thought of Kierkegaard* (Philadelphia: Muhlenberg Press, 1962) notes the distinction between "manly" and "womanly" despair but does not explore it in her analysis. Several Studies of

For a generation grown skeptical of sexual stereotypes, however, such a distinction is quite questionable and calls for critical examination. Beginning with a brief account of what Kierkegaard has to say about feminine and masculine despair, the following examination will focus on two areas of concern: 1) the congruence of his views with the general structure of selfhood and analysis of despair presented in *The Sickness unto Death*; and 2) the compatibility of his perspective with recent findings on sexual differences and personality development. From a determination of these correlations we can more readily assess the significance of these correlations of the sexual categories employed in Kierkegaard's analysis of despair.

As if anticipating objections to his classification of despair as feminine and masculine, Kierkegaard appends a lengthy note to the text that introduces this distinction, defending and commenting upon it in some detail. He claims that his classification is conceptually correct as well as true in actual life, although in exceptional cases masculine despair may occur in women, and conversely, feminine despair may appear in men (SUD, 49). The distinction is thus an ideal one that holds true largely, but not entirely, in actuality. It corresponds on the whole with the ways despair is generally experienced in human life. Women are more apt to manifest despair in weakness, while men are more prone to despair in defiance.

Kierkegaard goes on in this note to give a brief account of despair in weakness or feminine despair in women. Woman's nature, he says, is characterized by devotedness (*Hengivenhed*) or giving of herself in sub-

---

Kierkegaard's view of woman and man touch on or are relevant to the discussion of this distinction: Howard P. Kainz, Jr., "The Relationship of Dread to Spirit in Man and Woman, According to Kierkegaard," *The Modern Schoolman* 47 (1969): 1–13; Christine Garside, "Can a Woman be Good in the Same Way as a Man?" *Dialogue* 10 (1971), 534–44; Gregor Malantschuk, "Kierkegaards Syn paa Man og Kvinde," in *Den Kontroversielle Kierkegaard* (Copenhagen: Vintens Forlag, 1976), 30–61; Birgit Bertung, "Har Søren Kierkegaard foregrebet Karen Blixens og Suzanne Brøggers kvindesyn?" *Kierkegaardiana* 13 (1984): 72–83; Peter Thielst, *Søren og Regine: Kierkegaard, Kærlighed og Kønspolitik* (Copenhagen: Gyldendal, 1980), 129–31. Sylviane Agacinski, *Aparté: Conceptions et morts de Søren Kierkegaard* (Paris: Aubier-Flammarion, 1977) also contains some pertinent reflections on Kierkegaard's views of woman and sexual differences (see especially 152–62).

mission and abandonment to others (*Hengivelse*). Lacking a selfish concept of self and not possessing intellectuality in any decisive sense, woman is blessed by nature with an instinctive insight into that to which she ought to give herself. While she can be coy and particularly hard to please, her womanly nature first comes into existence through a metamorphosis or transfiguration of her boundless coyness into feminine devotedness (SUD, 49–50). Substantively, then, woman gains herself by losing herself; that is, she becomes a woman by giving herself in devotedness to others. Only when she gives herself thus is she herself, and only then is she happy. Not intending to demean woman by this characterization, Kierkegaard lauds her sensitive instinctiveness, against which, he says, "the most eminently developed male reflection is as nothing," and he hails her devotedness as a "divine gift and treasure" (SUD, 49). Nevertheless, later on in the main text he states that femininity constitutes a "lower synthesis" than does masculinity, which alone falls within the qualification of spirit (SUD, 67). The reason for this, presumably, is that woman lacks the reflection and internal orientation of man. As indicated in the note, she becomes herself instinctively, by giving herself to someone or something outside herself.

The crucial point in Kierkegaard's characterization of woman is that the devotedness (*Hengivenhed*) which is her nature also constitutes a mode of despair for her. If I read the Danish text correctly on this point, devotedness in itself is not despair, nor is the lack or loss of devotion, as is suggested by the new Princeton translation, which reads: "woman, with genuine femininity, abandons herself, throws herself into that to which she devotes herself. Take this devotion away, then her self is also gone, and her despair is: not to will to be oneself" (SUD, 50). The word "devotion," however, does not appear in the Danish version of the second sentence quoted above; only the demonstrative pronoun "dette" or "this" is used, and grammatically it refers to the "det" or "that" to which woman devotes herself in the previous sentence, not to devotion.[2] The meaning of the text, therefore, is that in abandoning or throwing herself altogether into that to which she devotes herself, woman tends to have a sense of

[2] The Danish text reads: "...Qvinden aegte qvindeligt styrter sig i, styrter sit Selv i Det, til hvilket hun hengiver sig. Tages nu Dette bort, saa er ogsaa hendes Selv borte, og hendes Fortvivlelse: ikke at ville være sig selv" (SKS, 11: 166).

self only in and through the *object* of her devotion. When that object is taken away, her self is also lost. Her despair, consequently, lies in not willing to be herself, that is, in not having any separate or independent self-identity.

Kierkegaard further points out that man, like woman, gives himself (and "he is a poor kind of man who does not do so," Kierkegaard remarks), but his self, unlike hers, is not defined by devotion; rather, it is constituted by a "sober awareness" of his giving that remains behind when he gives (SUD, 50). Thus, he does not gain his substantive or sexual identity by giving, as she does, but already possesses and retains a sense of self apart from it. His despair, therefore, is quite different from hers, as it is characterized by an unwarranted self-assertion rather than self-abandonment. In relation to God, however, sexual distinctions disappear, and it holds true for both woman and man that selfhood is constituted by devotion to God, although Kierkegaard observes that "in most cases the woman actually relates to God only through the man" (SUD, 50).

I. The Structure of the Self and Despair

When these views are considered in relation to the general structure of selfhood and analysis of despair presented in *The Sickness unto Death*, a number of questions, problems, and issues arise. In the classic description of the self with which the work commences, a human being is viewed as becoming a self by relating to oneself as a synthesis of the finite and the infinite, the temporal and the eternal, necessity (limitations) and freedom (possibility). Since the human self is established by a power other than itself, it becomes itself by relating itself not only to itself but also to that power which establishes it, namely God. No distinction is made between man and woman in this description. Since the general term for human beings (*Mennesker*) is used, the basic structure of selfhood is presumably the same for both sexes. From Kierkegaard's note on feminine and masculine despair, however, it would appear that substantive differences nevertheless exist between woman and man within this general structure. Woman's being, we may recall, is centered in relatedness, in self-giving, while man's is characterized by a self-awareness sustained apart from relations to others. Although he gives to others, his self-identity is not constituted by giving. It should be noted too that giving or relating to others is not a constitutive factor in Kierkegaard's general description of a self either, as that includes relating to oneself and to God but says nothing about relations to others as forming an essential ingredient in the structure of the self. Kierkegaard's characterization of man's being thus corresponds more closely to the general description of a self than does that of woman, since it stresses self-consciousness or relating to oneself rather than relating to others.

The absence of a relation to others in Kierkegaard's general description of the self is rather puzzling inasmuch as only a year prior to the appearance of *The Sickness unto Death* he published *Works of Love* (1847), which focuses on relating to others through self-renouncing love and envisions a triadic structure (the lover, the beloved, and love or God as a third party) of existence in love (WL, 124). One must conclude either that Kierkegaard does not follow through with a systematic and integrated development of his thought, or that the insights of the earlier work are somehow implied in the later one. If the last alternative is accepted, it is possible to interpret the general description of a self in *The Sickness unto Death* as incorporating a social dimension in and through the relation to God or as a component in the self-relation, under the rubric of giving the eternal concrete expression in love, faithfulness, and so forth.[3] Still, one wishes that Kierkegaard had addressed the matter of relatedness to others more directly in defining the structure of the self. If self-renouncing love is included in the structure of the self, the resulting character of selfhood would correspond more to the feminine devotedness associated with woman than to the self-conscious masculinity of man.[4] That, however, would contradict Kierkegaard's contention that

[3] John Elrod, in "Kierkegaard on Self and Society," *Kierkegaardiana* 11 (1980): 178–196, also notes that Kierkegaard's pseudonymous works "pay no attention to the ontological and the epistemological roles played by the other in the development of a concept of the self." He sees *Works of Love* and all the later literature as being concerned with that deficiency, so that Kierkegaard discovers in them "a social conception of human beings based on the phenomenon of love" (181). Elrod makes a similar point in his book, *Kierkegaard and Christendom* (Princeton: Princeton University Press, 1981), treating *The Sickness unto Death* as part of the earlier pseudonymous literature even though it actually appears after *Works of Love* (131–32).

[4] An important qualification should be noted here, however. Instead of devoting oneself exclusively to one other, as is the tendency in erotic love relations,

only the latter falls under the qualification of spirit; males, or at least those persons who are predominantly masculine in character, presumably have more spirit or self because they possess more self-consciousness ("the more consciousness, the more self") than do most females (SUD, 29).

Further problems appear in connection with Kierkegaard's claim that devotedness constitutes the proper mode of relating to God. Woman, as represented in the gospels by the woman who was a sinner (Luke 7: 36–50), is presented by Kierkegaard in an edifying discourse as the model of religiousness because of her absolute submission to God.[5] Yet, as Sylviane Agacinski has perceptively pointed out, woman is not considered truly religious, or at least not as religious as man, because she abandons herself by nature, whereas man does not; ironically, therefore, it seems "as if the man were capable of being *more* and *better* a woman than the woman, that is to say, religious."[6] Since the self has its ground in the eternal, which consists essentially in love, and one's chief task in life is to actualize that quality, it would seem too that devotion to the eternal would properly be given expression in and through one's relations to others. That, in fact, is how he sees it commonly working in woman's existence, but not in man's, which sustains a separate, direct relation to God.

When Kierkegaard's distinction between feminine and masculine despair is considered in the context of his analysis of the two types of conscious despair, some incongruence can also be noted in relation to the despair of weakness. As delineated in the text, this form of despair occurs in two basic forms: despair over the earthly (the totality of worldly things) or over something earthly (the particular), and despair of the eternal or over oneself. The first of these is the most common form of despair, Kierkegaard says, and is immediate in nature, containing no (or

---

in Christian self-renouncing love one is devoted to all, bestowing love equally on the basis of our common humanity. One must give up the type of devotion and boundless abandon that characterizes erotic love; such devotion, Kierkegaard maintains in *Works of Love*, is nothing more than a "devoted self-love" (cf. WL, 67–68, 78, 80).

[5] See "The Woman Who Was a Sinner" in WA, 135–44 and 149–60. See also "Prototypes of Piety: The Woman Who Was a Sinner and Mary Magdalene" in the present collection.

[6] Agacinski, 153–155. For a similar interpretation of Kierkegaard, see Garside.

only a measure of) reflection. In it there is no infinite consciousness of the self nor any awareness of despair as being despair. One seemingly suffers as a result of external circumstances, so that one's despair is not at all self-activated from within. With an increase of reflection, this form of despair becomes more internally motivated, and a greater distinction is made between oneself and the environment. As consciousness of the self increases, despair in weakness becomes despair *over* one's weakness, in which one shuts oneself off from the self (*Indesluttethed*) but becomes preoccupied with it, confessing in solitude one's weakness in willing to be that self.

Kierkegaard characterizes despair in weakness as feminine, but in his illustrations of it mostly male examples are used.[7] Indeed, if it is the most common form of despair, one would assume that it is more typical of males than is despair in defiance. Yet the latter is primarily associated with male experience, while despair in weakness is supposed to be representative of women. Kierkegaard's description of the first form of despair in weakness corresponds closely to his characterization of woman as instinctive, that is, immediate and unreflective, in contrast to man's self-consciousness and intellectuality. At the more conscious and intensive stage of despair in weakness, however, the introversion that arises in it concerns the masculine mode (one's relation to oneself) more than the feminine mode (one's relation to others). Thus his characterization of despair in weakness as feminine is not altogether consistent.

As Kierkegaard moves to an analysis of defiant despair, it is seen to presuppose a still higher level of self-consciousness and awareness of despair; but here the feminine mode is projected as the appropriate way to selfhood: "through the aid of the eternal the self has the courage to lose itself in order to win itself" (SUD, 67). Earlier this paradox was seen as characterizing woman's existence, but not man's. Now it is related to masculine or defiant despair in that the self "is unwilling to begin with losing itself but wills to be itself" (SUD, 67). Defiant despair thus results from an individual's unwillingness to adopt a feminine mode of selfhood. In what sense the self is expected to lose itself is not stated in the text.

[7] See SUD, 53, 56, 59, 63–65. However, excellent examples of females who manifest despair in weakness as described in SUD can be found in *Either/Or*, Vol. I, in the characters of Marie Beaumarchais, Donna Elvira, and especially Margaret in Goethe's *Faust* (EO, I: 175–213).

Essentially, however, despair in defiance comes to expression when one seeks to become the self one wants to be instead of the self one is intended to be by God. Its distinctiveness lies in the fact that one will not recognize one's contingent or derived status as a self; rather, the self wishes to create itself, to be its own master. Fundamentally, then, this form of despair has to do with one's relation, or more precisely, misrelation to God and to oneself in the expression of an inappropriate form of self-assertion.

The pathway to selfhood thus includes both masculine and feminine modes of relating, and the possibility of going astray on this path arises in corresponding forms of despair. Feminine despair reflects a lack of self-consciousness (the masculine mode), while masculine despair indicates a need for the feminine mode (submission to that which is the ultimate source of life). While woman's self is lost or misplaced in a finite object of devotion outside herself, man's self is internally misplaced in himself. If being a self were only a matter of relating to oneself, and thus only a question of willing to be oneself, there would be only the possibility of despair in weakness. But since the self is constituted not only by its relation to itself but also to the divine power that establishes it, one can only become a true self through orienting oneself in (devoting or submitting oneself to) that power. Thus the feminine mode is inextricably involved in the process of becoming a self. How much that includes relatedness to other human beings in self-giving remains unclarified in *The Sickness unto Death.* Inasmuch as masculine self-consciousness provides individuality or a sense of separateness and consciousness of the eternal, it also plays an important and indispensable role. These modes and their corresponding forms of despair in woman and man are not altogether integrated in Kierkegaard's thought, but they indicate a complementary wholeness toward which he aims.

II. The Appropriateness of Sexual Distinctions

Although the inclusion of both masculine and feminine categories in Kierkegaard's analysis of despair is preferable to defining selfhood in terms of one sex only, the appropriateness of the sexual distinction itself remains a matter of debate. While definite physiological differences obtain between men and women, it is now widely recognized that psychological characteristics distinguishing them are often culturally rooted rather than biologically determined.[8] Indeed, many apparent differences turn out upon inspection to be mythical, the product of cultural stereotyping, rather than real. Thus far, psychological measurements devised for determining sex differences have shown only four such differences clearly to exist: males exhibit more aggression, better quantitative skill, and greater spatial visualization, while females excel in verbal ability.[9] There is no evidence supporting a gender difference in general intelligence, particularly the frequently held notion that women are less intelligent than men.

Kierkegaard's views on woman and man reflect traditional stereotypes of the sexes, and to the extent that these continue to shape cultural perceptions and patterns of social development, his characterizations are compatible with popular viewpoints in contemporary society. Yet that does not necessarily make them valid or acceptable; indeed, his views on woman's intellectuality and spirituality, or lack thereof, are highly questionable. Insofar as woman's being is typically characterized by devotedness, as Kierkegaard claims, it may well not be an innate feature of her nature, but what she has been culturally conditioned to (generally at the expense of forming her own separate identity). Similarly, the egocentricity that Kierkegaard sees in males could be due to excessive encouragement of the individuation process in them at the expense of developing a sense of relatedness to others.[10] Thus many social critics view the identification of woman and man in terms of conventional sex roles and characteristics as inhibiting their full blossoming as human beings, as these sex roles permit only a one-dimensional development of personality. Instead, these critics point to "psychological androgyny" or cultivation of

---

[8] Janet T. Spence and Robert L. Helmreich, *Masculinity and Femininity: Their Psychological Dimensions, Correlates, and Antecedents* (Austin: University of Texas Press, 1978), 4–10, 121–22; Janet Shibley Hyde and B. G. Rosenberg, *Half the Human Experience* (Lexington: D. C. Heath & Co., 1976), 7 (emphasizing an interaction of biological and environmental factors); Janet Saltzman Chafetz, *Masculine/Feminine or Human: An Overview of the Sociology of Sex Roles* (Ithaca: F. E. Peacock, Publishers, Inc., 1974), 4, 27.

[9] Eleanor Emmons Maccoby and Carol Nagy Jacklin, *The Psychology of Sex Differences* (Stanford: Stanford University Press, 1974), 349–55.

[10] This possibility is suggested also by David Bakan in *The Duality of Human Existence: Isolation and Communion in Western Man* (Boston: Beacon Press, 1966), 107–09.

both "feminine" and "masculine" characteristics in women and men as contributing to higher self-esteem and positive social adjustment.[11]

In substance, Kierkegaard's analysis of feminine and masculine despair is in line with that of proponents of androgyny inasmuch as he diagnoses woman's despair as a lack of masculine self-identity and man's despair as defiance against feminine devotedness and submission in relation to God. Ironically, however, his use of stereotyped characterizations of the sexes contributes to the perpetuation of cultural identifications of women and men in terms of those stereotypes and thus reinforces the very despair which his analysis is designed to counteract. Insofar as Kierkegaard's analysis is congruent with the views of contemporary advocates of androgyny, however, it offers a philosophical perspective that may be helpful in elucidating a common structure of selfhood in terms of the basic components of individuality (masculinity) and relatedness (femininity).[12] In at least two important respects, however, some contemporary

---

[11] J. H. Block, "Conceptions of Sex Roles: Some Cross-cultural and Longitudinal Perspectives," *American Psychologist* 28: (1973) 512–26; June Singer, *Androgyny: Toward a New Theory of Sexuality* (Garden City: Anchor Press/Doubleday, 1977); Barbara Lusk Forisha, *Sex Roles and Personal Awareness* (Morristown: General Learning Press, 1978), 30–36; 87–105; Spence and Helmreich, *Masculinity and Femininity: Their Psychological Dimensions, Correlates, and Antecedents*, 109–110 (with references to others favoring an androgynous or dualistic approach); S. L. Bem, "The Measurement of Psychological Androgyny," *Journal of Consulting and Clinical Psychology* 42 (1974), 155–62; Judith M. Bardwick, *In Transition: How Feminism, Sexual Liberation, and the Search for Self-Fulfillment Have Altered Our Lives* (New York: Holt, Rinehart and Winston, 1979), 153–69, 177–78 (although retaining an appreciation of gender identity and differences).

[12] Although working primarily out of a Whiteheadian perspective, V. C. Saiving, "Androgynous Life: A Feminist Appropriation of Process Thought," in *Feminism and Process Thought*, ed. Sheila Greeve Davaney (New York: The Edwin Mellen Press, 1981), 11–31, seeks to develop a general model in which both individuality and relatedness are included. In an earlier, ground-breaking article, "The Human Situation: A Feminine View," published in *The Journal of Religion* (April, 1960) and reprinted in , *Womanspirit Rising*, ed. Carol P. Christ and Judith Plaskow (New York: Harper & Row, 1979), 25–42, Saiving analyzes masculine and feminine experience in a manner very similar to Kierkegaard, although without specific reference to his analysis of despair. Kierkegaard's analysis is explicitly discussed and appropriated in a feminist context in Wanda

social theorists differ from Kierkegaard. In contrast to his interpretation of despair as being essentially internally motivated or self-activated, they emphasize the need for, and impact of, change in the external structures of society so as to provide better opportunity for fuller personality development.[13] Second, whereas Kierkegaard analyzes masculine despair only in terms of man's relation to the divine, they point to man's need to develop more receptivity, intimacy, commitment, and giving in relatedness to other human beings, especially in relation to woman.[14]

It should be noted, too, that there is considerable disagreement among women concerning the notion of androgyny and its appropriateness for women's development. While some emphasize the need for women to be self-assertive and independent like men, others acknowledge and seek to preserve a distinctive character in woman. Labeling androgyny as a patriarchal construct that results in a pseudo-integrity for women, the radical feminist philosopher Mary Daly thinks woman can create a sense of selfhood that is not male-defined and will manifest genuine differences from man, not those of traditionally defined femininity, but of a kind yet to be determined by spinning "threads of connectedness" with her sisters.[15] Closer in line with Kierkegaard's asso-

---

Warren Berry, "Images of Sin and Salvation in Feminist Theology," *Anglican Theological Review* 60 (1978): 25–54. See also my discussion of individuality and relatedness in "Women in Love," *Soundings* 65 (1982): 352–68.

[13] Hyde and Rosenberg, *Half the Human Experience*, 275–78; Bardwick, 170–82. Critical of the dualistic origin of the term "androgyny" but endorsing the notion of wholeness associated with it, Rosemary Ruether, in *New Woman, New Earth: Sexist Ideologies and Human Liberation* (New York: Seabury Press, 1975), emphasizes the need for social, economic, and political change (24–31, 204–211). See also Maccoby and Jacklin, 374; Dorothy Dinnerstein, *The Mermaid and the Minotaur: Sexual Arrangements and Human Malaise* (New York: Harper & Row, 1976).

[14] Bardwick, *In Transition* 97–99, 125–29; Eugene C. Bianchi and Rosemary R. Ruether, *From Machismo to Mutuality* (New York: Paulist Press, 1976) 84–85, 96, 120; Nancy Chodorow, *The Reproduction of Mothering* (Berkeley: University of California Press, 1978), 218.

[15] Mary Daly, *Gyn/Ecology: The Metaethics of Radical Feminism* (Boston: Beacon Press, 1978), xiii, 382, 387. To Daly androgyny conveys an image of "something like John Travolta and Farrah Fawcett-Majors scotch-taped together" (xi). Naomi Goldenberg, in *Changing of the Gods: Feminism and the End of Traditional Religions* (Boston: Beacon Press, 1979), finds some value in the fig-

ciation of femininity with devotion, psychologist Carol Gilligan identifies "a different voice" of women evident from the centrality of attachment and care for others in their lives and from the importance of relationships for the formation of their identity.[16] Claiming that "we know ourselves as separate only insofar as we live in connection with others," she finds in women's development a fusion of separation and attachment, identity and intimacy.[17] If that is true, Gilligan provides an important corrective to Kierkegaard in pointing to an interdependence of self-identity and relatedness in women.

Although Kierkegaard stresses devotion to others in woman's being, he views it as being a potential mode of despair for her in that she tends to lose herself in the object of her devotion. Certainly that can and often does happen, but the possibility of despair does not negate the importance of relatedness in forming self-identity. It is the integral intertwining of these two components of selfhood that Kierkegaard does not sufficiently recognize and incorporate in his analysis. He rightly sees a need for both separateness and relatedness, but for him they appear to be separate categories, so that he fails to perceive the actual interconnection between them. Although Gilligan finds such an interconnection typifying woman's development, this possibility can be extended to males, for with them also identity and relatedness are undoubtedly connected, even if perhaps in a somewhat different way. Thus, without negating sexual differences, one can ultimately look beyond them to a common model of selfhood not defined by gender. Since Kierkegaard carries out much of his analysis of selfhood and despair without regard to the sexes and in other works emphasizes our common humanity, the thrust of his analysis is in this direction.

---

ure of androgyny if it is used to inspire the imagining of a plurality of sexual styles, but she envisions a distinctly feminine form of religion and identity of women in the return to Goddess worship (78–81).

[16] Carol Gilligan, *In a Different Voice: Psychological Theory and Women's Development* (Cambridge: Harvard University Press, 1982). See also Saiving, "The Human Situation: A Feminine View."

[17] Gilligan, 63, 156, 159, 164. See also Christine Downing, *The Goddess: Mythological Images of the Feminine* (New York: Crossroad, 1981), which envisions for woman an "Aphroditic consciousness" that is a "loving consciousness" and a "being conscious in relationship" (202–07).

How, then, shall we finally assess Kierkegaard's use of sexual categories in the analysis of human despair? While a distinction between the forms of despair can be made without them, they enable Kierkegaard to bring more concreteness and specificity into his analysis as well as to account for what he perceives as differences between the sexes in the experience of despair. Insofar as it is historically true that the lives of males and females have been characterized by patterns traditionally associated with masculinity and femininity, he provides an astute analysis of the connection between the forms of despair and these modes of sexual identity. In particular, his linking of despair with submissive self-abandonment on the part of women and defiant self-assertiveness by men illumines some of the dangers and limitations of traditional feminine and masculine modes. His pointing in the direction of androgyny within a common structure of selfhood for the sexes provides a conceptual basis for a fuller development of individuality and relatedness in both sexes. We can further appreciate the depth to which Kierkegaard's analysis goes in showing a fundamental connection of despair in woman and man with a misrelation to the divine. The idea of a relation to God coupling a high level of self-consciousness with devotion or self-giving establishes an ultimate matrix within which to affirm both individuality and relatedness in woman and man.

Despite these positive features, there are several aspects of Kierkegaard's analysis that remain unsatisfactory. First, it perpetuates stereotyped views of woman and man that are in some cases erroneous or unsubstantiated, in others perhaps historically accurate but largely the product of cultural conditioning unfavorable to the full development of both sexes. Second, it does not take sufficient account of the influence of external factors in occasioning and potentially overcoming despair. On a more theoretical level, his analysis fails to incorporate clearly or adequately relations to others besides God in the general description of a self and in particular as an essential dimension of male self-identity. Furthermore, it does not recognize the integral interdependence of individuality and relatedness to others in the formation of the self, particularly in female development. Finally, we may wonder whether feminine devotedness provides an appropriate model for the relation to God inasmuch as it traditionally involves a form of submissiveness that is often made the basis for male dominance over women. Indeed, Kierkegaard himself points to a less hierarchical model for the divine-human relation, and thus also for human relations, in *Philosophical Fragments*, where in the parable of the King and a Maiden (PF, 26–35), the two are made equal in love.

6

IF THE LILY COULD SPEAK: ON THE CONTENTMENT AND GLORY OF BEING HUMAN*

Taking Matthew 6: 24–34 as their text, the three discourses that make up Part Two of *Upbuilding Discourses in Various Spirits* (1847), "What We Learn from the Lilies in the Field and from the Birds of the Air," focus on the lessons these two forms of nature teach us in their role as "divinely appointed teachers" of humanity (UDVS, 157). Kierkegaard gives further consideration to the lilies and the birds in the seven discourses that make up Part One of *Christian Discourses* (1848) and in *The Lily in the Field and the Bird of the Air: Three Devotional Discourses* (1849), making them his favorite metaphors of human beings and instruments for our instruction (CD, 13–91; WA, 1–45).

Although Kierkegaard allots the lilies and the birds approximately equal consideration in Part Two of *Upbuilding Discourses in Various Spirits* and in the devotional discourses of 1849 (whereas the birds are favored in *Christian Discourses*), the present essay places its primary focus on the lilies in the field and what they would say to us as teachers if they were able to speak as humans do.[1] My reasons for privileging the lilies are twofold. First, in *Upbuilding Discourses in Various Spirits* Kierkegaard attaches gender associations to the lilies and the birds, correlating the lilies with the feminine and "woman's work" and the birds with the masculine and "man's work" in such a way as to make the figure of the lily in particular somewhat problematic as a metaphor and teacher for women (UDVS, 163). Since Kierkegaard's views on women in some of his other

---

*Reprinted by permission from *International Kierkegaard Commentary: Upbuilding Discourses in Various Spirits*, Vol. 15, ed. Robert L. Perkins (Macon: Mercer University Press, 2005), 129–52.

[1] In the first discourse on the lilies and the birds from 1849 Kierkegaard states: "Surely it is speech that distinguishes humanity above the animal and then, if you like, far above the lily" (WA, 10).

writings have been assessed by feminist interpreters, including myself, as being ambivalent at best and misogynist at worst, it is important to examine the gender associations in this text, especially those attached to the lily, in order to determine what their function and import are for the edification of women, if not for men also, in this work.[2] Second, despite the stereotyped and (as we shall see) troubling gender associations attached to these figures, the discourses of Part Two contain an upbuilding insight that is equally important for both sexes to grasp and to appropriate in light of the current emphasis on diversity or differences in contemporary society and the inevitable (favorable or unfavorable) comparisons they tempt us to make between ourselves and others. Far from supporting the individualism for which Kierkegaard (famously or perhaps infamously) is credited with championing, he contends in these discourses that diversity and comparison actually make us so discontented with ourselves as individuals that we forget what it means to be a human being. To make this point, Kierkegaard utilizes both the lilies and the birds, but especially the lily, to teach us contentment with and the glory of our common humanity, thus providing a second rationale for privileging the lily in the present essay.

To fully appreciate the incongruity of using such lowly figures as lilies and birds to remind us of what it means to be human beings, we shall begin with a look at the design of *Upbuilding Discourses in Various Spirits* as a whole and of Part Two in particular in order to determine where and how they fit into the schema of existence spheres outlined by Johannes Climacus in *Concluding Unscientific Postscript.* Such a comparison will help us not only to understand the fundamentally "humorous" character of the discourses of Part Two but also to locate that humor within Climacus' scale of existence spheres so as more clearly to discern the religiously upbuilding role these discourses play in the book as a whole.

---

[2] For a range of feminist critiques of Kierkegaard's view of women, see *Feminist Interpretations of Søren Kierkegaard*, ed. Céline Léon and Sylvia Walsh (University Park: The Pennsylvania State University Press, 1997). See also my essay, "Issues That Divide: Interpreting Kierkegaard on Woman and Gender" in the present collection.

I. Climacus' Schema of Existence Spheres and the Design of *Upbuilding Discourses in Various Spirits*

The three parts of *Upbuilding Discourses in Various Spirits* are related to one another in a manner that recalls the distinctions between the existence-spheres delineated in *Concluding Unscientific Postscript.* In that book the pseudonymous author, Johannes Climacus, identifies three existence-spheres—the aesthetic, the ethical, and the religious—and adds two *confinia* or border territories between them: irony and humor, with irony comprising the *confinium* between the aesthetic and the ethical, and humor the *confinium* between the ethical and the religious (CUP, I: 501–02). This schema is later expanded and further clarified by a note in the text which says:

> The spheres are related as follows: immediacy; finite common sense; irony; ethics with irony as its incognito; humor; religiousness with humor as its incognito—and then, finally, the essentially Christian, distinguished by the paradoxical accentuation of existence, by the paradox, by the break with immanence, and by the absurd. Therefore, religiousness with humor as its incognito is still not Christian religiousness. Even though this also is hidden inwardness, it relates itself to the paradox. Certainly humor is also involved in paradoxes, but it still continually constricts itself within immanence, and it continually seems to be aware of something else—hence the jest. (CUP, I: 531–32, slightly amended[3])

Correspondingly, Kierkegaard suggests in a journal entry from 1847 that the three parts of *Upbuilding Discourses in Various Spirits* are related to one another as follows: Part One ("An Occasional Discourse") is essentially ethical-ironic; Part Two (the three discourses on the lilies and the birds) is humorous; and Part Three ("The Gospel of Sufferings," subtitled "Christian Discourses"), while not explicitly designated as such in the journal entry, is obviously religious and more specifically Christian in design (JP, 5: 5975). Within this ethical-ironic / humorous / Christian-

[3] The Hong translation of *Concluding Unscientific Postscript* places commas after immediacy and irony in the passage quoted above, but the Danish edition of the text uses semi-colons (SKS, 7: 483). Consequently, I have amended the quotation to conform to the Danish version of the text.

religious structure of the book as a whole, Kierkegaard further distinguishes between the discourses of Part Two in terms of the basic triadic division of the existence-spheres in the authorship: "The three discourses [on the lilies and the birds] are again related to one another aesthetically, ethically, religiously" (JP, 5: 5975; cf. also JP, 5: 5970).[4]

---

[4] The design of the book as a whole and of Part Two in particular has frequently been misconstrued by scholars. In *Kierkegaard*, Vol. 2 (New York: Harper & Brothers, 1962), Walter Lowrie suggests that the three parts of the book as a whole respectively represent the aesthetic, ethical, and religious spheres; but, recognizing the obvious ethical content of Part One, he does not quite know how to indicate its "aesthetic" character except by pointing to a comment by Kierkegaard that the first part has a comical coloring which leads one to laugh ironically (370–71). Lowrie correctly notes that Part Two is humorous in character but incorrectly identifies the parable of the troubled lily in Part Two as occurring in Part Three (372). Jeremy D. B. Walker, in *To Will One Thing: Reflections on Kierkegaard's 'Purity of Heart'* (Montreal: McGill-Queen's University Press, 1972) also incorrectly characterizes "Purity of Heart" as an aesthetic work and then proceeds to consider its *ethical* insights in a Kantian framework (5). George E. and George B. Arbaugh, in *Kierkegaard's Authorship* (London: George Allen & Unwin Ltd., 1968) reverse the order so as to label Part One correctly as ethical, but they err in designating Part Two as aesthetic. As noted above, only the first discourse in Part Two is aesthetic, but in what sense it is to be understood as aesthetic is yet to be determined. Certainly it is not aesthetic by virtue of being "humorous," since that category, according to *Concluding Unscientific Postscript*, applies to the *confinium* between the ethical and the religious spheres and to the presence of humor as an incognito within the religious sphere of immanence, and not to the aesthetic sphere. Noting the triadic structure of Part Two in terms of the three existence spheres but not the ethical-ironic / humorous / Christian-religious design of the book as a whole, Gregor Malantschuk, in *Kierkegaard's Thought*, ed. and trans. Howard V. Hong and Edna H. Hong (Princeton: Princeton University Press, 1971) views Part Two as "an expression of Kierkegaard's law of repetition, according to which all the preceding levels are seen in the light of that which the person has most recently attained" (320). In Malantschuk's view, the first discourse "repeats the edifying within the aesthetic sphere from the new perspective," but he does not orient this process of repetition within the overarching humorous character of Part Two, which in my view needs to be taken into account in order to understand the upbuilding character of the three discourses of Part Two as a whole and of the first discourse in particular since it is regarded by Kierkegaard as being aesthetic in design.

Viewed in relation to the expanded schema of existence spheres outlined in *Concluding Unscientific Postscript*, the three parts of *Upbuilding Discourses in Various Spirits* fit structurally within that framework, and the upbuilding character or intent of the book as a whole is made apparent by the designation of its three parts as falling within the realm of the ethical-religious in general. What is not so immediately clear, however, is the sense in which the discourses of Part Two may be understood as being humorous in character and whether they should be regarded as falling within the *confinium* of humor between the ethical and the religious or as an expression of humor as an incognito within the religious sphere. As Climacus describes the *confinium* of humor, its function is to evoke contradiction by setting the God-idea into conjunction with something else without the humorist actually being passionately related to that idea (CUP, I: 505). But in "A Glance at Danish Literature," in his review of "Guilty?" / "Not Guilty?" in *Stages on Life's Way*, Climacus also characterizes humor as constituting "the final *terminus a quo* in relation to the Christian-religious" and "the last stage in existence-inwardness before faith" which "terminates immanence within immanence" (CUP, I: 291; cf. also 271–72). For him, therefore, humor serves as a *confinium* or boundary category in two places, both between the ethical and the religious (broadly conceived as incorporating both immanent religiousness and Christianity) and between immanent religiousness (Religiousness A) and Christianity (Religiousness B).[5] Moreover, humor in the second instance, that is, as the incognito of immanent religiousness, possesses a depth of seriousness or earnestness that is lacking in humor as a *confinium* between the ethical and the religious. In the latter instance the humorist jestingly revokes the essentiality or decisiveness of suffering in existence, opting instead to take refuge in the eternal by way of recollection rather than through repetition or existential striving (CUP, I: 242, 447). In contrast to this non-serious expression of humor, Climacus identifies another form of jesting which he calls "holy jest" that serves as the incognito or sign of an utmost earnestness toward existence in the

[5] On the role of humor in *Concluding Unscientific Postscript*, see also my book, *Living Poetically: Kierkegaard's Existential Aesthetics* (University Park: The Pennsylvania State University Press, 1994), 212–17, together with other works cited therein. One should add to this list the more recent work by John Lippitt, *Humor and Irony in Kierkegaard's Thought* (New York: St. Martin's Press, 2000).

religious sphere (CUP, I: 462, 471–72). In this form of jesting, the religious individual appears outwardly to be a humorist but inwardly is not, inasmuch as he or she is existentially committed to the religious ideal and uses humor to give indirect expression to this religious pathos.

Considered in light of these criteria, the designation of "humorous" as a characterization of Part Two in *Upbuilding Discourses in Various Spirits* is somewhat ambiguous. On the one hand, it would appear to be an indication of the first form of humor since in Climacus' schema of the existence spheres that form of humor immediately follows upon the ethical-ironic, or the ethical with irony as its incognito, which according to Kierkegaard's journal entry constitutes the design of Part One of *Upbuilding Discourses in Various Spirits*. On the other hand, Part Two seems more appropriately to be an example of the second form of humor, or humor that is the incognito of religiousness, since what follows in Part Three is explicitly Christian in design and that form of humor serves as the *terminus a quo* of Christian religiousness. Moreover, in another journal entry concerning the discourses of Part Two, Kierkegaard suggests that while "[s]ome may find that these discourses lack earnestness," such a judgment, in his opinion, only indicates a very shallow and misguided understanding of what earnestness is, associating it with making financial contributions, thinking up public works, and starting a new collection campaign, "all of which may be very praiseworthy but in the strictest sense is not earnestness" (JP, 5: 5976). According to Kierkegaard's own assessment, then, the discourses of Part Two definitely should be regarded as serious or earnest in intent. Within Climacus' schema they would thus clearly qualify as an instance of religiousness with humor as an incognito rather than as humor *per se*. That this assessment is the correct one will be borne out, I think, by an examination of the discourses themselves, to which we shall turn in due course.

First, however, it should be pointed out that Kierkegaard also provides a much simpler explanation of the humorous character of Part Two than the one determined by comparing it with Climacus' scale of existence spheres. In the first journal entry cited above, he says it is the reversal of the normal relation between the teacher and the learner that provides the basis of the humor and incongruity of Part Two:

> to learn means that the learner relates himself to the teacher as to his more ideal *genus proximum* [nearest genus]. As soon as

> the teacher takes a lower position within the very same genus and stands below the learner, the situation becomes humorous. For example, to learn from a child or from a dolt, for the child or the dolt can only humorously be called the teacher.
>
> But the situation becomes even more humorous when the teacher and the learner do not have even the same genus in common but in qualitative heterogeneity are related inversely to one another. This is the definitely humorous relation. The lilies and the birds. (JP, 5: 5975)

Fundamentally, then, it is the incongruity of human beings being taught by creatures so qualitatively heterogeneous to themselves as the lilies and the birds that gives the discourses of Part Two their immediately humorous character. But knowing where they stand structurally in relation to the other parts of the book and on the broader scale of existence spheres also helps us to discern the immanently religious and universally human context within which that humor is expressed and used for upbuilding purposes.

Still to be determined with regard to matters of design is the way in which the three discourses of Part Two respectively reflect the basic triadic structure of the existence spheres. Clearly, the fact that the discourses are humorous in character does not mean that any or all of them fall within the aesthetic sphere as such. As we have seen from Climacus' schema, humor as an existential standpoint belongs on a higher plane than the aesthetic, even though it may be used for aesthetic purposes. Neither is it the immediacy of the lilies and the birds that gives the first discourse its aesthetic flavor, since all three discourses employ these innocent creatures of nature as teachers of humanity. Rather, in line with Gregor Malantschuk's analysis of the discourses, the immanently religious (with humor as an incognito) character of Part Two as a whole suggests that the aesthetic is revisited and addressed in the first discourse from a higher standpoint that is carried forward and deepened in the ethical and religious discourses that follow.[6] A brief overview of the discourses will show how this is so.

True to the educational pedagogy employed from the beginning of his authorship, Kierkegaard starts where he most often finds his readers,

[6] See note 4 above.

which is in the aesthetic realm. Accordingly, in the first discourse he addresses "the worried person" who is in distress about some aspect of life or livelihood, and he tries to persuade this person to pay close attention to the lilies and the birds, who neither spin nor toil, as a means of coming to learn something about him- or herself as an individual human being (UDVS, 160–62). The second discourse, anchored in the ethical by virtue of its identification of the spiritual nature of human beings and the perfection of their humanity through work, seeks to create a "godly diversion" whereby the worried person may find something other than his or her worry to think about, namely how glorious it is to be a human being created in the image of God (UDVS, 184–85). The third discourse employs the "rigorous words of earnestness" in the biblical text ("No one can serve two masters") to impress upon the worried person the necessity of choosing to serve God rather than the world, through which choice he or she may find comfort in the promise of blessed happiness in being human, which is distinguished from nature by the determinant of freedom (UDVS, 204, 206, 212).[7] The three discourses thus reflect an overarching ethical-religious orientation in their progress and design even as they individually represent respectively the aesthetic, ethical, and religious spheres in their focus and content.

II. Gender Associations: Woman's Adornment vs. Man's Work

It is in the first and second discourses of Part Two that Kierkegaard introduces gender associations between the lilies and women, on the one hand, and between the birds and men, on the other, and uses these creatures as metaphors of human beings to address the problems of diversity and comparison in human existence. Having taken account of the humorous and aesthetic / ethical / religious design of Part Two within the

[7] The third discourse thus poses an either / or between the ethical-religious and the aesthetic that is mirrored in other writings of Kierkegaard. See, for example, the excellent discussion of the relation and complexity of the stages of existence in *Either/Or*, *Concluding Unscientific Postscript*, *Stages on Life's Way* and *Three Discourses on Imagined Occasions* in Andrew Burgess, "The Relation of Kierkegaard's *Stages on Life's Way* to *Three Discourses on Imagined Occasions*," in *International Kierkegaard Commentary: Stages on Life's Way,* Vol. 11, ed. Robert L. Perkins (Macon: Mercer University Press, 2000), 261–85.

overall ethical-ironic / humorous / Christian-religious structure of *Upbuilding Discourses_in Various Spirits* as a whole, we are now in a position to consider the specific nature of these gender associations and their significance for discerning the upbuilding insights to be learned from the lilies and the birds, especially the lily, on this occasion.

In the opening discourse of Part Two Kierkegaard invites the worried person to look first at the lilies in the field. It is not "the rare plants that a gardener raises in his garden and that are looked at by experts" but rather the common lilies in the field who grow "in profuse, multi-colored abundance, the one just as fine as the other" to which the worried person is asked to give attention (UDVS, 162–63). The worried person is thus immediately directed away from the extraordinary or different specimen of lily, whose cultivation requires a great deal of work on the part of a gardener, to the common lilies that share an essential, impartial equality with one another (UDVS, 166). Unlike the rare specimen, the lilies in the field are unattended, seemingly "abandoned, unappreciated, disregarded, without human solicitude" (perhaps like the worried person him- or herself), and do not work or spin, yet they grow and flourish in loveliness (UDVS, 162–63).

As Kierkegaard interprets the biblical text upon which these discourses are based, in referring to the lilies as neither working nor spinning the text is making an allusion to "woman's work" inasmuch as "[t]he woman stays in the house, does not go out to seek the necessities of life; she stays at home, sews and spins, tries to keep everything as neat as possible: her daily occupation, her diligent labor, is most closely associated with adornment" (UDVS, 163). Like a woman, the lily also "stays at home, does not leave the place," but unlike woman "it does not work, it does not spin—it only adorns itself or, more correctly, it is adorned" (UDVS, 163). Woman's place, then, is in the private realm of the household, and within that realm her labor or "work" is primarily concerned with adornment. But that is precisely what constitutes her essential likeness to the lily. For although the lily, unlike woman, is without worry, if it were to have one, its worry, like that of woman, "might femininely be about whether it was truly lovely and was adorned," Kierkegaard says (UDVS, 164).

Corresponding to this association of the lilies with femininity and woman's work, the biblical text makes a parallel allusion to "man's work," Kierkegaard suggests, when it refers to the birds as not sowing, reaping, or gathering into barns (UDVS, 163). Although the birds, like the lilies, do not worry, their worry, were they to have one, would be like that of men, "about livelihood" or making a living, since they must fly far and wide to find food, just as man's work is "to support himself and his family" by going out into the world to earn a living (UDVS, 163–64, 171, 197). Unlike the lilies and women, whose place is at home in the private realm, the sphere of the birds and men is the public realm, with the crucial difference between the two parties in the latter realm being that the birds are innocent and carefree while men, being spiritual in nature and thus characterized by consciousness, have the capacity to worry about making a living. This capacity to worry nevertheless constitutes a perfection in men (even though, like the birds, they should not worry) because "[t]o work is a human being's perfection" and is that activity by which they come to resemble God as co-workers with the divine (UDVS, 192–93, 196–199).

Although we may applaud Kierkegaard's appreciation of the equality, beauty, and spontaneity of the lilies in his interpretation of the biblical text, the gender allusions he also finds in it are troubling for many modern readers, especially women. For in suggesting that the biblical text itself intends these associations, Kierkegaard invests them with a divine authorization that reinforces and helps to perpetuate gender stereotypes which are detrimental to the upbuilding and advancement of women, if not for men also.[8] The identification of woman's place as being in the home and her "work" as consisting chiefly in adornment locks her out of the public sphere where real work takes place. Since for Kierkegaard work has to do essentially with making a living, only men really work ("women's work" is thus a misnomer) and consequently only men have the capacity to perfect themselves as human beings through work. Nothing is said in the discourses about women perfecting themselves as human beings through adornment. On the contrary, the suggestion that adornment is (and should be) their chief occupation in life is demeaning of women, intimating that they are self-centered, vain, and pre-occupied

[8] On the negative consequences of traditional gender stereotypes for males, see Dorothy Dinnerstein, *The Mermaid and the Minotaur: Sexual Arrangements and Human Malaise* (New York: Harper & Row, 1976) and Nancy Chodorow, *The Reproduction of Mothering: Psychoanalysis and the Sociology of Gender* (Berkeley: University of California Press, 1978).

with making themselves beautiful and well-clothed, even though Kierkegaard apparently intends to be complimentary rather than derogatory in his description of women's work. Moreover, his characterization contains an element of classism as well as sexism inasmuch as only women of the upper classes, certainly not peasant women and urban household servants, would have the leisure to devote most of their time and effort to sewing and personal adornment.

When the logic implied in the gender associations employed in these discourses is followed through, it becomes apparent that they are problematic with respect to what they suggest about women. Yet Kierkegaard identifies the lilies in the field not only with the feminine and women but also with the human being as such, so that they function as a metaphor for humanity as well. He suggests that when the worried person becomes calm enough to examine a lily closely (any will do, since all are essentially the same), that person will come to wonder more and more at the beauty and ingenious formation of the lily, which is a product of divine artistry rather than human craftsmanship and thus lacks the defects and imperfections characteristic of the latter (UDVS, 164). The lily stands there in all its natural loveliness and does not speak, but if it could, Kierkegaard muses, what would it say to the worried person? To this question he ventures the following answer:

> Suppose the lily could speak—would it not say to the worried one, 'Why are you so filled with wonder at me; should it not be just as glorious to be a human being; should it not hold true that all of Solomon's glory is nothing in comparison with what every human being is by being human, so that in order to be the most glorious thing he is and to be conscious of this Solomon must strip off all his glory and just be a human being! Should not what holds of poor me hold true of being a human being, who, after all, is creation's wonderwork!' (UDVS, 165)

What holds true of the lily also obtains for a human being, so that, were the silent lily to speak, which it does not, it is as if the human being is speaking to and about him- or herself and learning something about what it means to be a human being. Like the lily, and in exactly the same sense, the worried person—despite the worries and without working and spinning or any merit on his or her part—is more glorious in his or her bare humanity than all the glory of Solomon, and thus what he or she learns so humorously or incongruously from the lily is contentment with simply being human (UDVS, 165). Lamentably, however, that knowledge and contentment are easily lost or forgotten because of the diversity of human beings and the many comparisons made between them in the world. Thus, employing the lily once again as a metaphor for the human being, but this time imagining it in a state of worry rather than innocence, Kierkegaard constructs a little parable about the worried lily, together with one also about the worried bird, to illustrate for the worried person the potentially destructive effects associated with these factors in human life.

III. The Dangers of Diversity and Comparison: The Parables of the Worried Lily and the Worried Bird

Although the lilies in the field are regarded impartially without making any distinctions among them, the worried person is invited to suppose that there is diversity among lilies, just as there is among human beings. Indeed, diversity is a fact of life that cannot be denied, but in Kierkegaard's judgment it should not be regarded as supreme, that is, as something higher than our common humanity, nor as something to worry about (UDVS, 166–67, 170–71). On the contrary, as he sees it, worry is generated precisely by making too much of diversities through the introduction of comparisons between individuals, causing us to forget that we are human beings and leading us in despair to regard ourselves as being so different from others that we even regard ourselves as "different from what it is to be human" (UDVS, 169).

To make this point, Kierkegaard uses a parable about "the worried lily" (UDVS, 167–69). Briefly recounted, the parable goes like this: A carefree lily growing by a brook in an isolated spot in the country is visited one day by a capricious and naughty bird. The bird disturbs the lily's innocent bliss by chattily comparing it unfavorably to some gorgeous lilies growing in another place, making the lily in the field feel humiliated, inferior, insignificant, and hardly even a lily. The poor lily then becomes very unhappy with its condition in life and begins to wish that it could become a Crown Imperial, which according to the bird is regarded as the most beautiful lily and thus the envy of all other lilies. Offering to help the poor lily realize this seemingly not unreasonable or impossible desire (for after all the lily does not wish to become what it is not—a bird, for example—but only the most beautiful within its own species), the bird plucks the lily from the ground and flies with it to the place where the gorgeous lilies grow, in the hope that the change of place and new surroundings would enable the lily to become a gorgeous lily like the others, perhaps even a Crown Imperial. But alas, the worried lily withers and dies on the way.

The function of parables, it is generally acknowledged, is to illustrate a single point through the use of metaphors. In this instance, however, the parable of the worried lily can be interpreted metaphorically on two different levels, both in terms of the gender associations attached to the lilies and the birds and as a symbol of our common humanity. When the story is read on the first level, keeping in mind the gender associations of the lily with the woman and the bird with the man, it reveals a sad tale of male seduction, humiliation, and destruction of the female. Indeed, in offering his own explanation of the symbolism of the parable to the reader, Kierkegaard explicitly calls the naughty bird a "seducer" or representative of the seductive in human beings (UDVS, 169). Not only does the bird / man humiliate the poor lily / woman by comparing it / her unfavorably to other lilies / women on the all important feminine quality of beauty, it / she is made to feel imprisoned and bound by a lack of freedom through the bird's / man's boasting of its / his freedom to fly capriciously from place to place (UDVS, 167–68). The parable thus has the earmarks of a modern tale of male misogyny (à la "The Seducer's Diary"), but Kierkegaard clearly does not condone the malicious behavior of the bird / male in the story. On the contrary, the bird / man is called naughty because it / he does not put itself / himself in the lily's place, delighting in her loveliness and innocence instead of putting her down, and because it / he is not altogether truthful in its / his chatter about the other lilies / women, in comparison to which the poor lily / woman is made to feel like nothing (UDVS, 167). The bird / man thus is held responsible for seducing and inciting the lily / woman to worry, for making false and demeaning comparisons between it / her and other lilies / women, and ultimately for causing its / her demise.

To the extent that the parable exposes and condemns the maltreatment of women by men, the false concern over feminine beauty incited in women by men, and the potentially destructive consequences of worry over comparisons with other women for female self-identity and contentment, it contains a powerfully illuminating insight and warning for women in particular, but also for men in its depiction of male seduction of women as a pathology of their sex.[9] Nevertheless, the message for female readers that comes out of the parable interpreted at this level is not entirely edifying, inasmuch as it suggests that the lily / woman should be content with the place (in the home) to which it / she is assigned in life (UDVS, 169–70; cf. also 211). Moreover, in identifying woman's worry (although falsely imposed on her by the male) with concern over her degree of beauty vis-à-vis other women, the parable reinforces the gender stereotypes it assumes rather than challenging them for the greater edification of both women and men.

At the second level of interpretation, which is the one explicitly supplied and supported by Kierkegaard in the discourses, the worried lily and the naughty bird function as metaphors for the human being and "the restless mentality of comparison" respectively (UDVS, 169). Here the lily is not simply a metaphor for woman but stands for both woman and man in the beauty of their common humanity, while the bird is representative of the poetic and seductive tendency in human beings to make more of their diversities than is warranted by engaging in inhuman comparisons (UDVS, 169). By virtue of its capriciousness or ability to roam far and wide, the bird gains a knowledge of diversity, which is then falsely declared to be supreme (UDVS, 169). This elevation of diversity to a position of supremacy is deemed to be false by Kierkegaard because, as he sees it, "to be a human being is not lower than the diversities but is raised above them" (UDVS, 171). It is precisely when this status is reversed, with diversity being regarded as higher than our common humanity, that worry about diversity is generated through the making of comparisons, with the result that "the worried person finally goes so far that because of diversity he forgets that he is a human being, in despair regards himself as so different from other people that he even regards himself as different from what it is to be human" (UDVS, 169, 182). "All *worldly* worry," Kierkegaard claims, "has its basis in a person's unwillingness to be contented with being a human being, in his worried craving for distinction by way of comparison" (UDVS, 171). Kierkegaard does not go so far as to say that all earthly and temporal worry is "an invention

[9] On the pathology of male seduction of women in Kierkegaard's thought, see my essay, "Veni, Vidi, Vici: Immediacy and Reflection as Gendered Categories in Kierkegaard's Thought," in the present collection.

of comparison," since he admits that there are some circumstances, such as real need for food and clothing, in which that would not be the case, but certainly he thinks it is implicated "in countless ways," especially with regard to worry about making a living (UDVS, 171).

To show how comparison "lies at the root of the worry about making a living," Kierkegaard introduces a second parable parallel to that of the worried lily, focusing this time on the worried bird, more precisely a wood-dove, as a metaphor for the human being (UDVS, 174–77, 179). In this parable the wild wood-dove loses its carefree peace of mind as a result of engaging in conversation with some tame doves in the area.[10] Preening themselves in self-satisfaction and confidence that they are secure and well provided for by the rich farmer whose barn they inhabit, the tame doves provoke in the wood-dove an awareness of and anxiety over the uncertainty or lack of security with regard to making a living, which in the past it had always managed to do without any concern for the future. The wood-dove now becomes miserable over its insecurity and envious of the tame birds, lamenting to itself: "why did I become a poor wood-dove and not one of the wealthy doves!" (UDVS, 175). Seeking to change its situation so as to become a secure and wealthy bird like the tame doves, the wood-dove joins them on the farmer's roof, only to become trapped in the dovecote and killed the next day, thereby being "delivered from its worry about getting a living," Kierkegaard adds ironically (UDVS, 176).

Unlike the lily, which is seduced by the bird, the wood-dove is trapped by itself, both psychologically in worry and physically in the dovecote, and thus brings about its own demise as a result of becoming discontented with its given situation in life (UDVS, 176, 178). Initially, however, the wood-dove, like the lily, becomes worried as a result of comparing itself to others of its own species, contrasting its poor and insecure status to their seemingly rich and secure position. But whereas the worried lily / human being only compares itself to other lilies / humans,

[10] Earlier in the discourse Kierkegaard states that "[a] misapprehension, after all, stems from speech, more specifically from a comparison that is implicit in talking, especially in conversation" (UDVS, 160–61). Consequently, to avoid comparison, the worried person is encouraged to isolate him- or herself from others in order to speak with him- or herself in the presence of the silent lily (UDVS, 165, 190).

forgetting what it means to be a lily / human being as a result, the worried wood-dove / human being also compares itself to God, inasmuch as it seeks to become independent and self-supporting, making a living by itself rather than relying on the providence of the divine (UDVS, 177–78). Kierkegaard thus interprets the worried bird as being not only a metaphor for the human being but also a symbol of human independence, which in the worried person also signifies a forgetfulness of God (UDVS, 177,181). "It is certainly praiseworthy and pleasing to God that a person sows and reaps and gathers into barns, that he works in order to obtain food; but if he wants to forget God and thinks he supports himself by his labors, then he has worry about making a living," Kierkegaard observes (UDVS, 177). Regardless of whether one is rich or poor, if one forgets that God is the ultimate source of human support, one is not free from worry about making a living (UDVS, 177, 180–81). Thus the rich person has no advantage over the poor person in this regard, and it holds true of them equally and paradoxically that complete dependence on God is the only independence, for it was only when the worried wood-dove "foolishly feared to be completely dependent on God" that it ceased to be independent (UDVS, 181–82).

As in the parable of the worried lily, the worried person symbolized by the worried dove "is unwilling to be contented with being a human being but wants to be different or to have diversity, wants to be rich, independently wealthy, prosperous, fairly secure, etc. In other words, he does not look at the bird of the air—away from the diversity of human life—but looks comparatively at others, at the diversity, and his worry about making a living is a relation of comparison" (UDVS, 179). Instead of focusing on our diversity and comparing it with that of others, then, in Kierkegaard's estimation we ought rather to raise ourselves above diversity by looking away from it in contentment with our bare humanity, which we share in common with all other persons of our species.

But does not this compromise our status as individuals? Definitely not, according to Kierkegaard. On the contrary, the individual is secured as a separate and distinct individual in distinction from other human beings as well as animals not by comparing him- or herself with others but rather by becoming isolated from them in the recovery of those vital "first thoughts" about the glory of being a human being that have been forgotten in the modern emphasis on diversity and comparison (UDVS, 189–90). Taking issue with Aristotle and to some extent Plato as well on this matter, Kierkegaard expounds his views on what it means to be an individual human being in the second discourse of Part Two, to which we shall now turn.

IV. The Isolated Individual

In the second discourse on the lilies and the birds Kierkegaard returns to the metaphor of the lily, focusing this time on the significance of its being "clothed" by God for humans. Since for the lily there is no distinction between existing and being clothed, it follows that "to be a lily is its clothing" (UDVS, 188). A comparable equation obtains for humans, inasmuch as "[t]o be clothed…means to be a human being" (UDVS, 188, cf. also 190). The "first clothing" of humans, like that of the lily, is the clothing or being that is given to them from the hand of God. Consequently, the "first thoughts" appropriate for humans to have are "those great, uplifting, simple thoughts" about "how glorious it is to be a human being" (UDVS, 189). But in our preoccupation with external clothing, by which (through comparisons) we seek to distinguish ourselves as individuals, these first thoughts and our first clothing have been ungratefully forgotten and replaced by worldly worry (UDVS, 188–89). Indeed, Kierkegaard asks rhetorically, "[i]f worldly worry is to be defined with a single phrase, would we not have to say that it is worry about clothes, worry about appearances?" (UDVS, 194). Far from becoming an individual through worldly worry about clothes and appearances, however, the person who devotes him- or herself to such concerns on the contrary disappears and perishes as an individual and actually "regards himself [or herself] as a beast, no matter whether by way of comparisons he [or she] was distinguished or lowly" (UDVS, 190). It was precisely in order to distinguish human beings from animals, Kierkegaard claims, that "God isolated the human being, made every human being this separate and distinct individual, which is implied in the unconditional character of those first thoughts" that have been forgotten (UDVS, 190). In contrast to the isolated individual human being, "[t]he individual animal is not isolated, is no unconditionally separate entity; the individual animal is a number and belongs under what that most famous pagan thinker has called the animal category: the crowd" (UDVS, 190). Consequently, "[t]he human being who in despair turns away from those first thoughts in order to plunge into the crowd of comparisons makes himself [or herself] a number, regards himself [or herself] as a beast, no matter whether he [or she] by way of comparisons became distinguished or lowly" (UDVS, 190).

According to the Hongs, the "most famous pagan thinker" Kierkegaard has in mind here is Aristotle, who is later explicitly named in *The Sickness unto Death* as having identified the abstraction of "the crowd" with "the animal category" (SUD, 118; cf. also 180, n. 65). In *Upbuilding Discourses in Various Spirits* Kierkegaard is intent on refuting what he regards as a confusion of the individual human being with the individual animal and consequently the crowd on Aristotle's part, while in the later work he is primarily concerned with the way in which this confusion has led, in Christendom, to a further identification of the crowd with God, so that God and man or the mob are the same. Although it is not entirely certain which text by Aristotle Kierkegaard has in mind in these references, the Hongs refer the reader to Aristotle's *Politics*, where the ancient philosopher argues both for and against, but on the whole in favor of, the principle that the multitude, rather than the few best individuals, ought to have power in the state, since "the many, of whom each individual is not a good man, when they meet together may be better than the few good, if regarded not individually but collectively," whereas "each individual, left to himself, forms an imperfect judgment" (*Politics*, III, 11, 1281a, 40–43; 1281b, 1–2, 38–39). Aristotle goes on to contend that "this argument would equally hold about brutes," which perhaps provides the textual basis for Kierkegaard's association of the crowd with animals in Aristotle's thought. In any case, as Kierkegaard sees it, in privileging the crowd over the individual Aristotle has clearly misrepresented what it means to be a human being, which is to be a separate and distinct individual, not an individual animal or mere number in a crowd.

If Aristotle gets it wrong, in Kierkegaard's judgment his teacher Plato at least comes closer to getting it right about what it means to be a human being, inasmuch as Plato's own teacher and spokesperson in his early and middle dialogues, Socrates, understood the equation that obtains between being clothed and being human and in his wondering about "that *simple first thought*" of what it means to be human introduced the "distinguishing mark of being human," which for him was uprightness in mind and body (UDVS, 190–91). But since Plato attributes the human being's clothing, which in his view is the body, to the weaving of the soul rather than to God, Kierkegaard nevertheless regards his discourse as imperfect because, "although aware of the first thought, [it] is not really aware of God" (cf. *Phaedo*, 87, b-e; UDVS, 191).

Even more imperfect than Plato's discourse--indeed, from Kierkegaard's standpoint, the "[m]ost imperfect of all" as well as "simply foolish"—is "the discourse that so utterly forgets the solemn first thought that it summarily and thoughtlessly regards being a human being as if it were nothing, empties it, and promptly commences the foolishness about pieces of clothing, about trousers and jackets, about purple and ermine" (UDVS, 191). In other words, discourse which regards the human being and human clothing as something material and external or visible, a matter of outward appearance rather than spiritual and inner or invisible in character, as in the case of the worried person who compares him- or herself with others on the basis of appearances. Kierkegaard goes on to emphasize in this regard that, unlike the lily and the rest of nature, which do not resemble God, the human being is created in the image of God, who is spirit and thus invisible in and to the world (UDVS, 192). This distinction provides a second reason why Kierkegaard thinks Plato "spoke imperfectly about the human being," inasmuch as he "said nothing about the invisible God's creation of every human being in his image" (UDVS, 192–93).

To be spirit as God is spirit, then, is the human being's true glory and rightful clothing. But what does it mean to resemble or be made in the image of God? In line with the "inverse dialectic" that governs all of Kierkegaard's ethical-religious thought, Kierkegaard reiterates here that human beings do not resemble God directly, as in pagan attempts to be like God by becoming rulers; rather, resemblance to God occurs "only within the infinite diversity," that is, only in the context of the infinite qualitative difference that obtains between God and humans due to their sinfulness (UDVS, 193).[11] Consequently, "[t]he human being and God do not resemble each other directly but inversely; only when God has infinitely become the eternal and omnipresent object of worship and the human being always a worshiper, only then do they resemble each other" (UDVS, 193). It is also in the paradoxical posture of worship that human beings experience their greatest glory: "It is glorious to be clothed as the lily, even more glorious to be the erect and upright ruler, but most glori-

[11] On Kierkegaard's inverse dialectic, see my article, "Kierkegaard's Inverse Dialectic," *Kierkegaardiana* 11(1980): 34–54, and in *Living Poetically*, 227–28.

ous to be nothing by worshiping!" (UDVS, 193). This thought prompts a third and final criticism of Plato / Socrates in the observation that "the most grievous thing that can be said about [paganism] is that it could not worship—even that noble, simple wise man, he could be silent in wonder, but he could not worship" (UDVS, 193).[12]

In identifying the human being's essence as spirit and his or her proper posture toward the divine as worship, Kierkegaard brings the discourses on the lilies and the birds explicitly under the aegis of the religious and underscores even more strongly the (religiously) humorous incongruity of their roles as teachers of humanity. For the lilies and the birds, unlike humans, are not made in the image of God (in Kierkegaard's view at least) and thus cannot resemble or worship the divine as humans may do. Their glory is visible, while that of the human being is invisible, falling as it does under the qualification of spirit rather than nature. Even so, Kierkegaard suggests that nature can remind us to worship God, and of the lily in particular he states that "it bears a little mark by which it reminds one of God; it has witness, since God has not let himself be without witness in anything created" (UDVS, 192–93). That "little mark" of which he speaks is undoubtedly the physical beauty and loveliness that constitutes the glory of the lily, the appreciation of which can fill the worried person with wonder and lead that person to contemplate the nature and source of his or her own being in the recovery of those first thoughts of what it means to be a human being. It is toward this end that Kierkegaard has invited the worried person to pay close attention to the lilies, for "with the lilies the worried one is isolated, far away from all human or, perhaps more correctly, inhuman comparisons

---

[12] Some Plato scholars may take issue with Kierkegaard on this claim and criticism. Certainly Socrates believed in the gods or a god and understood his mission as a service to the divine and as an expression of piety, if not worship (see *Apology* and *Euthyphro*). But scholars are divided on the nature and role of religion in his life and thought. See, for example, C. D. C. Reeve, *Socrates in the 'Apology': An Essay on Plato's 'Apology of Socrates'* (Indianapolis / Cambridge: Hackett Publishing Company, 1989); Michael L. Morgan, *Platonic Piety: Philosophy and Ritual in Fourth-Century Athens* (New Haven: Yale University Press, 1990); and Mark L. McPherran, *The Religion of Socrates* (University Park: The Pennsylvania State University Press, 1996). Then, of course, there is also the perennial problem of distinguishing between Socrates and Plato on this and other matters.

between individuals" (UDVS, 190). In this isolation it is hoped that the worried person, whether female or male, may also discover the individuality that truly distinguishes him or her as a human being from other humans, animals, and the abstraction of the crowd.

Having identified the human being as the isolated individual in these discourses, Kierkegaard naturally provokes in his readers a question about the sociality of the human. Indeed, he even anticipates and addresses this very question in a journal entry from 1847 (JP, 5: 5972):

> Despite everything people ought to have learned about my maieutic carefulness, in addition to proceeding slowly and continually letting it seem as if I knew nothing more, not the next thing—now on the occasion of my new upbuilding discourses [*Upbuilding Discourses in Various Spirits*] they will probably bawl out that I do not know what comes next, that I know nothing about sociality. You fools! Yet on the other hand I owe it to myself to confess before God that in a certain sense there is some truth in it, only not as men understand it—namely, that when I have first presented one aspect sharply, then I affirm the other even more strongly. Now I have my theme of the next book. It will be called: "Works of Love"

Upbuilding Discourses in Various Spirits was published on March 13, 1847; *Works of Love* followed soon after on September 29 of that year.[13] In this deeply reflected book Kierkegaard continues to emphasize the need to lift ourselves above all earthly dissimilarities or differences between persons in the recognition of our eternal equality as individual human beings before God, and this equality or common humanity forms the basis upon which love of the other as a neighbor and individual is affirmed and made central to sociality in this work (WL, 68–73, 86–90, 141–43, 230). But that is another story, reserved for another essay.

V. Some Humorous Conclusions

[13] On *Works of Love*, see the essays in *International Kierkegaard Commentary: Works of Love*, Vol. 16, ed. Robert L. Perkins (Macon: Mercer University Press, 1999) and M. Jamie Ferreira, *Love's Grateful Striving: A Commentary on Kierkegaard's 'Works of Love'* (Oxford and New York: Oxford University Press, 2001). See also the two essays on *Works of Love* in the present collection.

In conclusion, let us briefly recap the results of these considerations and reflect a final moment upon the humorous lesson which the lily, were it able to speak, would teach us in the present age. In our structural considerations of the design of *Upbuilding Discourses in Various Spirits* as a whole and of Part Two in particular, we determined that—based on Kierkegaard's own statements about the design of the work and its parts and on comparisons with Climacus' schema of existence spheres in *Concluding Unscientific Postscript*—the three discourses on the lilies and the birds should be understood as being humorous in design, but humorous in two senses: 1) as the incognito of an immanent religiosity that, unlike the *confinium* of humor per se, is really an expression of earnestness in its humorous jesting, and 2) as the reversal of the normal relation between the teacher and the learner in placing the lowly lilies and the birds in the incongruous position of being teachers of human beings about what it means to be a human being. We have seen that the three discourses are also designed as recapitulations of the aesthetic, ethical, and religious spheres respectively from the higher standpoint of immanent religiousness, which is what gives them their upbuilding character individually and as a group.

Our consideration of the gender associations Kierkegaard introduces in Part Two between the lilies and women, on the one hand, and between the birds and men, on the other, has shown that the upbuilding potential of these discourses for women is rendered somewhat problematic by Kierkegaard's stereotyped, classist, and sexist characterization of women as belonging to the private sphere, where their chief occupation in life is with personal adornment. Yet some illuminating and upbuilding insights for women as well as men may be found in Kierkegaard's exposé of the male misogyny implied in the first level of metaphorical interpretation of the parable of the worried lily, and in his exposé of the potential dangers of diversity and comparison revealed in the parables of the worried lily and the worried wood-dove at the second level of interpretation, namely: the false elevation of diversity over our common humanity; the dissatisfaction with and loss of self-identity and true individuality through inhuman comparisons with others; the forgetfulness of what it means to be a human being, which is to be a single and distinct individual made in the image of God; and finally even forgetfulness of God in the desire to become independent beings in the denial of our ultimate dependence upon the divine for life and livelihood.

Certainly it is humorous for human beings to be taught what it means to be a human being by teachers as lowly as the lilies and the birds. In an age such as ours, however, preoccupied as it is with sexual, class, ethnic, and cultural differences, often in forgetfulness of our common humanity, which binds us together as human beings even as it isolates each one of us as single individuals before God, it is doubly humorous to learn from these flowered and feathered teachers that the very individuality we seek to affirm through our modern / postmodern emphases upon diversity and comparison is in danger of being undermined and lost by those very preoccupations. This does not mean that diversity should be denied in favor of unity or homogeneity; rather, it suggests that we should learn to value diversity without deifying it, affirm it without falling into abstraction or fragmentation, and embrace it without forgetting those first thoughts of our common humanity. For in our comparative efforts to emulate other human beings rather than to become ourselves as separate and distinct individuals in resemblance to the divine; in our tendencies to define ourselves as individuals by reference to membership in a particular sex, race, class, or culture, or what Kierkegaard, following Aristotle, has dubbed "the crowd;" and in the arrogant elevation of ourselves as autonomous beings independent of the divine, many persons in the present age are clearly in danger of forgetting what it means to be a human being or single individual as Kierkegaard understands it. The discourses on the lilies and the birds thus may serve as timely as well as "godly" or upbuilding diversions by which we may be humorously reminded of the contentment and glory of simply being human.

7

PROTOTYPES OF PIETY: THE WOMAN WHO WAS A SINNER AND MARY MAGDALENE*

Of all the female figures portrayed in Kierkegaard's authorship none receives greater attention from his pen than the biblical figure of the woman who was a sinner in Luke 7: 36–50. She first appears early in the authorship in the second discourse, "Love Will Hide a Multitude of Sins," of *Three Upbuilding Discourses* (EUD, 75–77).[1] Then *Philosophical Fragments* briefly alludes to her in passing as a "repentant prostitute" and "pardoned prostitute" (PF, 33). Paraphrases of a specific text (Luke 7: 47) from the biblical story relating to her also occur in the discourses on "Love Builds Up" and "Love Hides a Multitude of Sins" in *Works of Love*, although without explicitly naming her (WL, 219, 282). She then reappears as the main subject of two discourses in Kierkegaard's later religious writings: "The Woman Who Was a Sinner" (*Synderinden*) in *Three Discourses at the Communion on Fridays* (1849) and a discourse bearing the same title published singly in 1850 as *An Upbuilding Discourse* (WA, 135–44; 145–60). Finally, the first discourse in *Two Discourses at the Communion on Fridays* (1851) focuses on the second clause of Luke 7:47, "But One Who Is Forgiven Little Loves Little," but does not explicitly mention her (WA, 167–77). Either directly or indirectly, then, the woman who was a sinner constitutes a person of interest in a

---

* Reprinted by permission from *International Kierkegaard Commentary: Without Authority*, Vol. 18, ed. Robert L. Perkins (Macon: Mercer University Press, 2006), 313–42.

[1] A paragraph on a similar figure, the woman accused of adultery in John 8:3–11, appears in the first discourse on "Love Will Hide a Multitude of Sins" in this series (EUD, 67). Two other texts also refer in passing to this woman, who is identified as "the woman who was a sinner" in one (TDIO, 35) and as "a woman seized in open sin" in the other (CD, 289).

number of texts throughout the authorship, particularly in the collection of discourses that make up *Without Authority*.

Focusing on these various treatments of the woman who was a sinner in the authorship, this essay will examine the way in which she functions as a "prototype of piety" for Kierkegaard, e.g. the manner in which she constitutes an exemplar of the dialectic of confession and forgiveness in the Christian life. As a prototype of piety, this female figure also seemingly provides a positive image of woman in contrast to the negative portrayals of her that pervade much of Kierkegaard's authorship.[2] However, such a perception is thrown into question by the Christian tradition's identification of the woman who was a sinner with several other female figures in the New Testament, e.g. Mary Magdalene, whose positive role as a disciple of Christ and primary witness to his resurrection has been obscured in the process. I shall begin, therefore, with a brief account of the historical conflation of these biblical women in the Christian tradition as traced by Susan Haskins in her masterful study of Mary Magdalene,[3] with whom the woman who was a sinner displays some important differences as well as similarities in Kierkegaard's portrayals of her vis-à-vis Roman Catholic characterizations and artistic representations of the two women.[4] In contrast to Haskins, who favors the original

---

[2] For a range of essays criticizing the view of woman in Kierkegaard's authorship, see *Feminist Interpretations of Søren Kierkegaard*, ed. Céline Léon and Sylvia Walsh (University Park: The Pennsylvania State University Press, 1997).

[3] Susan Haskins, *Mary Magdalen: Myth and Metaphor* (New York: Harcourt Brace & Company, 1993). Henceforth references to this work will be designated by the siglum MM and placed in parentheses in the text along with page numbers. I am grateful to Mark Lloyd Taylor for introducing me to this study in a footnote to his article, "Practice in Authority: The Apostolic Women of Søren Kierkegaard's Writings," in *Anthropology and Authority: Essays on Søren Kierkegaard*, ed. Poul Houe, Gordon D. Marino, and Sven Hakon Rossel (Amsterdam: Rodopi, 2000), 85–98. Haskins uses a variant spelling of Mary Magdalene's name, which in Greek is "Magdalēnē," that is, "of Magdala," a town on the Sea of Galilee.

[4] Haskins reports that the Eastern Orthodox Church and Protestant reformers such as Calvin and Zwingli were opposed to the identification of these biblical women (MM, 26, 249–50). Thus the conflation of these figures was primarily a Roman Catholic phenomenon, although Bruce Chilton, in *Mary Magdalene: A Biography* (New York: Doubleday, 2005), points out that it be-

Mary Magdalene over the woman who was a sinner as a model for contemporary women of faith and recommends that Christianity dispense with its preoccupation with sin, I shall argue that, given the centrality of the dialectic of sin and forgiveness in Christianity, which is axiomatic and therefore indispensable in Kierkegaard's view, the woman who was a sinner as described in his writings provides an appropriate prototype of piety for women as well as men in the Christian community, and she does so *in spite of* as well as *because of* her checkered history as a repentant prostitute.

I. The Conflation of Identities

The biblical story of the woman who was a sinner tells of an occasion when Jesus is invited to eat at the home of a Pharisee. While he is eating, a woman intrudes, bringing with her an alabaster flask of oil with which to anoint him. *The New Oxford Annotated Bible* (New Revised Standard Version) identifies her only as "a woman of the city, who was a sinner," while *The New English Bible* describes her more specifically as "a woman who was leading an immoral life in the town" (Luke 7:37).[5] Taking her place behind Jesus, the woman wets his feet with her tears, wipes them with her hair, and then kisses and anoints them with oil. Seeing this, the dinner host says to himself that Jesus must not be a prophet or else he would have known that the woman was a sinner and would not have allowed her to touch him.[6] Sensing the man's thought, Jesus responds with a parable about two men whose debts are equally forgiven, even though one owes the creditor a large sum of money while the other owes him only a small amount. Jesus asks the Pharisee which debtor will love the

---

came "a key point of contention during the sixteenth century" in Catholicism after a Catholic humanist scholar, Jacques Lefèvre d'Etaples, refuted it in 1517, for which he was banned from teaching at the University of Paris and declared a heretic (59–60).

[5] *The New Oxford Annotated Bible with the Apocrypha / Deuterocanonical Books*, 3rd ed. (New York: Oxford University Press, 2001); *The New English Bible with the Apocrypha* (New York: Oxford University Press, 1976). Hereafter references to these editions will be placed in parentheses in the text using the sigla NOAB and NEB respectively.

[6] Jewish custom of the time associated sin in the form of sexual immorality with impurity or uncleanness and therefore as taboo or untouchable.

creditor more, to which the Pharisee answers: "I suppose the one for whom he canceled the greater debt" (Luke 7:43, NOAB). Contrasting the Pharisee's lack of attention to the care lavished on him by the woman who was a sinner, Jesus concludes: "Therefore, I tell you, her sins, which were many, have been forgiven; hence she has shown great love. But the one to whom little is forgiven, loves little" (Luke 7:47, NOAB). Turning to the woman, Jesus announces to her that her sins are forgiven, whereupon the dinner guests begin to ask themselves, "Who is this who even forgives sins?" (Luke 7:48–49, NOAB). The story then ends with Jesus saying to the woman, "Your faith has saved you; go in peace" (Luke 7:50, NOAB).

The New Oxford Annotated Bible is vague about the nature of the sinfulness of the woman in question inasmuch as, according to Haskins, the Greek word for "sinner" (*harmartolos*) used in the passage could apply in Jewish society to "someone who had forfeited his or her relation to God by disobeying the Law" or "to anyone who lived an immoral life, such as a murderer or thief, or who followed a dishonorable profession" (MM, 18).[7] In describing the woman as leading an immoral life, *The New English Bible*, unlike *The New Oxford Annotated Bible*, clearly opts for the latter connotation of the term. But the fact that she was "a woman of the town" (or "city" in the NOAB) lends credence to the view that took hold in the Christian tradition, namely that the nature of her immorality or sinfulness was *sexual* in nature, i.e., that she was a prostitute, which is further attested by the fact that she wore her hair loose, as a sign of her profession and / or fallen state (MM, 18).

Immediately following this story, the next chapter of Luke opens with a reference to "some women who had been cured of evil spirits and infirmities" that accompanied Jesus on his journeys and provided for him and his twelve disciples "out of their resources" (Luke 8:1–3, NOAB). First named among these female followers of Jesus is Mary Magdalene, from whom, according to Mark 16:9, he had exorcized seven demons. The close proximity of this reference to the story of the woman who was a sinner no doubt influenced the eventual conflation of these two figures in both popular and ecclesiastical minds, with the result that the most prevalent image of Mary Magdalene from the sixth century on was that

[7] See also Elizabeth Schüssler Fiorenza, *In Memory of Her: A Feminist Theological Reconstruction of Christian Origins* (New York: Crossroad, 1983), 128.

of a repentant whore (MM, 11–15). Initially, however, she was recognized and lauded in the early church for being a disciple of Christ who was present at his crucifixion and, according to Mark 16:9 and John 20:14, the first person to witness the resurrection, as well as, according to John 20:17, the first of Jesus' disciples to be charged with publicly proclaiming the good news of his resurrection and ascension (MM, 3–14). Hippolytus (c.170–c. 235), a bishop of Rome, not only accorded her apostolic status but elevated her to the position of being the "apostle to the apostles" (MM, 63–65, 88–90). Since the status of women in the church was already in decline by the second century A.D., this appellation was anachronistic and soon obscured by the association of Mary Magdalene with the woman who was a sinner.[8] Among the Christian Gnostic cults, however, she continued to play an important role, in correlation with the more egalitarian status of women in these groups.[9] One of their writings, *The Gospel of Mary*, written sometime in the late second or early third century, portrays her as more beloved by Christ than his male disciples (much to their envy) and as standing in a position of authority over them (much to their disgruntlement) (MM, 38–41).[10] Significantly, the Gnostic gospels nowhere refer to Mary as a sinner or prostitute, yet the dualistic nature of their religion, in which the opposition between spirit and

---

[8] According to recent biblical studies, women enjoyed an equality of discipleship in the early church, but by the beginning of the second century they were no longer allowed to teach, baptize, or have authority over men as a result of Eve's secondary creation and responsibility for original sin (MM, 86–89). See also Fiorenza, 130–54, 286–87, and *passim*.

[9] See Elaine Pagels, *The Gnostic Gospels* (New York: Random House, 1979) 60–61, 66.

[10] *The Gospel of Philip* also portrays her as a close "companion" [*koinonōs*] of Christ, who "used to kiss her often on the mouth." Haskins suggests that this word "is more correctly translated as 'partner' or 'consort,' a woman with whom a man has had sexual intercourse" (MM, 40), but Antti Marjanen, in *The Woman Jesus Loved: Mary Magdalene in the Nag Hammadi Library and Related Documents* (Leiden: Brill, 1996), points out that the term is used variously in the Bible to denote a marriage partner, a companion in faith, a co-worker in proclaiming the gospel, or even a business associate, and in this text it more likely connotes a spiritual consort than an illegitimate sexual partner (151–54). On the spiritual significance of kissing, which Jesus bestowed upon his male disciples as well, see Chilton, *Mary Magdalene*, 141–43.

matter, male and female, good and evil is ultimately overcome in a spiritual state of androgyny or sexual indifference, nevertheless led to the association of woman and sexuality with evil, requiring her to lose her femaleness and become a man in order to achieve spiritual perfection (MM, 38, 42–43).[11]

With the defeat of Gnosticism, the suppression of the positive image of Mary Magdalene began full force in the early church, and an association of her with sin and repentance began to take hold. Texts that lauded her were purged from the canon (MM, 56–57). St. Augustine's formulation of the doctrine of original sin linking hereditary sin to sexuality capped a preoccupation with the Fall from the second century on by both eastern and western fathers of the church (MM, 71). Eve was blamed and excoriated for the Fall,[12] and Mary Magdalene was dubbed the "Second Eve," whose penance for her sin—identified as the sexual sin of fornication—would undo the effects of the first Eve at the resurrection (MM, 65, 67). Penance, asceticism, and celibacy increasingly became the Christian ideal, with Mary Magdalene leading the way as the *model of repentance* through the association of her with the woman who was a sinner, and as the *model of contemplation* through the identification of her with Mary of Bethany, another female disciple of Jesus mentioned in Luke 10:38–42 and John 11:1–45 (MM, 26, 80–82, 90, 93–95).[13]

---

[11] In *The Gospel of Thomas* the Apostle Peter, manifesting an anti-female bias, says to Jesus, "Let Mary leave us, for women are not worthy of Life," to which Jesus replies, "I myself shall lead her in order to make her male, so that she too may become a living spirit resembling you males," and he adds, "[f]or every woman who will make herself male will enter the Kingdom of Heaven" (MM, 43).

[12] The most famous castigation of Eve—and by extension all women—was that of Tertullian (c. 160–c. 225): "And do you not know that you are [each] an Eve? The sentence of God on this sex of yours lives in this age: the guilt must of necessity live too. *You* are the devil's gateway: *you* are the unsealer of that [forbidden] tree: *you* are the first deserter of the divine law: *you* are she who persuaded him whom the devil was not valiant enough to attack. *You* destroyed so easily God's image, man. On account of *your* desert—that is, death—even the Son of God had to die" (MM, 79).

[13] Haskins notes that "[t]o a lesser extent she [Mary Magdalene] was also associated with the woman from Samaria (John 4:6–42) and to the woman taken

This latter figure, commended by Jesus in the Gospel of Luke for listening to him teach rather than helping her sister Martha with domestic service to their houseguests, is explicitly identified in the Gospel of John with Luke's woman who was a sinner, inasmuch as John 11:2 says (placed in parentheses in the NEB): "This Mary…was the woman who anointed the Lord with ointment and wiped his feet with her hair." Mary of Bethany is further identified in this text as the sister of Lazarus, whom Jesus raises from the dead after she falls weeping at his feet in grief over the death of her brother (John 11:33; 44). In *anointing* the feet of Christ and wiping them with her hair (see also John 12:3) and in *weeping* (albeit over her brother's death rather than over her own sin), Mary of Bethany shares two characteristics in common with the woman who was a sinner, so it is no wonder that the two were identified very early in the Christian tradition. Moreover, it was by way of Mary of Bethany that the woman who was a sinner came to be identified with Mary Magdalene. Mary Magdalene takes on the persona of Mary of Bethany through the sharing of a common name as well as the characteristics of anointing and weeping[14] and through the association of the latter Mary with the contemplative life. On the basis of Luke's account (see also John 11:20), Origen (c. 185–254), the great biblical scholar and theologian of the eastern church, identified Mary of Bethany and her sister Martha respectively with the contemplative and active forms of the religious life (MM, 22–23). Subsequently, through the growth of a legend from the fifth century on, Mary Magdalene was believed to have become a hermit who spent the last thirty to forty-seven years of her life devoting herself to a life of repentance and/or contemplation in France (MM, 111–33).[15]

---

in adultery (John 8:3–11) (MM, 26). As noted above, Kierkegaard also associated the latter figure with the woman who was a sinner in one text.

[14] In Luke's account of Christ's resurrection Mary Magdalene comes to the tomb along with other women bearing spices and ointments for his dead body (Luke 23:55–56; 24:1–11; cf. also Mark 16:1). In John's account she is found by the risen Christ weeping outside the empty tomb (John 20:11–15).

[15] In this legend she is further identified with another Mary in Christian folklore, Mary of Egypt, who was also envisioned as a prostitute who became an ascetic (see MM, 111 and Chilton, *Mary Magdalene*, 9). See also Benedicta Ward, *Harlots of the Desert: A Study of Repentance in Early Monastic Sources* (Kalamazoo: Cistersian Publications, 1987), 26–56. The most famous version of this

Although biblical support for linking Mary Magdalene to these women is scant,[16] consisting mainly in the fact that each is associated with the anointing of Christ at various points and for different purposes (MM, 16, 18, 20, 26),[17] the conflation and identification of them as the same woman was a matter of intense scrutiny and debate in both the eastern and western church from the fourth century on for two centuries (MM, 90–95). The issue was finally put to rest in 591 when in a homily on Luke's gospel Gregory the Great (c. 540–604) declared:

> She whom Luke calls the sinful woman, whom John calls Mary, we believe to be the Mary from whom seven devils were ejected according to Mark. And what did these seven devils signify, if not all the vices? ... It is clear, brothers, that the woman previously used the unguent to perfume her flesh in forbidden acts. What she therefore displayed more scandalously, she was now offering to God in a more praiseworthy manner. She had coveted with earthly eyes, but now through penitence these are consumed with tears. She displayed her hair to set off her face, but now her hair dries her tears. She had spoken proud things with her mouth, but in kissing the Lord's feet, she now planted her mouth on the Redeemer's feet. For every delight, therefore, she had had in herself, she now immolated herself. She turned the mass of her crimes to virtues, in order to serve God entirely in penance, for as much as she had wrongly held God in contempt. (*Homily* XXXIII; MM, 96)[18]

---

legend is *The Golden Legend* by Jacobus de Voragine in the thirteenth century (MM, 222–26).

[16] In fact, the annotation to Luke 8:2 in the NOAB states unequivocally that "[t]here is no evidence to identify her [Mary Magdalene] with the woman [who was a sinner] in 7:36–50."

[17] Interestingly, Haskins points out that one of the earliest images of Mary Magdalene in Christian art was as a myrrhophore or anointer of Christ (MM, 62–63). On the spiritual significance of anointing associated with Mary Magdalene, see Chilton, *Mary Magdalene*, 54–70.

[18] For a slightly different translation of the homily, see *Gregory the Great: Forty Gospel Homilies*, tr. Dom David Hurst (Kalamazoo: Cistercian Publications, 1990), 268–79.

Although demonic possession is nowhere equated with sin in the New Testament (with the possible exception of John 8:46–49), Pope Gregory clearly associates it here with the sexual sin of prostitution, thereby sealing Mary Magdalene's identity with that of the woman who was a sinner (cf. MM, 14–15 and n. 32).

With the unification of the three women firmly fixed in the eyes of the church, Mary Magdalene soon became the favorite female saint of the Middle Ages (MM, 134). Cults in her honor were established at Vézelay and Saint-Maximin in France, where according to legend she presumably was buried and her relics are preserved; many trade groups adopted her as their patron saint; hospitals, refuges for repentant prostitutes, etc. operated under her guardianship; and colleges at Oxford and Cambridge were named after her (MM, 113–16, 127–33, 135). Interestingly, Haskins also reports that "[d]aughters were given the name Magdalene for the first time in the late eleventh century" (MM, 135). Although Mary Magdalene functioned as a model of repentance and contemplation for both women and men in the Middle Ages, she especially served in that capacity for women, who by virtue of their sexuality were associated with sin and evil through the first Eve. The Virgin Mary was also much venerated in the medieval period as the ideal of perfect womanhood because of her sexual virginity or innocence (and thus sinlessness). But Mary Magdalene was associated with the ordinary woman, who like her was sexually impure and subject to sin. Unlike the Virgin Mary, then, Mary Magdalene was a figure to whom all women could relate, both in terms of their sinfulness and the possibility of redemption through repentance; consequently she became the symbol of Everywoman (MM, 137–41).

Although Mary Magdalene provided a feminine model of asceticism for a large number of female ascetics in England in the eighth and ninth centuries (MM, 111), it was primarily in her capacity as the model of repentance, i.e., in her persona as the woman who was a sinner, that she rose to the fore in the penitential mood that swept over Europe in the eleventh century (MM, 145–48, 157). It was during this time too that monks and friars from various orders produced anti-female diatribes against woman's sinful sexuality and inferiority (MM, 148–50). Lust, personified by a woman, was regarded as "the greatest filth," and fornication, deemed "a particularly female vice" because woman was considered to be more carnal than men, caused whores to be compared to dung

(MM, 152). The remedy envisioned for woman's sinful condition by these clerics was conversion and penance. Having moved from being a prostitute to becoming a penitent herself, the woman who was a sinner, a.k.a. Mary Magdalene, provided the model of penitence for two kinds of women in particular: 1) female mystics from the eleventh to fifteenth centuries who looked to her as a model for fasting, weeping,[19] chastity, and other aspects of the female ascetic life of piety (MM, 177–91); and 2) repentant prostitutes who like Mary Magdalene had rejected their former life in sin and entered convents under her patronage (MM, 170–76). The ubiquity of prostitution in the mid-thirteenth century, due to poverty, lack of education, and no other means of economic support for many women, testified to the widespread toleration of this social evil in medieval society (MM, 170–72). The classic rationale for regarding it as a necessary evil had already been provided by St. Augustine: "If you eliminate prostitution from society, you will disrupt everything through lust" (MM, 172). Following the Augustinian line of justification, St. Thomas Aquinas graphically characterized it as a "sewer" in a palace which, if removed and eliminated, would result in pollution and sodomy, a vice "infinitely more heinous" than prostitution (MM, 173). Nevertheless, salvation was possible for those prostitutes who were willing to renounce their profession and repent, and convents under the patronage of Mary Magdalene, the patron saint of prostitutes, were founded for their reformation. Similarly in the eighteenth century, also noted for its large number of prostitutes, "Magdalene-houses" were established as halfway houses or reformatories in England for the restitution of repentant prostitutes (MM, 309–16).[20] In the nineteenth century, which also had its

[19] Weeping, as we have already seen, was especially associated with Mary Magdalene. Haskins devotes a whole chapter to the many artistic representations of her in this posture (MM, 229–96). On the theology and iconography of Mary Magdalene's tears in the Christian tradition, see also Diane Apostolos-Cappadona, "'Pray with Tears and Your Request Will Find a Hearing': On the Iconology of Magdalene's Tears," in *Holy Tears: Weeping in the Religious Imagination*, ed. Kimberley Christine Patton and John Stratton Hawley (Princeton: Princeton University Press, 2005), 201–28.

[20] Kierkegaard refers twice to such an institution in *Either/Or*, Part I. In "Silhouettes" the esthete A suggests that Donna Elvira must elect one of two options: either enter a "home for fallen women" (*Magdalens-Stiftelse*), where after having previously known the religious she will now "have to return peni-

share of charitable institutions seeking to reclaim prostitutes from what was regarded as the "Great Social Evil," the theme of the fallen woman, whose paradigm again was Mary Magdalene, was popular in literary works, art, and sculpture of the period (MM, 318–26, 341–65).

Although less frequently portrayed in twentieth century art and literature, Mary Magdalene was celebrated rather than condemned for her sexuality by some female writers of this century, and Christian as well as non-Christian feminist writers regarded her positively as the representative of the liberated or independent woman (MM, 382–85). However, although no longer associated with sin and penitence, she was still portrayed primarily in terms of her sexuality in these works and thus was not accorded the full dignity of her person in the gospels. For the rectification of that one-dimensional misperception, Haskins credits feminist biblical scholars, historians, and theologians of the twentieth century, who restored the original figure of Mary Magdalene "in her New Testament role as chief female disciple, apostle to the apostles, and first witness of the resurrection" (MM, 392).

As a result of this retrieval, Haskins concludes that a "radical revision" of Christianity's view of woman may now be needed, along with a recognition of "the true feminine model, one which, according to the gospels, embodies strength, courage, and independence, all feminine qualities which the Church has attempted to suppress by subordinating women to the model it has created" (MM, 392–93). In spite of the fact that Roman Catholics under Pope John Paul II sought to restore the Virgin Mary to the position of importance she held in the church before the Second Vatican Council and to promote her as the model of Christian spiritual life instead of Mary Magdalene, Haskins notes that the latter figure "has become a figure-head for many women in the Church today," particularly for those seeking the right to be ordained (MM, 393, 397). Thus she "continues to travel with the times, once again a proto-

---

tently, in repentance and contrition," or take the easier course of continuing to love Don Giovanni, who has seduced and jilted her (198). And in "The Seducer's Diary," while contemplating Cordelia's calculated reaction to the dissolution of their engagement, Johannes says: "So one makes oneself and the neighbors believe that one is among the victimized, and, not qualified to be accepted into a home for fallen women [*Magdalens-Stiftelse*], one takes lodging next door as a wailer. People are duty-bound to hate me" (426).

type for women, but this time in her own guise, and as the symbol of women's right to resume their place and role in the Church" (MM, 397). As Haskins sees it, then, the repentant prostitute or the woman who was a sinner no longer serves as a symbol of Christian piety, and rightly so, inasmuch as she has long been used as a scapegoat for a Christian preoccupation with sin that, in Haskins' view at least, needs to be overcome in the affirmation of a more positive and accurate picture of women and their place in the Church (MM, 398).

Needless to say, the foregoing conclusions by Haskins present a challenge to Kierkegaard's view of the woman who was a sinner as a prototype of piety. Even more importantly, they constitute a challenge to the centrality of the consciousness of sin and forgiveness in his understanding of Christianity and the Christian life.[21] Before embracing Haskins' conclusions in a wholesale and uncritical fashion, therefore, we need to see how the woman who was a sinner is actually presented in Kierkegaard's writings and to consider the deeper question of whether Christianity can dispense with the notions of sin and forgiveness without losing the very heart of its identity as a religion. It is to these critical issues that we shall now turn.

II. The Woman Who Was a Sinner in Kierkegaard's Writings

When we first encounter the woman who was a sinner in Kierkegaard's authorship (in "Love Hides a Multitude of Sins," the second discourse in *Three Upbuilding Discourses* from 1843), it is in the context of a deliberation on the words of comfort offered by the apostle Peter in 1 Peter 4:7–12, in which he enjoins his readers "to have a heartfelt love for one another," since "love hides a multitude of sins" (EUD, 70, 72). The comfort to be found in these words, Kierkegaard suggests, consists precisely in the seemingly contradictory claim that "love is able to live in the same heart in which there is a multitude of sins and that this love has the power to hide the multitude" (EUD, 72, 77). Of course, love is not blind in that it does discover a multitude of sins in persons, even in those who are self-

[21] On the centrality of the consciousness of sin and forgiveness in Kierkegaard's later religious writings, see my book, *Living Christianly: The Dialectic of Christian Existence* (University Park: The Pennsylvania State University Press, 2005), Chapter 1.

deceived into thinking that they are perfect while others are not (EUD, 72). Love thus takes away self-righteous perfection, just as it takes away imperfections, and hides them both in love, which takes neither perfection nor imperfection into account (EUD, 74). But to be able to love in this way one must have "the courage to will to love" and a "humble bold confidence," Kierkegaard observes (EUD, 75). In his estimation, that is exactly what the woman who was a sinner displayed. In appearing at the Pharisee's house where Jesus was being entertained, she faced the "proud contempt," the "silent disapproval," the "sanctimonious anger" of the Pharisees gathered there, and their disdain only confirmed and heightened "the accusations of her own heart" against herself (EUD, 75). But she was not frightened away by their disdain and instead pressed on, placing herself at Jesus' feet, where "she forgot herself in her work of love" (EUD, 75). There her tears of repentance were transformed into tears of adoration as she was given the grace to "weep herself out of herself" and into "the peacefulness of love" (EUD, 76). Consequently, her many sins were forgiven because she loved much. That the person who loves much is forgiven much constitutes "love's blessed deception," Kierkegaard says, but also "love's perfection," in that much forgiveness indicates that one loves much (EUD, 76).

An interesting dialectic of concealment and disclosure in regard to the deceptiveness of love is introduced next as Kierkegaard proceeds to compare the world's judgment, which is never deceived and seeks to disclose everything, to love's judgment, which hides or conceals a multitude of sins while discovering what the world actually conceals—the presence of love in the woman who was a sinner (EUD, 76–77). In the first discourse of this series, which focuses on the same theme, Kierkegaard points out that "what one sees depends on how one sees" and that "observation is not just a receiving, a discovering, but also a bringing forth," so that "how the observer himself is constituted is indeed decisive" (EUD, 59). Thus one person may see one thing while another sees something different in the same thing or person, with the result that the one discovers what the other conceals and vice versa. With respect to observation of things in the external world, however, Kierkegaard admits that the internal constitution of the observer is less important than it is in the world of spirit, since "everything spiritual is appropriated only in freedom" and how things are seen there is determined from within (EUD, 60). Moreover, external observation is "irrelevant" to a person's "deeper nature," while everything that makes one's being and observation impure comes from within; for example, "an evil eye discovers much that love does not see" (EUD, 60). It is a person's inner being, therefore, that determines what that person discovers and hides. Thus, "[w]hen an appetite for sin lives in the heart the eye discovers the multiplicity of sin and makes it even more multiple," whereas "[w]hen loves lives in the heart, the eye is shut and does not discover the open act of sin, to say nothing of the concealed act" (EUD, 60).

To illustrate this difference, Kierkegaard uses another biblical example, the woman caught in "open sin" or adultery in John 8:3–11, in which the scribes and Pharisees quickly and easily discover her sin and are ready to condemn her to being stoned in accordance with Mosaic law (EUD, 67). Hoping to trap Jesus by asking his opinion on the matter, the Pharisees ironically are revealed in their own sinfulness by his answer: "Let anyone among you who is without sin be the first to throw a stone at her" (NOAB, v. 7). As they depart one by one, leaving Jesus alone with the woman, he looks up from the ground where he had been writing with his finger—not to judge but "to erase and forget" her guilt, Kierkegaard surmises (EUD, 67)—and asks whether anyone has condemned her. To her answer, "no one," he replies: "Neither do I condemn you. Go your way, and from now on do not sin again" (NOAB, v.11).

Kierkegaard returns to this biblical example of discovery and concealment in the second discourse, virtually identifying or eliding the woman caught in adultery with the woman who was a sinner, inasmuch as he quotes three different lines from Luke's story concerning the latter figure as if they were from John's story about the former (EUD, 77). This elision is undoubtedly conscious and calculated on his part, as the point he wishes to make here with respect to the adulterous woman is that "love discovered what the world concealed—the love in her," which through Jesus' love is made "even more powerful to hide a multitude of sins" because she, like the woman who was a sinner, loved much (EUD, 77). In his initial presentation of the woman who was a sinner, therefore, Kierkegaard refers to her in order to emphasize the non-judgmental character of love, the possibility of love existing simultaneously with a multitude of sins in persons, and the hiding or forgiveness of those sins by Christ in response to their love for him. Kierkegaard praises the woman who was a sinner in particular for her courage, bold confidence, and self-forgetfulness in expressing her love for Christ. Significantly, he does not identify the nature of her sins nor those of the woman caught in adultery—one has to go to the biblical stories themselves to learn that.

When Kierkegaard next alludes to the woman who was a sinner, in *Philosophical Fragments*, he refers to her explicitly as a "repentant prostitute" and as a "pardoned prostitute," in the context once again of a discussion of revelation, the possibility of deception, and concealment, only this time it is the god's (*Gudens*) love in the lowly form of a servant whose whole life is a story of suffering and self-denial for the sake of others that is revealed (PF, 33). A revelation of the god in any other way, Climacus contends, would be a deception, inasmuch as it would involve a change in the learner rather than the god, thus concealing from the learner his or her need for change, or else it would have to maintain a superficial ignorance of the delusory character of the understanding that exists between them, as in paganism (PF, 33). Thus, even if one were to plead with the god to alter his resolution and to assume a less ignominious condition, Climacus suggests that it would be of no avail:

> Though my eyes were more flooded with tears than a repentant prostitute's, and though each and every tear of mine were more precious than the copious tears of a pardoned prostitute, and though I could find a more humble place than at his feet, and though I could sit there more humbly than a woman whose heart's only choice was this one thing needful, and though I loved him more sincerely than the faithful servant who loves him to his last drop of blood, and though I were more comely in his eyes than the purest of women—nevertheless, if I pleaded with him to change his resolution, to manifest himself in some other way, to spare himself, then he would look at me and say: 'Man, what have you to do with me; go away, for you are of Satan, even if you yourself do not understand it!' (PF, 33)

Here Climacus hypothetically and poetically compares himself with the woman who was a sinner, alluding to her association with prostitution and repentance, her copious weeping, her place at the feet of Christ, and the pardoning of her sin. But in this imaginative scenario, feminine tears, humility, and love do not elicit hiding and forgiveness as in the biblical story of the woman who was a sinner, since Climacus employs them in opposition to the divine resolution and for that reason is associated with Satan, as was Peter when he rebuked Jesus for predicting Jesus' suffering, death, and resurrection (Matthew 16:23). In this poetic invention, then, it is the pseudonymous author himself, not the woman who was a sinner, who is associated with Satan, even though he exhibits the same qualities as she and even exceeds her in the expression of them.

In *Works of Love* we find two further brief allusions to the woman who was a sinner in paraphrases of what for Kierkegaard is the crucial text in the biblical story relating to her: "Therefore I tell you, her sins, which are many, are forgiven, for she loved much; but he who is forgiven little, loves little" (Luke 7: 47).[22] The first allusion is a paraphrase of the first clause of this passage in reverse order: "To him who loves much, much is forgiven" (WL, 219). The second is an even closer paraphrase of the same clause: "many sins are forgiven one who loved much" (WL, 282). In both paraphrases there is no mention of the woman who was a sinner; rather, they are now generalized so as to refer to any sinful person who loves much and thus is forgiven much. In an indirect way, then, the woman who was a sinner has already begun to function here as a prototype of piety for others, although that claim is not explicitly made until later in the authorship. In indirectly alluding to her through these paraphrases, however, Kierkegaard effectively expands upon his earlier portrayal of her by etching in greater detail the perfection and consequences of loving much and being forgiven much that she exemplifies.

The first paraphrase occurs in the context of a discussion of how love builds up, which Kierkegaard suggests is by presupposing love in others, not by discovering faults and weaknesses in them (WL, 218). By presupposing love, one draws out the good in others or "loves forth love," a lovely expression Kierkegaard had used previously in his writings.[23] This time he employs it in connection with the perfection of love to

---

[22] Here I am using the Revised Standard Version of the older *Oxford Annotated Bible* (New York: Oxford University Press, 1962) because it is closer to Kierkegaard's paraphrase and in my estimation offers a better rendition of the Greek in this instance than either the NOAB or the NEB. The NOAB says: "Therefore, I tell you, her sins, which were many, have been forgiven; hence she has shown great love. But the one to whom little is forgiven, loves little" And the NEB has: "And so, I tell you, her great love proves that her many sins have been forgiven; where little has been forgiven, little love is shown."

[23] See EUD, 38 and 61, and JP, 5: 5526, where Kierkegaard first uses this expression in a letter to Regine Olsen. See also my essay, "When 'That Single Individual' is a Woman" in the present collection.

point out that "the more perfect the loving one presupposes the love to be, the more perfect a love he loves forth," which establishes a "like for like" or correspondence between presupposing love and its result that, in Kierkegaard's view, is unparalleled in other relationships in the world (WL, 219). Earlier, the perfection of love was associated with the need for much forgiveness; here the focus is upon the first part of the paraphrase, namely what is involved in loving much, which is probably why the two parts of the biblical verse are reversed in the paraphrase.

The second paraphrase, as noted earlier, is closer to the original biblical text yet also lacks its specificity of reference to the woman who was a sinner. But Kierkegaard does give a specific reason why many sins are forgiven one who loves much, namely "because the love in him hides a multitude of sins" (WL, 282). Although the masculine pronoun is presumably used generically here to refer to anyone, male or female, who loves much, it at least has the virtue of including men as well as women among those who are sinners in need of much forgiveness and who are also capable of loving much. But Kierkegaard's primary interest in this discourse, "Love Hides a Multitude of Sins" (the third one thus far in the authorship devoted to this topic), is with the *works* of love or "love in its outward direction," not with the inward dialectic of love and forgiveness (WL, 282). Thus he cuts off further discussion of the latter topic in order to focus on how love hides a multitude of sins in others rather than in oneself. Yet this discourse is instructive with respect to our concern with the woman who was a sinner, since it was her love for Christ that led to forgiveness or the hiding of a multitude of sins in her.

Displaying a profound insight into the moral psychology of human beings in this discourse, Kierkegaard exposes our inclination to discover evil in others, which in turn is approved and regarded by the world as "sagacity," whereas the person who loves others discovers nothing, becoming as it were a child in relation to the evil in them by choosing not to see it, pretending as in a child's game not to see what is taking place right in front of one's eyes (WL, 285–87). Of course, the person who loves others is aware of evil or sin in them, but Kierkegaard points out that there is a difference between making a conscious effort to discover evil in others and becoming aware of it against one's will (WL, 285). Not only are we inclined to discover the faults of our neighbors, we are even more inclined to publicize them, to report their faults abroad by means of rumor and slander, which in Kierkegaard's view is more criminal and depraved than the acts of those whom society regards as criminals. Thus he laments: "Ah, there are crimes that the world does not call crimes, that it rewards and almost honors—and yet, yet I would rather, God forbid, arrive in eternity with three repented murders on my conscience than as a retired slanderer with this dreadful, incalculable load of crime that had piled up year after year" (WL, 291). In contrast to this "nervous debility" or weakness in people, as Kierkegaard mildly describes it, love hides a multitude of sins in others by not discovering them or, alternatively, by hiding what it cannot avoid seeing and hearing, either keeping silent about them, seeking a mitigating explanation of them, or forgiving them (WL, 289–90). Whereas the first two ways of hiding sins do not take them away or at most only reduces them by explaining some away, forgiveness actually removes or blots out sin and thus is "the most notable way" of hiding a multitude of sins, Kierkegaard observes (WL, 294–95). Since Christ is the "highest example" or prototype of discovering nothing and lovingly hiding the multitude of sins in forgiveness, the person who loves learns from him to do likewise (WL, 288). We are thus indirectly brought back to the woman who was a sinner, whose multitude of sins were hidden and forgiven by Christ's love. At this point in the authorship, however, she is not yet explicitly viewed as a prototype herself, inasmuch as Christ fills that role, but she is well on the way to becoming such because she loved much.

It is in Kierkegaard's communion discourses that the woman who was a sinner finally emerges overtly as a prototype of piety in his writings. In the third of three communion discourses published together in 1849, Kierkegaard once again focuses on the text from Luke 7:47 (WA, 137–44). In the Christological prayer that precedes the discourse he also returns to the theme of "loving forth love," suggesting this time that Christ is not indifferent to whether he is loved in return, nor is he judgmentally jealous about who does or does not love him; rather, he loves forth the love that loves him and encourages it to love him much (WA, 137). In loving Christ much, the woman who was a sinner thus illustrates first of all *the mutuality of love* that Christ seeks to elicit in relation to, as well as between, human beings. Unlike many sinners for whom coming near to Christ and being disclosed before him is "the most frightful annihilation," which they seek to flee or avoid as long as possible, the woman who was a sinner expresses her love for Christ most strongly in an inverse manner by hating herself, that is, by *being ashamed* of herself in her sinfulness (138).[24] According to Kierkegaard, woman has a stronger sense of shame than man, which is perhaps a major reason why the woman who was a sinner functions as a prototype of piety for him, that is, because she was not only a sinner but "[a]las, a woman," in whom "the power of the sense of shame is the strongest, stronger than life" inasmuch as "she would rather give up her life than give up her sense of shame" (WA, 138). Such a gender distinction seemingly reflects the nagging association of woman with sin and evil with which she has long been saddled in the Christian tradition and is quite dubious from a modern feminist perspective of gender differences. However, Kierkegaard does not regard the sense of shame in the woman who was a sinner as an indication of evil but rather as that sensitivity within her which ought to have kept her from sinning in the first place, and failing that, as an expression of love in the self-hatred and self-annihilation it engenders in her in going before Christ. Moreover, Kierkegaard does not indict her for her shame but rather the assembly of Pharisees who, he surmises, would have regarded the woman's audacity "to thrust herself forward with her sin" as the expression of a "disgusting vanity, especially for a woman," since from their viewpoint what she should have done was "to hide herself from the eyes of all people in a remote corner of the world" (WA, 138). Indeed, Kierkegaard suggests that "there perhaps is no suffering so designed to torture particularly a woman as the cruelty of the mockery that awaited her from the proud Pharisees in the house of the Pharisee" (WA, 138). Because she was a *woman*, then, her sin and subsequent behavior was particularly heinous to the Pharisees and deserving of their disdain and judgment, but not to Christ, who regarded her sense of shame as an expression of love.

However appalling, seemingly inappropriate, and disturbing the behavior of the woman who was a sinner may also seem to the reader, perhaps leading one to "shudder" and "shrink from following her," Kierkegaard suggests, to him her going forward to the dinner was equivalent to going to *confession*, and it is primarily in this capacity that she emerges as a prototype of piety in this discourse (WA, 138–39, 144). Nothing, not even the secrecy of sin, weighs more heavily upon a person than having to go to confession, he observes (WA, 139). Consequently, "human sym-

[24] On Kierkegaard's use of "inverse dialectic" see my article, "Kierkegaard's Inverse Dialectic," *Kierkegaardiana* 11 (1980): 34–54.

pathy" (i.e., the church) devised an alleviation for this burden by conveniently hiding the confessor in an enclosure and eventually doing away with the confessional altogether, so that confession might be made entirely in secret before God and therefore remain hidden in one's innermost being (WA, 139). The woman who was a sinner, by contrast, confessed openly, at a dinner, as a result of her own decision. Once again, then, a dialectic of concealment and disclosure comes into play, but this time the sins of the woman who was a sinner are not hidden, as in the earlier discourses, but fully disclosed through her own open confession.

As Kierkegaard continues to reflect on the woman who was a sinner in this discourse, he focuses primarily on what it means to say that she loved much. Two actions on her part are identified. First, in sitting at the feet of Christ and wiping them with her tears, she was expressing her ability to do *nothing* while inversely Christ is capable of doing *unconditionally everything* (WA, 139–40). To confess that one can do nothing, Kierkegaard says, is equivalent to loving much, while conversely to think that one is capable of doing something is to love less. Second, in the process of weeping the woman who was a sinner forgets what she was weeping over, or more precisely, she *forgets herself completely*, which in Kierkegaard's view is what constitutes "the true expression of loving much," while conversely the more one remembers oneself the less one loves others (WA, 140). In this way the woman who was a sinner becomes, as it were, a *symbol* or *picture* or *parable*, Kierkegaard says, inasmuch as she is lost in Christ in such a way as to seem *absent* even though she is *present* as he speaks *about* her rather than *to* her in the statement that "[h]er many sins are forgiven her, because she loved much" (WA, 141). In forgiving her sins, Christ also consigns them to an "infinite oblivion," so that they are not only *forgiven* but also *forgotten*—forgotten in such a way that immediately upon recollection her name or what she was called is forgotten: she is simply "the woman who was a sinner, neither more nor less" (WA, 142). In forgetting herself and becoming anonymous, however, the woman who was a sinner also becomes and remains a prototype or "eternal picture" for others through which they may be reminded of themselves (WA, 145). In a journal entry Kierkegaard explains:

> The prototypes are anonymous or eternal pictures: 'the tax collector,' 'the woman who was a sinner'—a name distracts so easily, sets tongues wagging, so that one comes to forget one-

self. The anonymous prototype constrains a person to think of himself insofar as this can be done (JP, 2: 1856).

Although the forgiveness of sin is offered to all persons in every generation, it must be made true in each person's life by loving Christ much just as the woman who was a sinner did. The test for that, Kierkegaard suggests, is not whether one loves Christ more than "father and mother, gold and material goods, honor and reputation" as one might expect, but whether one loves him more than one's sin (WA, 143). One may love Christ more than all of the former but still not love him more than one's sin. Moreover, loving one's sin more than Christ consists not merely in wanting to remain or continue in sin but in not wanting to confess it. *As long as one is unwilling to confess one's sin, one does not love Christ more than one's sin.* But that is often a hard and frightening thing to do. As Kierkegaard astutely notes, "there is nothing to which a human being so desperately clings as to his sin. This is why a perfectly honest, deep, completely true, completely unsparing confession of sins is the perfect love—such a confession of sins is to love much" (WA, 143). Traditionally, the place where that happens is at Holy Communion, where the pledge of forgiveness of sin is given at the communion table after the confessional.[25] As a prototype or eternal picture of piety, the woman who was a sinner is envisioned here as walking in the lead as a guide on the path to confession and forgiveness, inciting those who follow her to accept the invitation of Christ that calls each and all to the altar.

The second discourse devoted to the woman who was a sinner in Kierkegaard's authorship is not a communion discourse but an upbuilding discourse published singly in 1850 (WA, 149–60). Unlike the other discourse, therefore, it does not focus on the woman who was a sinner as a prototype of piety for *confession* but rather in her more general capacity as a *teacher*. Even though, according to 1 Corinthians 14:34, women are admonished to keep silent at worship and therefore may not teach, Kierkegaard maintains that silence belongs essentially to godliness and thus

---

[25] On the practice of confession and communion in the Danish Lutheran Church in Kierkegaard's time, see Niels Jørgen Cappelørn, "Søren Kierkegaard at Friday Communion in The Church of Our Lady," in *International Kierkegaard Commentary: Without Authority*, Vol. 18, ed. Robert L. Perkins (Macon: Mercer University Press, 2006), 255–94. See also Michael Plekon, "Kierkegaard and the Eucharist," *Studia Liturgica* 22 (1992): 214–36.

one may learn true godliness from a woman precisely through her silence. Indeed, he goes so far as to equate piety or godliness fundamentally with womanliness in this discourse (WA, 149). Thus one may learn various aspects of godliness from a woman. For example, from the Virgin Mary one learns the humble faith and proper hearing of the Word that does not doubt or demand to understand before believing but holds it fast with a "devout and beautiful heart" (WA, 149; cf. Luke 8:15). And from Mary (of Bethany), the sister of Lazarus, one learns concern for and choice of "the one thing needful" (WA, 149; cf. Luke 10:42). What the woman who was a sinner teaches us is *proper sorrow over our sins*. According to Kierkegaard, a woman is particularly qualified to teach this lesson because woman's element is fundamentally one: one wish, one thought, one sorrow so deep within her heart that it is "immensely much more" than a multitude of sorrows (WA, 150). This single sorrow is the sorrow over sin, which the woman who was a sinner exemplifies. While man may exhibit more earnestness with regard to thought, which he has in greater abundance (although many are only half-thoughts, Kierkegaard adds critically) than woman, she possesses more earnestness with respect to "feeling, passion, decision" and does not thwart herself or the decision with "thoughts, intentions, resolutions" nor deceive herself by coming close to making a decision without actually deciding (WA, 150). Since decision, "especially in the godly sense and, again, especially in relation to sorrow over her sin," is precisely what constitutes earnestness, the woman who was a sinner is particularly suited to serve as our teacher and prototype in this regard (WA, 150).

As Kierkegaard sees it, there are essentially three things we may learn directly or indirectly from the woman who was a sinner in her role as a teacher: 1) to become *indifferent* to everything except sorrow over our sin and finding forgiveness for it; 2) to recognize that we are *able to do nothing at all* with regard to finding forgiveness; and 3) to *enjoy a comfort* she did not have, namely Christ's atonement as the pledge of forgiveness. With respect to the first lesson, Kierkegaard points out that it is rare to see someone who has a single concern, and even more rare to see someone who is unconditionally concerned over his or her sin, although sin is "the one thing" that is common to us all (WA, 150–52). While it is possible to sorrow unconditionally over sin in such a way that sorrow becomes an expression of despair, Kierkegaard contends that true sorrow over sin is "far from being a sickness unto death," inasmuch as life and happiness are to be found precisely in forgiveness—the one thing that is unconditionally important to the person who sorrows unconditionally over his or her sin (WA, 152). Correspondingly, the woman who was a sinner was indifferent to everything else—"everything temporal, earthly, and worldly, honors, esteem, prosperity, the future, relatives, friends, people's opinion"—which had become unconditionally unimportant to her (WA, 153). Over against an unconditional concern and sorrow over her sin, other concerns, which often weigh one down in dejection, became as nothing or were *borne lightly*, thereby providing "an opportunity to express genuine sorrow" over her sin (153). This indifference also extended to the opposition and mockery of the Pharisees toward her, emboldening her to dare "to do what perhaps no other woman...would have dared to do" (WA, 154). In this she exhibited the *courage* and *energy* of despair but truly was not in despair; rather, she was a believer and therefore "so quiet, modest, and humble, so unnoticeable in her infinite indifference to everything, that she does not draw any attention to herself by her entrance" (WA, 154). Yet it was not to express indifference toward everything else but rather to find forgiveness for herself that she found her way into the Pharisee's house.

The second lesson to be learned from the woman who was a sinner is awareness of our *inability to do anything at all* with regard to receiving forgiveness. This lesson is one which Kierkegaard had already touched on in the communion discourse devoted to the woman who was a sinner. There, we may recall, such awareness was correlated with loving Christ much. Here it is associated with two factors relating to the woman who was a sinner, first of all the awareness of her *unworthiness*, which impels her to Christ; and second, the practice of "the true feminine art" of *doing nothing at all* (WA, 157). Concerning the first factor, Kierkegaard points out that the woman who was a sinner did not wait until she felt worthy to go before Jesus, for if she had done that she would have waited a long time or perhaps would never have gone before him at all. On the contrary, it was precisely her feeling of unworthiness that not only drove her to him but was the expression for the awareness that she could do nothing to merit or make herself worthy of forgiveness. Thus she did not abandon herself to self-accusation and self-torment as a means of coming closer to salvation or making herself more pleasing to God (WA, 155–56). Rather, ironically affirming the opinion of Judas in John 12:3–4 regarding the anointing of Christ's feet with costly ointment by Mary of

Bethany (who in this instance is identified with the woman who was a sinner), Kierkegaard suggests that she "squanders" the ointment in a festive, worldly manner (WA, 155). This festiveness on her part, however, is dialectically coupled with silent weeping, which forms the appropriate expression for her sorrow over her sin. In weeping and anointing Christ with oil, she may appear to be doing something, but Kierkegaard points out that these actions are really expressions for doing nothing, inasmuch as they are immediate, unreflective actions on her part and in any case are of no avail with regard to procuring forgiveness, which is received only by devoutly remaining silent or still, doing nothing, and letting God do everything in that regard (WA, 157). While doing nothing may seem easy, Kierkegaard contends that it is really a "sublime, rare, exceedingly difficult" art, inasmuch it is more difficult, and therefore a greater achievement, to conquer oneself than to conquer a city (WA, 157). Moreover, everything one is able to do, even if it is something good, is "infinitely nothing" with regard to gaining forgiveness of sin and places one in a new debt of gratitude to God, since "one is capable of nothing except *through* God" (WA, 157–58).

The third lesson the woman who was a sinner teaches us is an indirect one that is gained by comparing our situation with hers. Revisiting the issue of the advantages and disadvantages of contemporaneity with Christ discussed earlier in *Philosophical Fragments*, Kierkegaard denies that it was easy for the woman who was a sinner to believe in the forgiveness of her sins because of her immediate contemporaneity with Christ (WA, 158). On the contrary, he claims that, in a sense, immediate contemporaneity with Christ makes believing the "most difficult of all," for although this woman had the advantage of hearing Christ's words from his own mouth and thus could not possibly be in doubt as to whether his words of forgiveness were meant for her, she did not enjoy the *comfort and pledge of forgiveness that was wrought through his death as the atonement for sin* (WA, 158). With that, everything is changed inasmuch as his death becomes "the infinite comfort," "the infinite headstart," "the ultimate pledge" of satisfaction, so that doubt now becomes impossible because it is impossible to find "anything more reliable" or any "stronger assurance" of the forgiveness of sins, inasmuch as the atonement is now a matter of the past rather than the future (WA, 159).

In her paradigmatic roles as *confessor* and *teacher*, then, the woman who was a sinner is presented in a positive, non-judgmental fashion, in spite of her sense of shame and unworthiness, which is interpreted inversely and indirectly by Kierkegaard as an expression of love for Christ on her part. In another communion discourse published in 1851, however, the subject of judgment is taken up through the discourse's focus on the second clause of Luke 7: 47, "But One Who Is Forgiven Little Loves Little." Although the biblical passage constituting the theme of this discourse is taken from the story of the woman who was a sinner, she is nowhere explicitly mentioned in it, and for good reason. For here Kierkegaard focuses on the *obverse* side of love and forgiveness, namely the instance of *not loving* Christ and therefore of *not receiving* forgiveness aright at the communion table, in which case the word of forgiveness spoken at the altar becomes a word of judgment rather than one of salvation. In the prayer with which the discourse opens, Kierkegaard addresses Christ, saying: "Lord Jesus Christ, you who certainly did not come to the world in order to judge, yet by being love that was not loved you were a judgment upon the world" (WA, 169). Christ's judgment falls upon those who respond to the invitation to come unto him (Matthew 11:28), namely those who call themselves Christians but do not love him in return. His judgment, then, is that they love little. Consequently, anyone who does not receive forgiveness upon taking communion has only oneself to blame, since one is forgiven little because one has loved little. Yet even here the biblical admonition contains a word of comfort in that, even though "we are all more or less guilty of the guilt of loving only little," nothing is said in the passage to indicate that divine love has changed or loves us less as a result (WA, 174). Since the sacred scriptures do not suppress the truth or lie, one can take comfort in the fact that "God is unchanged love" (WA, 175). One can also take comfort in the fact that Christ's judgment concerns only the *present*, in which one loves little; for unlike God's love, human love is subject to change, that is, loving little can become a thing of the past, replaced in the next instant by a love that loves much (WA, 175).

The typical way of presenting words of judgment, however, is to pit justice against love or severity against leniency, suggesting that one is forgiven little because one has *sinned too much* to merit forgiveness or leniency (WA, 171–72). But Kierkegaard suggests that love is more severe than justice, inasmuch as love forgives everything, so that, if there is little or no forgiveness, it is because one *loves little*. Does this not mean, then, that the forgiveness of sins is after all *merited* through love? Kierkegaard concludes the discourse with a brief discussion and denial of this possibility. Referring back to the parable of the two debtors in the biblical story of the woman who was a sinner, he reminds the reader that both were forgiven even though one owed much and the other little. In response to Jesus' question as to which would therefore love the most, the Pharisee correctly answers that it was the one who was forgiven most. Thus, as Kierkegaard sees it, the matter of forgiveness does not revert to "the baleful region of meritoriousness" but remains in the sphere of love, where forgiveness is given in response to loving much and "loves forth" even more love in the one who is forgiven much (WA, 176). The woman who was a sinner remains unmentioned to the end, but Kierkegaard's final statement in this regard surely applies to her: "The love that loves much and then is forgiven much is strong, divinely strong in weakness, but even stronger in love's second time, when the same love loves again, loves because much has been forgiven" (WA, 176).

III. The Woman Who Was a Sinner and Mary Magdalene: Similarities and Differences

Having surveyed the historical conflation of these two biblical figures in the Christian tradition and the treatments of the woman who was a sinner in Kierkegaard's authorship, we are now in a position to make some comparisons between them and to consider whether one or both would qualify as a prototype of piety for women in particular and perhaps for men as well in the contemporary church. Implied in the latter consideration is the deeper question of whether Christianity should any longer be preoccupied with the notions of sin and forgiveness or whether the focus should now be on more positive qualities that may help to enhance women's position in the church.

The first thing to note is that, unlike the Roman Catholic tradition, Kierkegaard does not conflate these two women, although we have seen that in a couple of instances he is guilty of identifying the woman who was a sinner with Mary of Bethany and with the woman in John 8:3–11 who was caught in open sin. Mary Magdalene's name does not appear at all in these discourses; indeed, in addition to the two references to Magdalene houses mentioned above,[26] it occurs only one other place in the

[26] See n. 20 in this chapter.

authorship,[27] in "Guilty?"/"Not Guilty?" of *Stages on Life's Way*, where, interestingly enough, the editors of the English translation refer the reader to Luke 7:37–50 when Quidam says:

> Suppose that Mary Magdalene had had no witness to her shame and she could have sneaked through life with honor and in death sneaked out of the world with a myrtle wreath upon her brow—it seems to me that through her courage she won another honor; it seems to me that in death she lies more honored without the myrtle wreath than with it. (SLW, 353–54)

In referring to Mary Magdalene's "shame," this passage seemingly alludes to the woman who was a sinner, thus suggesting an identification of the two women on the part of Kierkegaard's pseudonym. But even here the emphasis is upon her *courage* rather than her shame, which is entirely consistent with the way the woman who was a sinner is generally described in Kierkegaard's writings. Like the original or reclaimed Mary Magdalene whom Haskins recommends as a prototype of piety for women because of the "strength, courage, and independence" she displays, the woman who was a sinner is praised by Kierkegaard for her courage, bold confidence, audacity, lack of fear, strength, energy, perfect love, self-forgetfulness, godliness, festiveness, unconditional concern or sorrow over sin, and open confession of it. She is not condemned for the multitude of sins she has committed nor castigated for her shame; rather, her sins—the nature of which are unspecified in his writings except in *Philosophical Fragments*—are seen as hidden, forgiven, and forgotten in and through Christ's love, and her shame and sense of unworthiness are interpreted inversely as an expression of love. In manifesting these positive characteristics, therefore, she qualifies in much the same way as Mary Magdalene does to be a prototype of piety.

But some significant differences between these two figures emerge as well from the historical and Kierkegaardian treatments of them. Whereas Mary Magdalene has a name, a specificity of person with whom others, especially women, may identify, the woman who was a sinner is an anonymous prototype. That the latter lacks a name, of course, is not Kierkegaard's fault, but he turns it to good use by suggesting that this

---

[27] See Alastair McKinnon, *Index Verborum til Kierkegaards Samlede Værker* (Leiden: E. J. Brill, 1973), 699.

very anonymity is conducive to self-reflection in others, thereby encouraging them to inspect their own lives rather than maliciously discovering evil in others. Second, whereas Mary Magdalene was the symbol for Everywoman in her association with female sexual sin and repentance and even in her rehabilitated image as a prototype only for women, the woman who was a sinner is a symbol for Everyone, male and female alike, in the commonality of our human sinfulness and in the expression of true godliness through unconditional sorrow over sin and open confession of it. Third, whereas Mary Magdalene was seen in the Roman Catholic tradition as the model for a female ascetic life in which various acts of penance (for example, fasting and chastity) formed the appropriate expression of religious piety, Kierkegaard views the woman who was a sinner as a prototype of piety precisely because she was able to do nothing at all with respect to meriting forgiveness.

In emphasizing grace rather than works in his understanding of Christian forgiveness, Kierkegaard reflects the traditional Protestant divide from Roman Catholicism on this issue. In maintaining the centrality of the consciousness of sin and forgiveness as the fundamental concern of the Christian gospel, however, he stands squarely with the New Testament and Christian tradition. But in Kierkegaard's estimation, people in his age had a confused, inadequate, and superficial understanding of sin and forgiveness. Thus in his religious writings he sought to present a proper understanding and expression of this central dialectic in Christianity and the Christian life. This state of affairs is no less prevalent in the present age. Haskins' desire to do away with a "preoccupation" with sin in the Christian church through the promotion of Mary Magdalene as a positive image for women, minus the baggage of sin and penance with which she traditionally has been saddled, reflects just the sort of attitude and trend Kierkegaard sought to counter and correct in his religious writings. Certainly biblical scholars have done the Christian community a great service in restoring the image of Mary Magdalene to her rightful position among the first disciples of Christ and in separating her persona from that of other female figures in the New Testament. It is altogether proper as well that she be regarded as a prototype of piety for women in the church today, especially in light of their continuing struggles for ordination and other positions of leadership in the Christian church as a whole. But that does not nullify the equal importance and authority of the woman who was a sinner as a prototype of piety for Christians as well. Given the enormous evil, inhuman, intolerant, and judgmental attitudes and actions toward others in the world today, Christianity cannot and must not forego the doctrine of sin and the gospel of forgiveness through Christ which constitute its very essence as a religion. Moreover, to the extent that it has engaged in and perpetuated such attitudes and actions itself, the Christian church stands in need of a recovery of its own essence. Kierkegaard's religious writings can make a substantial contribution in that regard. His interpretation of the woman who was a sinner in particular emphasizes the non-judgmental, loving, forgiving attitude of Christ toward her in her sorrow over sin, but it does not obscure the fact that she was a sinner. Mary Magdalene was no doubt a sinner too (especially if demon possession is regarded as sinful), but the biblical narratives do not present her in that guise as they do the woman in Luke 7. Thus the latter figure has a vital role to play, as Kierkegaard has discerned, in representing the proper posture of sorrow over sin and the open confession that is required for a genuine reception and appropriation of forgiveness in Christianity. Moreover, she functions as a prototype of piety for Christians not merely *in spite of* but precisely *because of* her sinfulness and sorrow over sin, constituting in her person both saint and sinner of the Lutheran tradition. For if the central dialectic of Christianity is the consciousness of sin and forgiveness as Kierkegaard claims, the exemplars of this dialectic must be individuals who manifest its operation in their own lives. In the case of the woman who was a sinner, however, her exemplary status surely has less to do with the fact that she was a woman who had mastered the peculiarly "feminine art" of doing nothing, as Kierkegaard thought, than with the fact that in confessing her sin she loved Christ much, which any person, male or female, with equal earnestness and sorrow over his or her sin can do.

8

IRONIC LOVE: AN AMORIST INTERPRETATION OF SOCRATIC EROS*

In Plato's *Symposium* Socrates makes the remarkable claim that the only thing he understands is "the art of love" (*ta erotica*) (177d-e). Since Socrates generally professes to know nothing at all, this pronouncement comes as a surprise and should perhaps be taken ironically, with the implication that no more than truth, goodness, or beauty can love be adequately defined and understood by finite human beings.[1] The art of love as exemplified in the person of Socrates nevertheless forms the phenomenological starting point for the formulation of a concept of love in Kierkegaard's doctoral dissertation, *The Concept of Irony*. Although this work is primarily concerned, as its title suggests, with an exposition of the concept of irony, I hope to show that the hermeneutical method employed to illumine that concept in the text also yields a concept of love. But it is an abstract concept of only the negative element in love, and hence an ironic concept of love that is really no concept inasmuch as the positive nature of love remains undisclosed and indefinable in its Socratic manifestation.

That there is a close, even integral connection between interpretation and the erotic is apparent in the hermeneutical method set forth and followed by Kierkegaard in *The Concept of Irony*. In fact, this method may aptly be described as an *erotic hermeneutics* inasmuch as in it the observer / interpreter, or "philosophical knight" as Kierkegaard calls him, is an *amorist* (*Erotiker*), that is, an interpreter who pays close attention, in a

---

* Reprinted by permission from *International Kierkegaard Commentary: The Concept of Irony*, Vol 2, ed. Robert L. Perkins (Macon, GA: Mercer University Press, 2001), 123–40.

[1] An ironical reading of Socrates' claim is reinforced by the fact that he later retracts it (198d). Still later in the text, however, he claims that Diotima "is the one who taught me the art of love" (201d), with the result that the claim remains ambiguous.

deferential and enthusiastic fashion, to every feature and facet of the phenomenon (CI, 9). In this way the philosophical concept is allowed to come into existence in and with the phenomenon rather than being imposed upon it by the interpreter in a violent and domineering fashion. The erotic character of Kierkegaard's hermeneutic is heightened by the fact that the phenomenon, identified as feminine in gender, surrenders itself by nature to the stronger, masculine power of the amorist interpreter, whose predominance over the phenomenon is to be used only "to help the phenomenon obtain its full disclosure" (CI, 9). This way of construing the relation between phenomenon and interpreter undoubtedly constitutes an advance over patriarchal modes of interpretation which, in Kierkegaard's estimation, rely too much on "the jingling of spurs and the voice of the master" (with an obvious allusion to the phenomenological method of Hegel).[2] But it is debatable, from a feminist standpoint at least, whether Kierkegaard's erotic hermeneutics really abandons this patriarchal framework or merely tempers it. For on the one hand, stereotyped notions of gender and male / female relations endemic to patriarchy are preserved and perpetuated in his method, which does not appear to go beyond a paternalistic understanding of the relation between the phenomenon and interpreter. Thus one could conclude that while Kierkegaard's erotic hermeneutic does away with intellectual rape and incest on the part of the interpreter, it falls short of a radical re-visioning of the hermeneutical method itself (CI, 9).

On the other hand, the assistance of the amorist interpreter in the self-disclosure of the phenomenon bears a close likeness to Socratic midwifery, in which Socrates metaphorically assumes the same role as his mother, Phaenarete, who is reported to be a midwife—"like mother, like son," one might say (*Theaetetus*, 149 a–b, 150 b–d). Thus the masculine interpreter may be said to appropriate the feminine in a kind of gender reversal on his part. On this basis one could argue that Kierkegaard's erotic hermeneutic not only transcends the worst features of patriarchy

---

[2] An instance of the intellectual violence Kierkegaard associates with Hegelian interpretation may be noted in a footnote to the text in which Kierkegaard accuses Hegel of "a bold act of rape" in interpreting the Sophistic thesis that man is the measure of all things as meaning that "man is the goal toward which everything strives" (CI, 207n).

but is actually revolutionary in its conception of the erotic and the feminine as constituting the very essence of interpretation.[3]

Just as there is an integral connection between the erotic and interpretation in *The Concept of Irony*, so too one may observe an intimate relation between the erotic and irony as exemplified in the figure of Socrates in this text. Not only is Socrates described as an ironist who sustains a negative relation to the established order or state but also as "an amorist [*Erotiker*] of the highest order" who is ironic in his personal relations as well (CI, 187). Kierkegaard even goes so far as to identify the erotic love embodied by Socrates as an ironic love, with the result that, just as Socratic irony is distinguished from Platonic irony in the text, so too Socratic eros is revealed to be significantly different from Platonic eros in it.[4]

---

[3] Whether such a method would constitute a feminist hermeneutics, however, is highly debatable, inasmuch as feminists more often than not tend to view the traditional concept of the feminine itself as a patriarchal construct. See, for example, Simone de Beauvoir's classic analysis in *The Second Sex*, tr. H. M. Parshley (New York: Vintage Books, 1989). Moreover, feminist assessments of Kierkegaard's use of gender categories and his attitude toward women and the feminine vary considerably. For a range of feminist approaches to his writings, see *Feminist Interpretations of Søren Kierkegaard*, ed. Céline Léon and Sylvia Walsh (University Park: The Pennsylvania State University Press, 1997). My own assessment is both critical and commendatory, as I find him quite ambivalent on the topic of woman and gender, reflecting in many ways the prejudices and presuppositions of his time while also pointing the way to the possibility of true selfhood for both women and men. See my essays in the volume cited above as well as in the present collection. One may note a range of conflicting feminist assessments of Plato's use of feminine imagery as well in *Feminist Interpretations of Plato*, ed. Nancy Tuana (University Park, PA: The Pennsylvania State University Press, 1994). While some interpreters in this volume view the image of Socratic midwifery negatively as an attempt of male philosophers to appropriate female reproductive powers to themselves (duBois, Tuana), others read Plato's dialogues more positively as using such imagery (the personification of truth and philosophy as female, for example) to mount a Socratic critique and / or subversion of masculinist features of Greek culture (Brown, Hampton) and Platonic philosophy (Nye).

[4] On the difference between Socratic eros and Platonic eros, see also Gregory Vlastos, *Socrates: Ironist and Moral Philosopher* (Ithaca: Cornell University

To substantiate these claims it will be necessary to attend the development of Kierkegaard's textual analysis rather closely, adopting, as it were, the manner of an amorist interpreter myself in order to allow the concept of erotic love to emerge in its essential connection with Socratic irony. We shall begin with an examination of Kierkegaard's attempt as an amorist interpreter to construct a "reliable and authentic view" of the "historical-actual, phenomenological existence" of Socrates from ancient accounts of the philosopher by Xenophon, Plato, and Aristophanes (CI, 9, 13).

Lacking a sense of the importance of situation for Socrates and an ear for the irony, or "reverse echoing," of his rejoinders, Xenophon's account, in Kierkegaard's estimation, portrays him erotically as an ordinary, repulsive pederast who brags about the love potions with which he lures young men to himself (CI, 16, 18–19). The general reaction to such pedestrian behavior, Kierkegaard observes, is that "we are just as disgusted with him as with an aged coquette who still believes herself capable of captivating—indeed, we are even more disgusted, because we cannot perceive the possibility of Socrates' ever having been capable of it" (CI, 24; cf. *Memorabilia* III, 11).[5]

Plato, for whom Kierkegaard confesses to harbor a "somewhat youthful infatuation" himself, presents a much more complex, duplex picture of Socrates (CI, 27). In Plato's account Socrates is portrayed as an original or primitive personality whose impact upon the race and individuals was "not merely inciting but epoch-making" in both positive and negative ways (CI, 28–29). Like Christ, Socrates communicates life and spirit to individuals as well as indirectly aids them, in the manner of a midwife, "to come to" or give birth to themselves as individuals (CI, 29). The latter activity, Kierkegaard points out, is the one most often accen-

---

Press, 1991), 38–39. Noting that the two are often conflated by interpreters, Vlastos identifies four major differences between them.

[5] Contra Kierkegaard, Vlastos finds both "simple" (what is said is not what is meant) and "complex" (what is said both is and is not meant, in that it is meant to be true in one sense, false in another) irony in Xenophon's account (Ibid., 31). Thus, where Kierkegaard interprets Socrates' remarks in the *Memorabilia* as an indication that he engages in carnal pederasty, Vlastos reads him ironically on this score. In line with Vlastos, K. J. Dover, in *Greek Homosexuality* (Cambridge: Harvard University Press, 1978), contends that both Xenophon's Socrates and the Platonic Socrates "condemn homosexual copulation" (160).

tuated with respect to Socrates. In Plato's dialogues Socratic midwifery is characterized as a relation of love in the form of a spiritual pederasty (as opposed to Xenophon's carnal pederasty) in which young men are awakened to spiritual development through their relationships with Socrates (CI, 29n). As for Plato's own love relation to Socrates, Kierkegaard finds it to be so symbiotic that one has difficulty distinguishing the actual Socrates from the poetic Socrates who is a product of Plato's spiritual unity with him (CI, 30). Nevertheless, Kierkegaard believes it is possible to differentiate between them and to detect the genuine or "unalloyed" Socratic elements in Plato's dialogues (CI, 40). This may be done by paying close attention, first of all, to the method of dialectic—the art of asking questions or conversing—in the dialogues. As Kierkegaard analyzes it, this questioning may be either *speculative* (Platonic) or *ironic* (Socratic) in intent, seeking a fullness or plenitude in the answer or interested only in sucking out its apparent content so as to leave an emptiness behind (CI, 36). This distinction "appears in a more definite form," he claims, "as the relation between the *abstract* and the *mythical* in Plato's dialogues" (CI, 40). The former terminates in (Socratic) irony, while the latter heralds "a more copious [Platonic] speculation" (CI, 40–41).

Kierkegaard engages in a close analysis of these elements in five of Plato's dialogues: *Symposium*, *Protagoras*, *Phaedo*, *Apology*, and *Republic*, Book I (CI, 53). He begins with the *Symposium*, a dialogue especially important for our purposes since it focuses on the concept of love. Only a cursory review of the speeches leading up to Socrates' oration in the dialogue is given, since in Kierkegaard's opinion none of them stands "in any necessary relation to the final one" and together they constitute merely a collection of "heterogeneous viewpoints found in life" (CI, 42).[6] More importantly, in Kierkegaard's opinion they reveal nothing about the nature of love, which remains invisible in them. Kierkegaard thus moves on quickly to the speech of Socrates, which takes up and further

---

[6] Briefly, Kierkegaard notes the eternal, victorious character of Eros, the god of love, in the speech of Phaedrus. In the oration of Pausanias he finds a concentration on the god's dual (heavenly / vulgar) nature. In Eryximachus' speech the unity of dichotomous factors in love is emphasized. In Aristophanes' mythological account it is the negative element in love's yearning for union that stands out. And in Agathon's speech the perpetually youthful, delicate, and lovely demeanor of the god is eulogized (CI, 42–44).

develops the theme of love as desire and longing for union in the speech of Aristophanes.

Noting the reputation of Socrates as an ironist, which in Kierkegaard's estimation is based on far more than a knack for the use of rhetorical irony, our amorist interpreter focuses his analysis of Socrates' speech on the way in which the dialectical method functions in it (CI, 45). Unlike the method of Hegel, which moves from an abstract universal constituting everything to its unfolding in the concrete, the Socratic method, he observes, moves in the opposite direction, from the concrete to the abstract, "simplifying life's multifarious complexities by leading them back to an ever more abstract abbreviation" (CI, 32, 41, 46; cf. 267). In this instance the Socratic method yields a negative, abstract definition of love as "the want of and desire for what one does not have" (CI, 32, 41, 45). But this is a definition of love which, in Kierkegaard's estimation, is really no definition, since it lacks substance or content, denoting "a relation to a something that is not given" rather than the fullness of divine or infinite love (CI, 45–46). It thus constitutes an ironic definition of love, or to state it more precisely, erotic love is defined here as ironic love, the opposite of what love is in its fullness or positive definition.

This dialectical, negative, ironic, purely abstract view of love is complemented by another development in the *Symposium* which in Kierkegaard's view establishes a point of conjunction between Socrates and Plato, or between the ironical (the dialectical) and the speculative (the idea in its fullness), by having the idea of love exemplified in the person of Socrates (CI, 46–47). This development may be observed in the speech of Alcibiades, which Kierkegaard proceeds to examine next, bypassing for the moment the speech of Diotima as reported by Socrates. The reason for overleaping Diotima's speech at this point is because it introduces the element of the mythical and thus is deferred until consideration of that factor in the dialogue.

In the speech of Alcibiades, Kierkegaard notes that, unlike the previous speakers, who groped for the idea of love like blind men, Alcibiades is able to grasp it "with immediate certainty" because he is in a heightened state of immediacy due to alcoholic intoxication (CI, 47). Although Alcibiades becomes attached to Socrates with "vehement passion" in an ambiguous love relation that is at once enslaving and painful to him, their relation is characterized as an *intellectual* one by Kierkegaard (CI,

48). But it is not a normal intellectual relationship involving a mutual exchange of ideas or a process of give and take between teacher and student in which the idea is present as a third term binding them together. Rather, it is one in which the idea remains hidden, masked by irony, as "it is essential for the ironist never to articulate the idea as such but only casually to suggest it, to give with one hand and take away with the other, to hold the idea as personal property," Kierkegaard maintains (CI, 48–49). He thus concludes that "even in Alcibiades' view of Socrates irony is his essential aspect," with the result that nothing can be learned about the nature of love from their relation (CI, 49). Even in moments of Socrates' transfiguration, when Alcibiades is able to behold the divine images, or a divine fullness, in his soul, this fullness is hidden in such a way as not to function as a positive source of inspiration for his pupil. What attracts Alcibiades and incites his love is Socrates' personality, which stands ironically in a "negative self-relation to the idea," that is, turned in upon himself in a kind of "omphalopsychic staring" at himself, Kierkegaard observes (CI, 50). Thus, even in the exemplification of love in his own person Socrates provides only a negative or ironic manifestation of an intellectual love equivalent to "what lovers' games and quarrels are in the realm of baser love" for the incitement of love (CI, 51). While our amorist interpreter is willing to admit that the ironist possesses an *Urgrund* (primordial ground) or intrinsic value in himself, this fullness is a determination of nature or vitality of being that never discloses itself in the ironist's dealings with the world (CI, 51–52).

This view of Socrates will re-appear and receive further treatment in Kierkegaard's analysis of Aristophanes' portrayal of the ironic philosopher. Before moving on to that account, however, we must attend to the second factor by which Kierkegaard thinks Plato's thought may be differentiated from that of Socrates in the early dialogues, namely the mythical. Whereas the dialectical prevails in Plato's earliest dialogues, which end either indeterminately without a conclusion or else ironically with a negative conclusion, the mythical element is more prominent in the *Symposium* and *Phaedo*, Kierkegaard claims (CI, 54–55, 62). Moreover, these two dialogues bear a certain kinship with one another inasmuch as longing constitutes the substance of both (CI, 62, 72n). In the *Symposium* this longing takes the form of a desire to possess, while in the *Phaedo* it is manifested as a desire to lose, as in the philosopher's apathetic wish for death, which Kierkegaard regards as a "snobbish sickness found only in the highest social circles" (CI, 72n, 75–77). In his judgment, however, both forms of longing are negative inasmuch as they signify an ignorance of "the what" into which the subjects would either hurl or volatilize themselves (CI, 72n).

However, the thoroughgoing negativity of Socratic dialectic in these and other early dialogues of Plato is complemented by the contrasting presence of the mythical, or the imaginative representation of ideality in the form of actuality. As Kierkegaard sees it, the mythical belongs to Plato rather than to Socrates, for whom the dialectical is characteristic. If the dialectical may be understood erotically as a desire or craving for the idea, the mythical corresponds to an erotic "embrace" of the idea (CI, 103). It appears in the early dialogues as an unconscious, poetic reaction on Plato's part to Socrates' negative dialectic, and in the later dialogues as a conscious mirroring of the idea in the form of metaphor. In the *Symposium*, which is the dialogue of primary interest to us here, the mythical makes its appearance, Kierkegaard observes, in the speech of Diotima, which contains two mythical components. The first emerges in Diotima's attempt to let the negative element in thought, that is, its eternal restlessness, be *seen* under the qualifications of time and space in the figure of Eros, who is characterized by the Mantinean priestess as an intermediate being neither divine nor human, immortal nor mortal, rich nor poor, wise nor ignorant (*Symposium*, 203c–204b; cf. CI, 106). In Kierkegaard's opinion, however, the mythical element in Diotima's speech does not consist in its reference to the myth of Eros as such but to the way in which the speech seeks "to maintain something that actually is not" in the form of an ideal reality concocted by the imagination that gives positive content to the idea of love (CI, 106).

The second mythical component of Diotima's speech may be discerned in its advancement of the beautiful as the object of Eros. First, the concept of beauty is stripped of all physical and psychic qualifications by an increasingly abstract dialectical movement from beautiful bodies to beautiful souls, beautiful observations, beautiful knowledge, and finally to the beautiful in itself. A mythical dimension is then added to this abstract dialectical movement by Diotima's suggestion that the essence of beauty, or "'beauty itself, sheer, pure, unalloyed, not clad in human flesh and hues or other mortal vanity,'" may be "*beheld*," that is, grasped in determinate form (CI, 107). As with the figure of Eros, Kierkegaard emphasizes that the mythical presentation does not consist in its being put into the mouth of Diotima, who is believed by most Plato scholars to be a fictional figure.[7] Rather, it consists in the object—in this instance the beautiful—being placed outside of thought only to be brought back again under the aegis of the imagination—a feature that is intrinsic to the mythical, Kierkegaard claims (CI, 108).

In focusing on the mythical elements in Diotima's speech and in associating them with Plato rather than Socrates, Kierkegaard considerably downplays the importance of Diotima's philosophic characterization of Eros as a lover of wisdom (*philosophon*) in the dialogue. But a passion for wisdom is everywhere assumed as the basis of Socratic eros in his account, as in, for example, the use of a passage from the *Phaedrus*—"passion for a loved one joined with the love of wisdom"—to explain what is meant by calling Socrates an amorist in an intellectual sense (CI, 191). On the whole, however, it is not Plato's view of Socrates that most informs Kierkegaard's phenomenological interpretation of him, but rather that of Aristophanes, who is credited by our amorist interpreter with opening up "the possibility of a new approach" to the Greek philosopher by depicting him dramatically in *The Clouds* as a comic figure (CI, 128). As Kierkegaard sees it (following Rötscher), the essence of comedy consists in "viewing actuality ideally," that is, in construing a personality or character as the representative of an idea or principle (CI, 129).[8] The principle Socrates represents for Aristophanes is the principle of subjectivity—but only in its barest, most abstract, negative or ironic form. Thus, as the representative of subjectivity Socrates provides merely a glimpse of the idea, not a representation of it in its positive fullness (CI, 132).

In his analysis of Aristophanes' dramatic presentation of Socrates, Kierkegaard pays close attention to three items considered to be "of primary importance" in the play: the understanding of Socrates as a person-

---

[7] For a discussion of whether Diotima is a mythical figure or an actual historical person, see David M. Halperin, "Why Diotima Is a Woman," in *One Hundred Years of Homosexuality and Other Essays on Greek Love* (New York: Routledge, 1990), 119–24. See also K. J. Dover, *Greek Homosexuality*, 161, n.11.

[8] It should be noted that Kierkegaard views both Aristophanes and Plato as providing an ideal, as opposed to an empirical, interpretation of Socrates, but the former portrays him ideally as a comic figure, while the latter presents him as a tragic ideality.

ality, the priority of the dialectical in his teaching, and his position vis à vis the principle of subjectivity (CI, 145, 147). Concerning the first item, Socrates is understood as a *personality* or individual because he is an ironist, a figure who falls under the rubric of personality by virtue of the fact that he is "always singular" and takes everything back into himself (CI, 147). The latter characteristic, in Kierkegaard's estimation, constitutes the primary qualification of personality, although an ironist qualifies as only an "abbreviation" or "outline" of a complete personality since his life lacks any positive content (CI, 147, 149, 220n). In consonance with Plato's characterization of Socrates as omphalopsychically staring at himself, therefore, Aristophanes portrays Socrates as an ironic personality who is totally immersed in himself (CI, 141, 145–46). His *dialectic* is described in like manner as a purely negative one that "continually remains in itself" and is self-sufficient, desiring nothing, never going out "into the qualifications of life or of the idea," and thus entirely without content (CI, 135–36, 145, 149–151, 154). As for his *position*, Socrates is graphically portrayed by the Greek dramatist as suspended in a basket, hovering between ideality and actuality, in a position of "complete isolation" (CI, 146, 152). Socrates has pupils but is not attached to them or involved in any real relationship with them. Rather, like the clouds symbolizing his ethereal position, he "continually hovers freely above them, enigmatically attracting and repelling" young men while remaining detached and seemingly indifferent to them (CI, 137, 146).

In spite of the fact that Kierkegaard thinks Aristophanes' portrayal of Socrates' ironic position is "entirely correct," as an amorist interpreter he understands himself to play the role of a neutral "third party" whose hermeneutical task is to mediate between opposing views or interpretations, reconciling their differences through an explanation of the phenomenon that can account for the discrepancies between them (CI, 146, 155). In this way there comes into existence the possibility of a "final view" that offers not merely a view or interpretation (*Opfattelse*) of the phenomenon, as in the accounts of Xenophon, Plato, and Aristophanes, but in a stricter sense of the word a reproduction or reconstruction of the phenomenon, which is the goal of Kierkegaard's hermeneutics and dissertation (CI, 155; SV XIII, 239–240). Ironically contrasting his approach to "the now widespread and in so many ways meritorious scholarly method" of the time, which in his estimation begins with, rather than arrives at, a final view, Kierkegaard criticizes the scholarly approach for its loss of the element of contemplation in relation to previous views, which are merely assigned a place in the final view (CI, 156). Contemplation is always important to interpretation, he maintains, but in this instance it is doubly important because that is the only way the phenomenon, not being present for immediate observation, may be regained (CI, 156).

Kierkegaard proceeds to construct or "actualize" a final—presumably his own—view of Socrates by taking into account certain historical phenomena which may be explained, he suggests, by keeping them, in an amorist fashion, "in their inviolate innocence" (CI, 156). These phenomena consist of two facts: 1) that Socrates assumed he possessed a daimon and 2) that he was condemned to death for not accepting the gods of the state and for seducing the youth (CI, 157, 168, 183). With regard to the daimon of Socrates, Kierkegaard notes that it is something abstract, divine, beyond definition, indescribable, and wholly negative, having the effect of making him relate polemically to actuality or the state (CI, 158–60). In agreement with Hegel, who views the daimon as separate from Socrates yet as something inward that confirms his position as subjectivity, Kierkegaard regards the daimon as a qualification of subjectivity. But in opposition to Hegel he maintains that in Socrates subjectivity did not disclose itself in its fullness via a positive relation to the idea (CI, 163–65). Rather, the idea was a "boundary from which Socrates turned back into himself in ironic satisfaction," egotistically closing himself off from the established order as well as from close relationships with others (CI, 165–66, 168–69).

As Kierkegaard interprets it, therefore, the Socratic maxim "know thyself" did not signify the attainment of any positive content on the part of Socrates but only meant "separate yourself from the other" (CI, 177). Although Socrates lived in "lively contact" with others and entered into personal relations with them, these relations were always loose and momentary, never developing into anything deeper or permanent (CI, 180–182). Thus he is aptly described by Kierkegaard as "a virtuoso in casual contacts" (CI, 181). "No relationship was strong enough to bind him," Kierkegaard contends, nor did he exhibit the earnestness and pathos required of a teacher toward his pupils (CI, 182, 187). Standing aristocratically above every relationship, sufficient unto himself in ironic contentment, Socrates freed others from their substantial ties to family and state but gave them nothing to put in the place of these relations (CI, 176, 182). As Kierkegaard expresses it:

> One could not think of Socrates as someone who under the celestial vault of ideas elevated his pupils through the intuition of their eternal essence, as someone who impregnated youths with the rich fullness of a vision, as someone who ethically laid an enormous responsibility upon his own shoulders and watched them with fatherly concern, reluctantly let them go but never lost sight of them, as someone who, to recall a previous expression, loved them in the idea. (CI, 187)

Although Socrates possessed "an extraordinary enthusiasm for knowledge," in Kierkegaard's opinion he harbored "no deeper speculative craving" as a result of the negative freedom he attained (CI, 176, 188). His pupils, however, were unable to enjoy their emancipation with the same ironic satisfaction as he. A longing was thus awakened in them that was not satisfied by him, precipitating the charge of Alcibiades—with which Kierkegaard here concurs—that Socrates was a seducer who attracted youths and deceived them into believing that he loved them when it was really they who loved him (CI, 176, 188). An ironic reversal of roles thus took place, with Socrates becoming the beloved rather than the lover in relation to his pupils (CI, 188, 191). In his role as the beloved, however, Socrates remained detached and seemingly indifferent to his lovers, as may be witnessed in his relation to Alcibiades, whose sexual advances were continually spurned by him (CI, 189–90, 47).

Kierkegaard's characterization of Socrates as the beloved thus corresponds closely to the *eromenos* (beloved) of Greek homosexual tradition who, according to Kenneth Dover and Martha Nussbaum, was also self-absorbed and self-sufficient, in need of nothing beyond himself.[9] But whereas the Greek *eromenos* engaged in carnal pederasty with his admirers, allowing them to touch and hug him physically without his being sexually aroused, Socrates' pederasty is understood metaphorically by Kierkegaard as the symbol of an intellectual love of possibility (CI, 191–92). As in Greek pederasty, Socrates' relations to his lovers never went

[9] See Martha C. Nussbaum, *The Fragility of Goodness: Luck and Ethics in Greek Tragedy and Philosophy* (Cambridge: Cambridge University Press, 1986), 188; K. J. Dover, *Greek Homosexuality*, II, Ch.5.

beyond the category of possibility inasmuch as they were only the beginning of relationships that never achieved any deeper meaning (CI, 189, 192). The same or worse may be said of Socrates' relation to his (supposedly) shrewish wife Xanthippe, whose main significance for Socrates, according to Xenophon, consisted in serving as "an exercise in controlling mankind"—which "does not indicate much conjugal love" on his part, Kierkegaard notes (CI, 192n).

Kierkegaard thus concludes that Socrates was "far too personally isolated" and his relations "too loosely joined" to result in anything more than casual contacts with others (CI, 182). However, this does not signify a depreciation of Socrates in Kierkegaard's interpretation. On the contrary, he is hailed as a hero in the (Hegelian) sense that he knew what was required for his time—that is, the next, necessary step for progress—and dedicated himself to promoting it (CI, 211, n. 497).[10] As Kierkegaard evaluates it, therefore, Socratic irony was world-historically justified inasmuch as Socrates served as a turning point in world history: He did not bring the new principle of subjectivity in its fullness but was the obstetrician (*accoucheur*) who delivered it in others (CI, 199–200, 211).

In like manner, we may conclude that just as irony is only the beginning or possibility of subjectivity, so too Socrates' ironic love represents only the beginning or possibility of love, not love in its fullness. As reconstructed in Kierkegaard's final view, Socratic eros hardly qualifies as the model of erotic love in either its Platonic or modern understanding, since these require a sustained, positive relation to the idea and through that to others which is altogether lacking in its Socratic manifestation. It is not surprising, therefore, that in the conclusion of *The Concept of Irony* Kierkegaard calls for the mastering of irony so as to make it a "controlled element" and "serving spirit" in one's personal life—something Socrates, having been overwhelmed by irony, was not able to do (CI, 264, 325). Along with controlled irony Kierkegaard also looks forward to the emergence of an erotic longing for a higher actuality that will constitute "a sound and healthy love," one that embraces actuality rather than rejects it, thereby making "life's content...a genuine and meaningful element in the higher actuality whose fullness the soul craves" (CI, 328–29). Far

[10] In Kierkegaard's opinion, however, Socrates is not a tragic hero, who stands in contrast to the ironist by virtue of the fact that he advances the new, whereas an ironist does not possess the new (CI, 260–61; 271).

from embracing Socratic irony and eros, then, as some interpreters think, the concluding irony of *The Concept of Irony* is the negation of both in their unmitigated negativity toward actuality and total self-isolation from others.[11]

In light of Kierkegaard's later writings, it can be seen too that the "final view" of Socrates set forth in this text turns out not to be his final view after all. For he later criticizes his own earlier interpretation of Socrates and views him in a substantially different light, as not simply an ironist but an ethicist who uses irony as an incognito of his inner relation to the ethical requirement (see CUP, 503–4).[12] Kierkegaard thus comes to view Socratic irony more like Plato and Hegel, as a controlled element in service to the idea rather than as absolute infinite negativity, although he continues to assert that "Socrates lacked the positive" (PF, 23). This modification is already anticipated in *The Concept of Irony*, inasmuch as in irony which is world-historically justified, such as that of Socrates, the emancipation of subjectivity is carried out, Kierkegaard claims, "in service to the idea, even if the ironic subject is not clearly conscious of this" (CI, 263). By the time of *Concluding Unscientific Postscript*, however, he has come to see more clearly that Socratic or "essential irony" signifies "the cultivation of the spirit" or the infinite within the subjectively existing

---

[11] For some perspectives that offer an ironic, as opposed to an amorist, interpretation of *The Concept of Irony*, see Sylviane Agacinski, *Aparté: Conceptions and Deaths of Søren Kierkegaard*, tr. Kevin Newmark (Tallahassee: Florida State University Press, 1988), 33–78; Louis Mackey, "Starting from Scratch: Kierkegaard Unfair to Hegel," in *Points of View: Readings of Kierkegaard* (Tallahassee: Florida State University Press, 1986), 1–22; and John Vignaux Smyth, *A Question of Eros: Irony in Sterne, Kierkegaard, and Barthes* (Tallahassee: Florida State University Press, 1986), 101–222.

[12] See also *Philosophical Fragments*, 23–24 and 30, where the relation between Socrates and his pupils is viewed as constituting the highest in human relations, and the charge that Socrates is a seducer is explicitly denied; rather, it is Socrates' pupils who are regarded as unsuccessfully employing the arts of seduction to entice Socrates into seducing them. Moreover, Socrates' ironic love is characterized in this text as an "assisting love" that is sympathetic as well as autopathic in nature, providing an occasion for both the teacher and the learner to acquire self-understanding. For a fuller discussion of Kierkegaard's revised view of Socrates, see my book, *Living Poetically: Kierkegaard's Existential Aesthetics* (University Park: The Pennsylvania State University Press, 1994), 211–12.

individual (CUP, I: 504). The form of the subjective thinker, like that of its paradigm, Socrates, is continually negative in the cognizance of the illusiveness of the infinite in existence, but at the same time the subjective thinker, again like Socrates, is passionately, positively related to the infinite as his or her ethical telos (CUP, 84).[13]

The problem with an ironic interpretation of *The Concept of Irony*—and with Kierkegaard's own "final view" or ironic interpretation of the phenomenon Socrates—is that it is not ironic enough, inasmuch as the irony of Socrates is taken literally rather than ironically. That is, Socrates' "seeming indifference" to others may be just that, a seeming indifference rather than an actual one, and thus the mask or incognito of a genuine ethical concern for others. In that case, the incongruence of *The Concept of Irony* with the later authorship's interpretation of him would not be as great as it at first seems. Furthermore, what appears to be an ambivalence or inconsistency in Kierkegaard's view of Socrates in *The Concept of Irony* itself would be resolved, for if Socrates is truly indifferent toward others, he must be interpreted as narcissistic and malevolent, not as an amorist at all.[14]

In one important respect, however, Kierkegaard's view of Socrates never changes, namely as continually turning into himself. In *The Concept of Anxiety*, for example, Vigilius Haufniensis specifically identifies Socratic irony as inclosing reserve (*Indesluttethed*) or the attempt of a person to close him- or herself off from others so as to become shut up within him- or herself (CA, 134). Ordinarily this phenomenon is understood as being demonic in nature, expressing an anxiety about the good or a state of unfreedom with respect to communication or disclosure of oneself to others (CA, 118–36).[15] In contrast to this demonic form of shut-upness, however, Vigilius also speaks of a "lofty inclosing reserve" which should

---

[13] On the relation between the positive and the negative in *Concluding Unscientific Postscript* and in Kierkegaard's later religious writings, see my article, "Kierkegaard's Inverse Dialectic," *Kierkegaardiana* 11 (1980): 34–54.

[14] In one passage of the text Kierkegaard actually admits that "by bringing others into the same situation [of a negative relation to the state] he [Socrates] actually did do evil" (CI, 183; cf. also 185n), and Socrates' self-immersion is characterized as "egotistical" several places in the text, although it is not as egotistic (and sickly) as that of the later romantic ironists (CI, 166, 213n).

[15] Cf. SUD, 61–66, where this phenomenon is identified with despair in weakness in its most intense (suicidal) form.

be encouraged and developed in persons. This can be done, he thinks, by leaving others to themselves "in the very highest degree and on the greatest possible scale," letting them learn, like a child, to walk alone (CA, 126; cf. CUP, 74, 80). From Vigilius' perspective this kind of inclosing reserve, like that of Socrates, is not negative or abstract but rather signifies a certitude or inwardness that is synonymous with a concrete subjectivity, earnestness, or religious self-consciousness, and thus with an actual personality, in whom anxiety, like irony, becomes "a serving spirit" (CA, 134, 138–54, 159).

Similarly, in *Works of Love* Kierkegaard asserts that the greatest or highest beneficence one individual can do for another is to help that person stand alone and become independent without being aware of being helped, and he specifically alludes to "that noble rogue," Socrates, as being "a master in this wisdom" (WL, 276; cf. also PF, 24 and CUP, 80). "In this understanding of what it is to help another human being, the one who truly loves and that noble rogue agree," Kierkegaard contends (WL, 276). But there is one crucial difference between them: "however noble and magnanimous and unselfish that rogue was, he still did not in the sense of concern love the one he wanted to help" (WL, 277). For one who truly loves understands that it is only through God's help, not by one's own assistance, that others are enabled to become wholly free. Thus, in helping the other the true lover is "God's co-worker" who works invisibly and without reward, annihilating himself or herself in self-sacrifice so as to become "completely and wholly transformed into simply being an active power in the hands of God" (WL, 279; cf. 364, 405–6).

While Socrates may not qualify as a true lover from Kierkegaard's later, more specifically Christian perspective, or even from the standpoint of his ironic interpretation of Socratic eros in *The Concept of Irony*, an amorist interpretation of the phenomenon may yet conclude that ironic love is to be commended inasmuch as it opens up the possibility of subjectivity or inwardness for both the lover and the beloved, enabling each to stand alone as an independent personality. Does such independence compromise a relational, and thus traditionally feminine, understanding of subjectivity and love as envisioned in Kierkegaard's erotic hermeneutics? I think not, since one of the distinguishing characteristics of irony, as Kierkegaard understands it, is that phenomenon and essence are not the same (CI, 247). Thus, what appears to be egotism and indifference toward others may not, in essence, be the case. To become true lovers we must become freestanding individuals ourselves as well as encourage that in others. Just as "one must warn against irony as against a seducer," therefore, one may also commend "diving into the sea of irony, not in order to stay there, of course, but in order to come out healthy, happy, and buoyant" (CI, 327).

9

KIERKEGAARD'S PHILOSOPHY OF LOVE*

In the preface to the first edition of his book, *The Nature of Love*, Irving Singer rightly observes that "in the last sixty years or so the analysis of love has been neglected more than almost any other subject in philosophy."[1] While his three-volume study makes a major contribution toward remedying this deplorable situation, it is sometimes superficial in its treatment of philosophers selected for the study. This is especially true of the nineteenth-century Danish philosopher Søren Kierkegaard. Although Singer rightly notes that Kierkegaard "writes book after book about the nature of love" (Singer, 3: 38), his thought receives only twelve pages of consideration in a chapter shared with and devoted mostly to Tolstoy and Nietzsche. In this essay I propose to rectify this imbalance and to reverse the priority Singer gives to Nietzsche, who wrote comparatively little about love, by providing a more thorough—though by no means comprehensive—analysis of Kierkegaard's philosophy of love. As a result I hope not only to demonstrate the importance of love in Kierkegaard's thought but also to secure his rightful place as a major thinker and perhaps the most significant modern Christian thinker in the history of the philosophy of love.

As indicated in Singer's comment on Kierkegaard quoted above, love is a major theme in Kierkegaard's writings. It forms a central concern of the pseudonymous works *Either/Or, Repetition,* and *Stages on Life's Way* and is integral to other Kierkegaard writings. In the pseudonymous works one can discern several different philosophies of love being worked out consistent with the esthetic, ethical, and religious life views of the authors to whom Kierkegaard ascribes these writings. Although

---

*Reprinted by permission from *The Nature and Pursuit of Love*, ed. by David Goicoechea (Amherst: Prometheus Books, 1995), 167–79.

[1] Irving Singer, *The Nature of Love*, 3 vols. (Chicago: University of Chicago Press, 1984 (vols. 1 and 2) and 1987 (vol. 3), 1: xi. Hereafter references to this work will appear in parentheses in the text as Singer with the volume and page numbers.

these works contribute in important ways to the formation of Kierkegaard's philosophy of love, the views they set forth cannot be unequivocally identified as his own. For that we must turn to a later work, *Works of Love* (1847), a collection of Christian discourses published under Kierkegaard's own name and thus indisputably representing his own point of view. This work constitutes by far the most important treatment of love in Kierkegaard's thought. As I have claimed elsewhere, it is "perhaps the most deeply reflective of all Kierkegaard's writings and surely one of the most profound meditations on love ever written."[2] Unfortunately, however, Singer allots only two and a half pages to it, regarding it as one of Kierkegaard's "religious tracts that need not detain us long" and quickly concluding that the book is "too remote from human experience to be convincing" (Singer, 3:45, 48). That such an estimate constitutes a gross misjudgment of this work is one of the points I shall seek to establish in this essay. Concentrating on *Works of Love*, my analysis will center on the dialectical identification of Christian love and self-denial in Kierkegaard's thought, with its consequent implications concerning the relation between human love and divine love, self-love and self-denial, neighbor love and erotic love and / or friendship, and finally love and suffering.

LOVE AND SELF-DENIAL

Kierkegaard was first and foremost a Christian thinker and thus in his philosophy of love he sought primarily to clarify the nature of Christian love. In *Works of Love* Kierkegaard understands Christian love in a traditional manner as involving love of God, one's fellow human beings, and even oneself, but as he sees it, Christian love must be distinguished from a merely human conception of love and understood in terms of its dialectical expression in self-denial. The dialectical relation between Christian love and self-denial is such that the first is not possible without the second, for Christian love *is* self-denial's love.[3] Part of the problem Kierkegaard wishes to address in *Works of Love* consists in his belief that Christian love and self-denial have been confused with and subsumed under purely natural, pagan, universal-human, and worldly conceptions of love

[2] See "Forming the Heart: The Role of Love in Kierkegaard's Thought," in the present collection.

[3] *Works of Love*, 55–56. All subsequent references to this work will be given in the text with siglum and page number.

and self-denial. A common error, he points out, is to regard Christian love as the highest expression of human love. Kierkegaard agrees that Christian love is the highest form of love, but in his view it is not the highest in direct continuity with purely human forms or expressions of love. Rather, Christian love is qualitatively different from, even the opposite of, merely human love and is distinguished by being placed against, not on, the comparative scale with natural, pagan, purely human, and worldly expressions of love. Far from being the highest expression of merely human love, it constitutes an offense to that understanding. Natural or merely human forms of love consist in immediate, spontaneous feelings or inclinations toward others such as erotic love and friendship. Christian love, too, is a passion that is grounded in inwardness, but one that seeks expression as action rather than as mere feeling. Christian love is what it does, i.e., it is a passion or form of inwardness that reduplicates itself inversely in outwardness and thus is known by its fruits, the works of love.[4] Although works do not provide any direct or unconditional demonstration of love, they at least indicate indirectly the presence of love. Still, one must believe, for one cannot know, that such works are expressions of love. Belief in love is possible, Kierkegaard thinks, only when one is a loving person oneself. By abiding in love one is able to recognize love in others, and one's own love becomes recognizable in the same manner. The important task, however, is not to seek recognition but simply to produce the fruits that manifest love, which make it knowable even if it cannot be unequivocally known.

Christian love is also distinguished from natural, human, and pagan forms of love by the fact that it is eternal, whereas these other forms of love are essentially transient, perishable, and subject to change even if change does not occur. For this reason temporal forms of love are always uncertain and require continual reaffirmation of their existence between

[4] Thus it is not sufficient, and even promotes the very confusion Kierkegaard hopes to dispel, to characterize Christian love simply as hidden inwardness. Whereas true religiosity is identified in *Concluding Unscientific Postscript* as consisting in hidden inwardness which can find no satisfactory outward expression of its pathos, in *Works of Love* Kierkegaard claims that Christian love, although ultimately hidden in inwardness, is not "such a hidden feeling that it is too exalted to bear fruit, or such a hidden feeling that the fruits demonstrate neither for or against" (WL, 15).

lovers. Christian love, by contrast, is love that has won not merely continuance (*Bestaaen*) without change but enduring continuance amid change (*Bestandighed*) (WL, 31–32). Enduring continuance is gained by love's having undergone the transformation of the eternal so as to become consciously grounded in the eternal through the Christian command to love. Christian love is thus a passion that is no longer simply immediate or spontaneous but one that has become a matter of conscience and duty.[5] When love is a duty it is forever decided that one shall love and that love shall abide.[6]

The qualitative heterogeneity of Christian love from merely human or pagan forms of love is most evident in the latter's view of what constitutes genuine love and self-love. As Kierkegaard understands it, paganism rejects self-love in favor of erotic love and friendship, which are regarded as genuine expressions of love inasmuch as they are passionate preferences for other persons (WL, 53). In his view, however, even erotic love and friendship are secretly forms of self-love. He points out that even when pagan love devotes itself to another and admires that person the relationship has the effect of turning back to the lover's advantage, for just as the loved one is the lover's object of admiration, so too the lover forms the beloved's object of admiration in return (WL, 54). To relate oneself to others in such a way as to expect or require reciprocity in love and to make demands upon them, to use them or try to get something from them, Kierkegaard contends, is really self-love.

In Kierkegaard's view, then, it is the selfishness in erotic love and friendship, not the immediacy or spontaneity as such, that Christianity directly opposes and excludes (WL, 23, 361). Christianity presupposes

---

[5] By becoming consciously based on the eternal love does not lose its immediacy but rather becomes a new form of immediacy after reflection or a "second immediacy," a phrase that does not appear in *Works of Love* but is used in several other works by Kierkegaard. On love as duty and second immediacy, see my essay "Forming the Heart" in the present collection.

[6] Kierkegaard recognizes that it is still possible for an individual to fall away from love, in which case that person becomes guilty in relation to the one who is forsaken. But in his view, the true lover never falls away from love, even if, in an external sense, the relation to the beloved is broken. An excellent example of this is Kierkegaard's own love relation to Regine Olsen, to whom he broke an engagement to marry but never stopped loving. For further discussion of the problem of falling away from love, see "Forming the Heart."

that persons naturally love themselves. It thus sets out to do away with selfish self-love, using natural self-love in such a way as to rid it of selfishness by requiring that one love one's neighbor as oneself. Selfish self-love is mastered by reduplication, that is, by the duplication of oneself in the other as neighbor. Erotic love and friendship also involve reduplication, Kierkegaard admits, but in a quite different manner from what takes place in Christian reduplication. For in erotic love and friendship duplication of oneself in the other means that the beloved becomes one's "other-I" (WL, 53–54). It is not really the other person who is loved but oneself as projected into and benefiting from the relation. Erotic love and friendship culminate in two becoming one in the creation of "a new selfish self" (WL, 56). In contrast to this, Christian redoubling involves reduplication of oneself in the neighbor in such a way as to transform love for oneself into love for the other. Every demand in the relationship is placed upon oneself rather than upon the other, and one desires for the other what one would have desired for oneself. In Christianity, therefore, one regards the other not as an "other-I" but as a genuine "other-you" who is distinct from oneself and who is loved first and foremost not on the basis of preferential love but because that person is a human being like oneself.[7]

In Christian redoubling or reduplication, therefore, one renounces oneself, or more accurately, one renounces self-love in the form of selfishness or egocentricity in oneself by loving others as oneself. Only Christian redoubling is real duplication, Kierkegaard claims, for selfish self-love cannot abide two, and even in its projection to the other it essentially maintains a single concern for itself (WL, 21, 280–81). The "as yourself" in the Christian command, however, implies two, that there is another whom one loves just as one loves oneself. At the same time it also implies that self-denial in Christian love does not entail a total renunciation of oneself but only a renunciation of selfishness. Christian reduplication, in fact, produces a proper form of self-love. As Kierkegaard understands it, Christianity is not opposed to love of self *per se* but only demands that one love oneself in the right way, that is, in a way that does not, for example, squander one's time and energy in vain or frivo-

[7] On Kierkegaard's view of genuine alterity see also my essay, "The Philosophical Affirmation of Gender Difference: Kierkegaard versus Postmodern Neo-Feminism" in the present collection.

lous activities or give in to despair and self-destruction (WL, 23). If one cannot do this, then neither can one love one's neighbor. Kierkegaard explains:

> To love yourself in the right way and to love the neighbor correspond perfectly to one another; fundamentally they are one and the same thing. When the Law's *as yourself* has wrested from you the self-love that Christianity sadly enough must presuppose to be in every human being, then you have actually learned to love yourself. The Law is therefore: You shall love yourself in the same way as you love your neighbor when you love him as yourself (WL, 22–23).

In Kierkegaard's view, Christianity also preserves erotic love and friendship, but the requirement is that we must express neighbor or spiritual love within and in addition to these relations. To love only selectively and to call this "loving one's neighbor" is to make Platonic and erotic special relations the highest and to confuse them with Christian love. First and foremost one must love all persons as neighbors. For Kierkegaard the category of neighbor is equivalent to the category of human being, which is the fundamental qualification of every individual (WL, 141). The Christian rule, according to Kierkegaard, is that "what is the eternal foundation must also be the foundation of every expression of the particular" (WL, 141). Being a friend, beloved, or spouse is a narrower definition of one's position in a special relation. Every special relation must be informed by the broader conception of the other party as a neighbor. Thus, while one certainly loves one's mate differently from the way one loves others, this difference is not essential, since fundamentally one loves one's mate as one loves others, that is, as a human being or as a neighbor. If one does not love one's spouse, beloved, or friends as a neighbor, then one does not love one's neighbor. For to love one's neighbor, as Kierkegaard understands it, is to love all persons without exception and to love them first and foremost as human beings, which we all are equally. A person's particularity or distinguishing characteristics are secondary and cannot serve as a basis for making that individual an exception to the Christian command of neighbor love.

As Kierkegaard sees it, therefore, the Christian task is first of all to love all persons on the basis of our common humanity without making any distinctions between them. This means that one must learn, as it were, to shut one's eyes and allow the "outer garment" of dissimilarities between persons to "hang loosely," to become blind to them and to look away from them (WL, 68, 88). Christianity does not literally do away with earthly dissimilarities between persons but seeks instead to make us victorious over the temptation of dissimilarities by teaching us to lift ourselves above them (WL, 71–72). Nor does it attempt to reduce everything to one distinction as does "well-intended worldliness" (WL, 71–72). In Kierkegaard's view, worldly similarity (*Lighed*), or the establishment of one social condition or class for all, is not the same as Christian equality (*Ligelighed*) (WL, 72). Christianity "allows all the dissimilarities to stand," he argues, "but teaches the equality of eternity" and locates the decisive change in the way one views dissimilarities (WL, 72). For the Christian, differences between persons begin to "hang loosely," enabling that which is common to all persons, their essential humanity, their "eternal likeness," to show through (WL, 68, 88). Then, while making no distinction between those whom one will love, one must at the same time make infinite distinctions between them. That is, one must love each according to his or her own individuality or personal differences. For Kierkegaard this consists primarily in helping persons become authentic selves or individuals by enabling them to become independent and stand on their own as individual selves before God. This is, Kierkegaard says, "the greatest beneficence" one person can accomplish for another (WL, 274).

GOD AS THE OBJECT OF LOVE IN CHRISTIAN TRANSFORMATION

Central to the possibility of Christian love is the requirement that one allow the God relation to penetrate and become a middle term in every love relation. In Kierkegaard's view, Christianity recognizes only one kind of love—spiritual love—and insists that this "lie at the base of and be present in every other expression of love" (WL, 143–44, 146). Before God the lover learns what it means properly to love oneself, to love the beloved, and to be loved in return. Initially in *Works of Love* Kierkegaard defines proper self-love as love for self that excludes selfishness. Later on he further qualifies this definition by adding that the "true conception" of what it is to love oneself is to love God (WL, 113). In Kierkegaard's view God is the only proper object of love. This does not mean that one should become occupied solely with love of God or that the love of others is effaced by one's individual relation to God. On the contrary, as Kierkegaard understands it, the true conception of what it means to love another person is to help that person to love God, and vice versa, to be loved means to be helped by another human being to love God. Since, in Kierkegaard's view, "love is God" and "God is love," this means that the true object of every genuine love relationship is love itself (WL, 190, 265). Christianity seeks to transform every love relation into sacrificial love, that is, to help each party learn to love rather than seek to be loved in and through their relationship. Christian transformation consists finally in being made wholly into an active power in the service of God or love, of becoming dedicated to the well-being of others rather than to one's own self-elevation and promotion in the world.

In Kierkegaard's view, this is how Christianity proposes to spiritually qualify and transform erotic love and friendship. It does not seek the discontinuation or modification of special relationships but rather seeks to inform all human relationships with a third dimension by making God or the neighbor a middle term in them.[8] In his view, all human love is fundamentally grounded in divine love and contains the possibility of manifesting that love by consciously centering personal relations in God, thereby bringing about a transformation of love. This change which Christianity brings about in love relations is internal rather than external in form. Externally, everything remains the same, but it has been internally purified, sanctified, and made new (WL, 145). This is the paradox of Christian transformation, that love is the same yet infinitely different, old yet marvelously new. Christianity seeks to change all forms of love into spiritual love, but it allows the outward distinctions between these forms to persist, simply requiring "the change of infinity" to take place in them (WL, 139). Christian transformation, then, is a transformation of one's former mode of existence in the world. Christianity does not require one to cut oneself off from one's former relationships and flee the world but rather to express Christian love in the context of one's ongoing relationships in the world. In Kierkegaard's view, Christianity's goal is to

[8] The notion of a third factor in love relations appears very early in Kierkegaard's thought, for he writes in his journal in 1837: "All true love is grounded in this, that one loves another in a third" (JP, 3: 2380).

bind the temporal and the eternal, to make the temporal a reflection of the eternal, not to negate or exclude it (WL, 6).[9]

This ethic of transformation has the effect of significantly qualifying the Christian dialectic in relation to the immediate, natural, pagan, worldly, and merely human conceptions of love. While Christianity stands uncompromisingly opposed to these conceptions in their unqualified, selfish forms, the intent of the dialectic points beyond mere differentiation and opposition to an eventual or ultimate union of the natural and the spiritual, the temporal and the eternal, the human and the Christian through the transforming power of self-denying love. Unlike some analyses of love that distinguish between various forms of love such as *eros, philia,* and *agape* (e.g. Nygren, C. S. Lewis, Tillich, and Singer), and in certain perspectives, most notably Nygren's, which regard *eros* and *agape* as unalterably opposed to one another, Kierkegaard recognizes only one genuine form of love, which is spiritual or Christian love.[10] In his view, spiritual love is not separate from or higher than natural forms of love such as erotic love and friendship but rather an altruism or concern for others that comes to expression precisely in and through those forms

[9] Kierkegaard's thought is frequently misinterpreted as calling one away from temporality and finitude. For example, K. E. Løgstrup in *Opgør med Kierkegaard* (København: Gyldendalske Boghandel, 1967) claims that Kierkegaard does not offer any observation on what is required in action by individuals in their milieu or temporal situations, only the action which eternity outside of all temporal and worldly requirements demand of the individual (p. 133). Similarly, T. W. Adorno, in "On Kierkegaard's Doctrine of Love," *Studies in Philosophy and Social Science* 8 (1940), 413–29, accuses him of being "socially conformist," of leaving the world to the devil, and of advocating a "fictitious, merely inward doctrine of equality" severed from social concern and insight. While it is true that Kierkegaard does not provide a "social ethic" in the form of a specific program for the implementation of the Christian command to love in society, one is not relieved from the duty and responsibility of implementing the command to love in one's everyday life. This is not made easy, nor does Kierkegaard attempt to tell us specifically how to do it, because in his view there is no direct and unconditional expression of love and self-denial in outward forms.

[10] Cf. Anders Nygren, *Agape and Eros*, tr. Philip S. Watson (New York: Harper & Row, 1969); C. S. Lewis, *The Four Loves* (New York: Harcourt Brace Jovanovich, Inc., 1960); and Paul Tillich, *Love, Power, and Justice* (London: Oxford University Press, 1954).

of love when the element of selfishness has been rooted out of them (WL, 55).

LOVE AND SUFFERING

Finally, an account of Kierkegaard's philosophy of love would not be true or complete without some consideration of the element of suffering in Christian love. In his view Christian love always involves "double danger" and the possibility of offense on the part of others as well as oneself, inasmuch as it involves a different conception of love than is normally held (WL, 72–73, 76, 81–82, 192, 194) . Serious consequences may result from the attempt to mediate one's temporal relationships with Christian love. Thus the possibility of suffering is always present in love and becomes, in Kierkegaard's later thought, the inverse sign of love by which it becomes indirectly recognizable in the external world. Although reciprocity in love would seem to be an ideal in human love, spiritual love, Kierkegaard claims, does not depend on it and may even express itself in ways that could appear to the other as hatred rather than love. This is just the point where outright collision between the divine conception of love and the merely human conception of love develops, and where Christian love must be expressed and made recognizable through a second form of self-denial. If to love another person means essentially to help that person love God, the extreme implication of this is that if only one party in the relation understands this, then that person may need, as it were, to hate the beloved out of love, even break off the relationship so as not to permit the beloved to reciprocate love as if one were God or meant everything to the beloved. In the context of love, this is what Kierkegaard understands by Christ's teaching that the Christian shall, if necessary, hate father and mother and loved ones. Christianly understood, such an extreme action is not really hate—"far be this abomination from Christianity!" Kierkegaard exclaims—but it would be regarded as such by others (WL, 108).[11] From the world's point of view, to call such

[11] K. E. Løgstrup manifests precisely this sort of misunderstanding in his work cited above. He accuses Kierkegaard of turning love into hate, of transforming it into something evil and isolating the beloved, whereas, in Løgstrup's opinion, love that is really for the neighbor's sake would do and say everything in order to win the neighbor's acceptance (pp. 144–45). From Kierkegaard's point of view, however, this way of proceeding would turn the relation back into self-

an act the expression of love and to sacrifice one's own happiness and that of the beloved is sheer madness. Thus the double inversion develops, namely that precisely what Christianity regards as the ultimate expression of love is looked on by the world as self-love and unkindness, while conversely what the world regards as genuine love Christianity considers to be the expression of self-love. There is, then, an infinite difference between the divine and human conceptions of love. What the world understands and approves as sacrificial love, Kierkegaard claims, is a kind of personal sacrifice to a larger group-selfishness and does not constitute true sacrifice because it seeks and has as its reward the approval of society. In Kierkegaard's view, true sacrifice has no reward, or rather, it has as its reward precisely the opposite of what could be expected through the performance of sacrifice. For the Christian discovers that as a reward for love one is sometimes hated by the beloved and abominated by the world. But voluntary submission to being hated and scorned in return for love is precisely the decisive distinction of Christian love and the "double mark" of Christian self-denial (WL, 195, 204). The Christian not only expects opposition from the world but "knows in advance that this will happen to it and freely chooses it" (WL, 195). In the purely human expression of self-denial one gives up one's own selfish desires, longings, and plans, but with the expectation that for doing so one will become appreciated, honored, and loved by the world (WL, 196). In *Judge for Yourself!* Kierkegaard cites as an example of this the medieval practice of self-denial in which persons were accorded worldly esteem for their acts of sacrifice (JFY, 205). The Christian concept of self-denial, by contrast, is to give up one's selfish desires, longings, and plans in order to work disinterestedly for the good and then to submit by free choice to being abominated, scorned, ridiculed, and perhaps even executed, for this action (WL, 196). From the world's point of view, however, to be willing to be forsaken and treated in this way is stupid and insane. It hardly warrants admiration and approval.

Thus Kierkegaard cautions: "if your ultimate and highest goal is to have life made easy and sociable, then never become involved with Christianity, shun it, because it wants the very opposite; it wants to make

---

ishness and would not have the best interest of the neighbor at heart, whereas in true sacrificial love one is willing to sacrifice everything, even one's own positive relation to the beloved, for the sake of the beloved's highest good.

your life difficult and to do this by making you alone before God" (WL, 124). He even advises ministers of the gospel that they should be prepared to preach against Christianity, if need be, so as to warn people of the dangers to expect in becoming a Christian instead of enticing them to Christianity by a fraudulent depiction of the Christian life (WL, 198). Christianity, Kierkegaard thinks, should not be directly recommended to people; on the contrary, sermons should open with the possibility of offense contained in Christian existence (WL, 198–99). The common practice in the preaching of Christian love, however, is to leave out the added danger that if one ventures to express such love in one's relations to others "it will go badly with him in the world" (WL, 192). In Kierkegaard's estimation such a presentation of Christian existence is deceptive and false. Opposition between Christianity and the world is essential, not accidental (WL, 194). If one ventures to express Christian love unconditionally in one's relations to others, then opposition from the world will surely result, since the Christian and worldly concepts of love are converse to one another and qualitatively heterogeneous. Thus Kierkegaard suggests that the Christian who gets through life without any opposition should be suspicious of him / herself. One must at least expect and be willing to accept opposition, not enter upon the Christian life with the thought of avoiding it and leading a happy life as a consequence of one's decision. The earnest Christian does not seek to avoid danger but willingly chooses it. A Christian does not seek worldly happiness in Christianity but conversely chooses to be unhappy—doubly unhappy—by constraining self-love and then, as a reward for not acting like the crowd, by reaping the world's derision, hatred, and scorn and probably losing one's life (WL, 196).

Kierkegaard's definition of Christian love and self-denial in terms of double danger thus has the effect of significantly qualifying his understanding of love. The Christian conception of love posits an ethical task, making it a duty to love and to make every sacrifice in order to help others become loving persons too. Whereas the worldly person's aim is to have life made easy and happy, Christianity makes life difficult, dangerous, and unhappy. At the same time, however, in coming to love God and neighbor, one finds true meaning in life and truly lives. In the conclusion of *Works of Love* Kierkegaard imagines the beloved apostle John as saying:

> The commandment is that you *shall* love, but ah, if you will understand yourself and life, then it seems that it should not need to be commanded, because to love people is still the only thing worth living for; and without this love you are not really living. Moreover, to love people is the only blessed comfort both here and in the next world; and to love people is the only true sign that you are a Christian"—truly, a profession of faith is not enough either. (WL, 375)

CONCLUSIONS

It is this strong conviction of the ultimacy of love in the form of spiritual or Christian love for God and other human beings, I would contend, that makes Kierkegaard's philosophy of love so deeply profound and so eminently important for the construction of a modern as well as postmodern theory of love.[12] To be sure, Kierkegaard presents an idealization of love that is extremely high and uncompromising, perhaps to an unbearable degree for most human beings, but it is tempered by an equally strong doctrine of grace and forgiveness in the realization that no human being other than Jesus Christ—who in Kierkegaard's view is not merely human but the God-man or God-human being—can express the Christian life of love fully and boundlessly. That does not exempt us, however, from assuming the ethical task of striving to fulfill it. In the definition of this task Kierkegaard delineates a perspective that tackles the age-old problem of selfishness or narcissism in a way that exposes its presence even in those expressions of erotic love and friendship where it is presumably overcome.

[12] For an attempt to formulate a postmodern expression of the altruistic life of self-denying love and compassion for the Other, see Edith Wyschogrod, *Saints and Postmodernism: Revisioning Moral Philosophy* (Chicago: The University of Chicago Press, 1990). Typical of postmodernism, however, is the negation or rejection of the concept of self in the affirmation of an excessive desire for the Other that leaves no room for personal individuality or particularity in the form of a fixed identity or ego on the part of the one who loves or in the Other who is the recipient of love. Over against this extreme expression of altruistic love Kierkegaard's thought offers a more dialectically balanced position affirming both the self and the other, an authentic form of self-love, as well as unbounded self-renunciation in disinterested love for the other.

Although Kierkegaard does not discuss the issue of sexuality in relation to love as directly or centrally as one might wish in *Works of Love*, certainly there are some profound implications in his thought for the expression of sexuality in love and vice versa. For as we have seen, Kierkegaard does not reject sensuousness in favor of a non-corporeal expression of spiritual love but rather seeks to transform the expression of sensuousness or erotic desire in human relations so as to eradicate the element of selfishness in them. In contrast to Irving Singer, who concludes in his own attempt to formulate a modern theory of love that appraisive love—that is, love of others on the basis of their appraised value or utility in relation to our own interests or needs—is a crucial ingredient of love (Singer, 3: 396), Kierkegaard believes in the possibility of human self-transformation via a relation to the eternal that does away with selfishness or self-centeredness while preserving individual self-identity and an authentic form of self-love. Like Singer, he rejects any notion of a "shared identity" or communal "ours," which in Kierkegaard's view constitutes only an augmented form of self-love (WL, 274–78; cf. Singer, 3: 406–417). But unlike Singer, who rejects any form of transcendentalism in favor of a naturalistic account of love, Kierkegaard views human love in the context of the divine, which for him constitutes the only true object of love. One of the chief criticisms Singer brings against both Platonic and Christian concepts of love in the first volume of his trilogy on love is that they advocate a transcendent idealization of love in the Good (Plato) or in God (Christianity) as the object of human love, with the consequence that love of persons is either neglected or used instrumentally as a means to this higher end (Singer, 1: 84, 343–63). Assuming that this criticism is justified in the cases of Augustine, Aquinas, and Luther, the three giants of Christian thought against whom Singer principally makes this charge (and that is certainly a debatable contention which space does not permit me to challenge here), I want finally to suggest that part of the profundity and importance of Kierkegaard's position lies in the way he deals with this problem. Since for Kierkegaard God is identified with love, and God or love is itself projected as the object of human love relations, it would appear that he, too, is subject to Singer's fundamental criticism of Christian views of love. But Kierkegaard's position is immune to this charge, I think, on at least two grounds. First of all, for Kierkegaard a genuine love of persons is secured on the basis of the Christian doctrine of human equality, which requires the recognition of human value bestowed upon all persons by God, not merely upon a human bestowal or creation of value in the love of selected individuals as Singer would have it (Singer, 1: 3). Second, since for Kierkegaard love is the object of love relations, love for the other person comes to expression precisely in helping that individual become an independent and loving person. As the true object of love, God is not conceived as a transcendent entity that directs us away from love of persons in the world but rather is understood in a relational context as the transcendent ground and matrix of love within which love of all persons is affirmed and expressed in the world. For Kierkegaard, then, love of God and love of persons are integrally connected; one cannot have the one without the other.

In these and other ways, Kierkegaard has plumbed the depths of love to a degree unmatched in modern literature on love. While there are shortcomings and limitations in his thought, as is true of every other philosophy of love, Kierkegaard has much to offer for our individual edification and scholarly reflection on the nature of love.[13]

[13] For an indication of what I perceive to be some weaknesses in Kierkegaard's views on love, see my essay "Forming the Heart: The Role of Love in Kierkegaard's Thought" and other studies on Kierkegaard's view of love cited in it.

10

FORMING THE HEART: THE ROLE OF LOVE IN KIERKEGAARD'S THOUGHT*

> It is said of certain plants that they must form hearts; the same must be said of a human being's love: if it is really to bear fruit and consequently to be recognizable by its fruit, it must *form a heart*. Love, to be sure, proceeds from the heart, but let us not in our haste about this forget the eternal truth that love forms the heart.[1]

Love is rooted in that innermost part of our being which we figuratively call the heart. Signifying far more than a vital organ of the body, the heart is a metaphor for inwardness, the passionate, subjective realm of the human spirit. Although love is a passion that comes from the heart, it is Kierkegaard's contention that love plays a formative role in shaping the human heart or inwardness. If, therefore, we look to Kierkegaard for an understanding of the grammar or morphology of the heart, we shall see that in his thought this grammar is construed fundamentally in terms of a grammar of love.

The role of love in forming the heart is probed by Kierkegaard primarily in *Works of Love*, a volume of Christian discourses written at the midpoint of his authorship and published under his own name as author. This work is perhaps the most deeply reflected of all his writings and surely one of the most profound meditations on love ever written, yet it is

---

* Reprinted by permission of HarperCollins Publishers from *The Grammar of the Heart: New Essays in Moral Philosophy & Theology*, ed. Richard H. Bell (San Francisco: Harper & Row, 1988), 235–56.

[1] Søren Kierkegaard, *Works of Love*, tr. Howard Hong and Edna Hong (New York: Harper & Row, 1962), 29. Future references to this work in this essay will be given in the text in parentheses with the siglum WL.

a work that is not well known or much studied until recently.[2] This misfortune is due in part to the fact that attention has been focused primarily on Kierkegaard's early pseudonymous authorship rather than his later religious writings, but it may also reflect a general lack of interest in the subject of love among thinkers of the present century. In a history of the nature of love in Western philosophical and religious thought from Plato to modern times, Irving Singer points out that "in the last sixty years or so the analysis of love has been neglected more than almost any other subject in philosophy."[3] Thinkers such as Santayana, Peirce, Scheler, Buber, and Simone de Beauvoir have incorporated some reflection on love in their philosophies, but to a large extent the analysis of love has been left to the field of psychology. In theology, too, we have seen the development of the neo-orthodox theologies of faith, the theology of hope, the theology of play, process theology, black theology, feminist theology, metaphorical theology, and lately the birth of deconstructionist "a/theology," but very little on the theology of love.[4]

---

[2] For recent studies focusing wholly or in part on *Works of Love*, see L. Brøndum, "S. Kierkegaard om 'Kjerlighedens Gjerninger,'" *Dansk Teologisk Tidskrift* 20 (1957), 242–51; Linell E. Cady, *The Conception of Love and the Self in the Thought of Søren Kierkegaard and Josiah Royce* (Ph.D. dissertation, Harvard University, 1981); Claude Edward Deyton, *The Idea of Love in the Work of Søren Kierkegaard* (Ph. D. dissertation, Drew University, 1981); Hans Friemond, *Existenz in Liebe nach Sören Kierkegaard* (Müchen: Anton Puslet, 1965); Leonard I. Holbein, *Kierkegaard's Understanding of Love, Particularly as Presented in 'Works of Love'* (Ph. D. dissertation, DePaul University, 1979); Valter Lindström, "A Contribution to the Interpretation of Kierkegaard's Book 'The Works of Love,'" *Studia Theologica* 6 (1953): 1–29, and "Eros och agape i Kierkegaards äskadning," *Kierkegaardiana* 1: 102–112; Paul Müller, *Kristendom, Etik og Majeutik i Søren Kierkegaard's "Kjerlighedens Gjerninger"* (Copenhagen: Kobenhavns Universitet Institute for Religionhistorie, 1976); Gene Outka, "Equality and Individuality: Thoughts on Two Themes in Kierkegaard," *Journal of Religious Ethics* 10 (1982): 171–203; Mark C. Taylor, "Love and Forms of Spirit: Kierkegaard vs. Hegel," *Kierkegaardiana* 10 (1977): 95–116.

[3] Irving Singer, *The Nature of Love*, 2 vols. (Chicago: University of Chicago Press, 1984), vol. 1: xi.

[4] Most notable among twentieth-century scholarship on the theology of love is Anders Nygren, *Agape and Eros,* tr. Philip Watson (New York: Harper & Row, 1969).

This state of affairs reveals how out of touch much of contemporary philosophy and theology is with one of the primary concerns of the human heart, where the experience of love has always been important and constitutes for many the ultimate value in life. Certainly, if the grammar of the heart is to be addressed in contemporary thought, attention needs to be given to the analysis of love. With the recent rise of interest in virtue ethics and the logic of the emotions, it is particularly timely that such an analysis be carried out. I cannot possibly do justice to that task in the present essay, but I shall try to sketch the contours of the grammar and language of love, using Kierkegaard's understanding of these as a model and guide for stimulating our own reflection on and schooling in the grammar of love and the heart.

THE GRAMMAR OF LOVE

Love is often thought to be a vague, elusive, indefinable passion that does not conform to the dictates of reason. But love has a logic, a structure, a "grammar," if you will, of its own by which it is known and understood. For Kierkegaard this grammar is informed by Christian love, which in his view constitutes the only true or genuine love and is the love that properly forms the heart. As he sees it, Christian love does not exist as a separate type of love in contradistinction to other types (WL, 77, 144, 146). It is not a "higher love" that is affirmed alongside of or in addition to other forms of love such as erotic love and friendship (WL, 59, 70). Rather, Christianity recognizes only one kind of love—spiritual love—and insists that it "lie at the base of and be present in every other expression of love" (WL, 144, 146). Spiritual or Christian love is characterized by Kierkegaard as a transcendent, transforming, inclusive, edifying, abiding, and spontaneous love that expresses itself in an indirect, inverse form and fashion. To master the grammar of that love, we must gain an understanding of its distinguishing features. In this section, therefore, the primary terms by which Christian love may be identified will be sketched and scrutinized.

Transcendent

Kierkegaard recognizes that human beings have a need both to love and to be loved and that this need for community in love is rooted in the hidden, "most inward depths" of their being, where it is grounded even more deeply and mysteriously in divine love (WL, 26–27, 78, 153). All human love thus has a transcendent matrix in the eternal, whether that is acknowledged or not, but Christian love is distinguished by the fact that it is love that has become *consciously* grounded upon the eternal or God through a command to love. Central to the possibility of Christian love is the requirement that we explicitly relate ourselves to the eternal and allow God to penetrate and become a third or "middle term" in our relations to others (WL, 70, 112–13, 117, 123). Ordinarily we think of love relationships as dyadic in nature; "three is a crowd" we are accustomed to say when a third party becomes involved. But God is not like other third parties. What might it mean to give our love relations a triadic structure by including God? Kierkegaard means something more, I think, than the divine sanction commonly sought and given in the saying of marriage vows, although that is an important aspect of coming to refer conjugal love to God. What the presence of a God-relationship within human love relations means is that God—or love, since for Kierkegaard love is God and God is love (WL, 124, 247)—becomes the object of love; that is, love itself, rather than either lover in the relation, becomes the focus of the relation.

Now, this is a very profound but deeply disturbing idea, for it seems to deflect love away from concrete others as well as ourselves to an abstract principle or transcendent reality that binds us. Who wants to love love? Love for love's sake, like art for art's sake, may be a noble idea, but it does not satisfy our deep human need to love and to be loved by other human beings. Moreover, within the context of the stages of life that Kierkegaard describes in his authorship, it even appears to be aesthetic in nature—a romantic flight from entering into real relations with others.[5] But that is not the intent or desired effect of Kierkegaard's view. On the contrary, love forms the proper object of love relations precisely by putting the focus of those relations on helping one another learn *to love rather than seek to be loved* in and through their relation. In other words, the ultimate goal of a love relation should be to assist both parties in learning to love themselves, each other, and other persons in a proper manner.

[5] For aesthetic interpretations of love as the object of love compare Roland Barthes, *A Lover's Discourse: Fragments*, tr. Richard Howard (New York: Hill and Wang, 1978), 31–32, and Denis de Rougemont, *Love in the Western World*, tr. Montgomery Belgion (New York: Fawcett World Library, 1969).

That is what it means to love God. Kierkegaard writes: "For to love God is to love oneself in truth; to help another human to love God is to love another person; to be helped by another human being to love God is to be loved" (WL, 113).

This conception of self-love, love of others, and love of God is quite different from the usual understanding of these concepts and requires a fundamental transformation of both the mind and the heart in order to understand and to love ourselves, others, and God in this way. It brings us, therefore, to the second term in the grammar of love.

Transforming

Fundamental to Kierkegaard's understanding of Christian love is the claim that it brings about an alteration in love—a "change of heart" we could say—by requiring our natural expressions of love to undergo "the transformation of the eternal" so as to eradicate the element of selfishness in them. We are all well acquainted with the problem of selfishness in human existence, especially as it is manifested in ourselves. There is nothing novel in the idea that we need to overcome narcissism. But Kierkegaard extends the charge of selfishness beyond self-love as we normally experience and understand it to cover also those forms of love, namely friendship and erotic love, wherein we seek naturally to overcome, or at least to modify, the expression of selfishness in ourselves. The problem, as Kierkegaard sees it, is not merely that we continue to act selfishly in obvious ways in our erotic relations and friendships, but that these relations are themselves a form of self-love and a means of perpetuating selfishness. The friend or beloved is an "other-I" with whom we selfishly unite to create a "new selfish self" modeled on our common likenesses and differences from others (WL, 68–69). Friends and lovers are chosen on the basis of our passionate preferences, and although we are (or are expected to be) concerned with their desires and needs in the relation, we expect them to satisfy ours in return. Reciprocity and mutuality in love are essential to friendship and erotic love, but in Kierkegaard's view these qualities are precisely what make these forms of love selfish in character. Kierkegaard is relentless in his exposé of selfishness in them. Even boundless devotion—an expression of erotic love stereotypically associated with and culturally encouraged in women's relations to men—is revealed as self-love in the "tremendous willfulness" with which it makes the beloved mean "everything" to the lover (WL, 67–68).

Unmasked at every attempt to masquerade as unselfishness and shown to be self-centered in their very makeup, can friendship and erotic love be saved? In Kierkegaard's opinion, Christianity is opposed to these forms of love only insofar as they are characterized by selfishness. Thus it does not stand *simply* opposed to them but seeks instead to purify, sanctify, and make them new through self-renunciation, or more properly speaking, through the renunciation of selfishness in them. This transformation is envisaged by Kierkegaard as being entirely internal in nature, except for certain marks (to which we shall return later) that may serve to elicit the possibility of offense on the part of the world (WL, 145–46). Thus the outward forms of erotic relations and friendships remain the same, though infinitely changed within, where love becomes, like other affairs of the heart, a matter of conscience (WL, 139).

This insistence on the totally inward character of Christian transformation has brought strong criticism of Kierkegaard, in particular the stinging charge that he lacked a social ethic. Although he was in many ways an astute and penetrating social critic of his time, I think we can see something of the limitation of his view as it applies to sexual equality. In *Works of Love* he writes:

> Outwardly in a way the old remains—for the man shall be the woman's master and she shall be submissive to him, but in inwardness everything is transformed, transformed with the aid of this little question to the woman, whether she has deliberated with her conscience about having this man—for a master, for otherwise she does not get him. Yet the question of conscience about a matter of conscience makes her in inwardness before God absolutely equal with the man. (WL, 139)

On a spiritual level we have in the last sentence the beginnings of a theological underpinning for a doctrine of equality between the sexes, but unfortunately no corresponding call for a change in social structures to make them commensurate with that doctrine. In the present century we have to some extent gone beyond Kierkegaard in recognizing that a change of external structures is needed to give outward expression to the ideals of sexual equality that we espouse. We have learned, too, that such changes, even when forced upon us by law, may actually facilitate the inner transformation of minds and hearts. In the area of personal relations, however, outward change cannot be legislated to any great degree, and we still live largely in the patriarchal structure of male-female relations to which Kierkegaard subscribes. To the extent that is true, many of us are no further along than him and perhaps not as far. This is not to say that Christian love cannot be expressed within a patriarchal structure, but such a pattern of relations, I would contend, is structurally incompatible with Christian love and equality. Certainly it is not an ideal structure for expressing them.[6]

A second issue that arises with respect to Kierkegaard's conception of transformation is whether the "erotic" element can be preserved in the metamorphosis of erotic love into spiritual love. Are we left with the mere skeleton of an erotic form, stripped of its distinguishing characteristics of sensuous desire, passionate preference, and reciprocity in love? Has Kierkegaard so identified the erotic with selfishness, or selfishness with the erotic, that it cannot be saved? Kierkegaard explicitly says in *Works of Love* that Christianity is not opposed to the sensuous as a physical drive and he distinguishes it from sensuality that is an expression of selfishness and egocentric self-love (WL, 65). Selfishness is thus to be understood as the *willful* and *demanding* assertion of our passionate preferences in relation to others and is not to be equated with our natural inclinations, needs, and desires themselves. Presumably, then, the sensuous can be taken up into Christian love, just as Judge William in *Either/Or* envisages its preservation in marriage, and given expression in the form of what I have described elsewhere as "spiritual sensuousness."[7] But is this sufficient to save the erotic? Do not erotic relations, as well as friendships, continue to be expressions of passionate preference and thus remain fundamentally selfish in nature? To address this question in the context of the grammar of love as Kierkegaard understands it, we need to

[6] Kierkegaard himself explores the possibility of a nonhierarchical model for the divine-human relation, and thus by implication also for human relations, in the parable of the king and the maiden in *Philosophical Fragments*, where the two are made equal in love (PF, 26–30). On this point see my essay "On 'Feminine' and 'Masculine' Despair" in the present collection.

[7] See Sylvia Walsh Utterback, "Don Juan and the Representation of Spiritual Sensuousness," *Journal of the American Academy of Religion* 47 (1979): 627–44.

consider the next term of that grammar, which introduces the decisive category of "the neighbor."

Inclusive

Central to the Christian concept of love is the requirement that we love others as neighbors. In Kierkegaard's view, "neighbor" reflects "eternity's mark" or that which is shared by all persons (WL, 96–97). Neighbor is an expression for human being or the fact that being a human being is the fundamental characteristic of all human beings. It further expresses our absolute equality before God. To love others as neighbors means to love them first of all on the basis of our common humanity, as fellow human beings, rather than on the basis of personal preference. Secondly, it means to exercise an eternal equality in loving by existing on an essentially equal basis for every person. Christian love, more specifically identified as neighbor love, is thus inclusive in nature and has as its task the love of all human beings, although one person is sufficient, Kierkegaard claims, to test our ability to love others in this manner (WL, 37). Only when others are loved as neighbors are they truly loved as an other, that is, as an "other-you" rather than an "other-I," for in love of neighbor the selfish desires and demands that we customarily exact in our relations to others are turned back and placed on us instead.

In Kierkegaard's opinion, the inclusiveness of neighbor love does not require doing away with distinctions between persons nor with the leveling of them to a classless society. In an apparent allusion to socialist views becoming prominent on the European continent at that time, he makes the point through a play on words that earthly likeness (*Lighed*) is not synonymous with Christian equality (*Ligelighed*) (WL, 82). Rather, we are to lift ourselves above distinctions and let them "hang loosely" so as to be able to perceive the "essential person" or fundamental humanity of others (WL, 82–84). Neither does neighbor love prohibit us from entering into or continuing in special relationships with one or more individuals. But the friend or beloved should be loved first and foremost, like others, as a neighbor. The Christian view, Kierkegaard claims, is that "what is eternally basic must also be the basis of every expression of what is special" (WL, 141). Thus, while we certainly love persons in our special relations differently from the way we love others, this difference is not essential, since we love them fundamentally as we love others, that is, as a neighbor, and do not exclude love of others in addition to those relations. This seems to be for Kierkegaard the decisive factor in the transformation of erotic love that rids it of selfish exclusivity and establishes equality in love while preserving special relations. If neighbor love is present in erotic love and friendship, then the relative distinctions of passionate preference are allowed to stand. Thus, while we may admire our loved ones for their intellect, wit, sexual attractiveness, and many other fine features, were they to lose any or all of these in the course of life, Christianly we should still love and respect them as human beings.

While such a view of love relations might appear (somewhat oddly, in the case of Kierkegaard) to undermine the particularity of others, Kierkegaard also stresses that persons are to be loved as they are, not as we want them to be, and each in his or her own individuality (WL, 252–53). Although we should seek in our love relations to strive against imperfections and to conquer deficiencies, the emphasis should lie on loving the persons we see, whether we see imperfections or perfections in them. The task is to find others lovable as given, no matter how they may change (WL, 157–58, 164, 169). Kierkegaard puts it even more strongly by characterizing the neighbor as "the ugly," in relation to whom the task is not to love the beautiful, but to love the unlovable, or rather, to find the unlovable in a person to be lovable (WL, 342–43). In this way Christian love becomes edifying, or love which "builds up."

Edifying

Kierkegaard devotes the whole second part of *Works of Love* to the many ways in which Christian love is edifying or upbuilding. We can only take note of some of them here. First of all, Christian love believes in love on the part of others and seeks to bring out the good in them. Kierkegaard denies that any person can implant or create love in the heart of another. Only God can do that. Thus we must presuppose love in others and seek to "love forth love" in them—a beautiful expression that Kierkegaard first used in a note to his fiancée Regina Olsen which reveals the fundamentally *reciprocal* nature of Christian love as well as erotic love, even though

Kierkegaard insists in other passages of *Works of Love* that reciprocity cannot be required or demanded (WL, 206, 226–27).[8]

Christian love also hopes in the possibility of the future for ourselves and for others; it hopes not simply in the manifold of possibilities that we long for in life but more specifically in the possibility of the good, which is the eternal. Love seeks as well to build up others by searching for a "mitigating explanation" of their sins and hiding them in silence and forgiveness (WL, 261–78). Most of all, it seeks to help others become authentic persons in their own right by encouraging them to become independent, to stand on their own as individuals before God. That, Kierkegaard claims, is "the greatest, the only benefaction one human being can accomplish for another" (WL, 258–59). There are many other ways love can be mutually supportive in special relations and upbuilding of others in general. One of these is through the language of love, which we shall examine in the second part of this essay.

Abiding

One of the crowning virtues of Christian love is that it abides. Merely human or natural love, as we are well aware, is transient, perishable, and subject to change even if it does not change. For this reason merely temporal love is always uncertain and requires continual reaffirmation of its existence between lovers. Its continuance is dependent on the test of time. Christian love, by contrast, is like "sterling silver," which one knows in advance and without testing will endure (WL, 47). It is secured by the commandment to love and thus is love that has been made a duty. When love is a duty, Kierkegaard maintains, it is forever decided that one shall love and that love shall abide (WL, 49). In love that has undergone the transformation of the eternal by becoming duty, therefore, there is no question of "falling out of love" or of breaking off relations with others, only of "falling away from love," which makes the ones who do it guilty. Here we can see the advantage of understanding love relationships in terms of three parties instead of two, for if one person forsakes another, the relation still is not broken, since the injured party may continue to hold onto the love that binds them and be strengthened by it. Although

[8] On Kierkegaard's use of the expression in relation to Regina, see JP, 5: 5526.

Kierkegaard entertains this as a possibility in Christian love of the utmost seriousness, since it involves not only breaking with another but also falling away from love or God, he nevertheless maintains that "the true lover never falls away from love" (WL, 283). The true lover never allows matters to reach the breaking point and continues to abide in love. Even if, in an external sense, a break does occur, the true lover still abides in love and turns the break into a possibility of reconciliation in the future.

There is another side of this notion of abiding love that Kierkegaard does not articulate but which is implied, I think, by his viewpoint. As we have seen, even when love is referred to God and recognized as a duty, there is no guarantee that we shall abide in love for others, for we may still fall away from love. But even then, a Christian standpoint would hold, I think, that love abides, for even if we fail in love, the love of God abides in us, with us, and for us. We may fall away but we are not cast away from that love. It continues to be extended to us in the form of forgiveness, for God, too, hides a multitude of sins and seeks a mitigating explanation for them. If that is not so, then love does not abide.

Spontaneous

If Christian love abides, does it also preserve the spontaneity of erotic love? In our natural human experience there is nothing quite so exhilarating, so heady, so heartwarming, so rejuvenating and enlivening as falling in love. At no time of our lives does the spirit of Dionysus overtake us more than in the early days of erotic love, whether we experience it in our youth, in middle age, or in later years. Then, as time begins to take its toll with the weight of responsibilities to family, work, and other commitments in life, our loves become routine, a matter of habit, and perhaps troubled as we discover and fail to tolerate the human limitations of our loved ones. If we manage to abide in love, much, if not all, of the early spontaneity of that love is gone out of it. What happens to love to cause it to lose that quality of its youth? Is spontaneity merely a romantic illusion that quickly disappears in reality? Can spontaneity be retained in love? Indeed, is not love itself a spontaneous passion, a free and autonomous feeling or inclination, so that when the spontaneity is gone, love has gone out of our relations too? The problem of spontaneity is seemingly intensified if we hold, with Kierkegaard, that love is a duty, for that, he admits, is "an apparent contradiction" (WL, 40). Commanded love, it would seem, stands in irreconcilable tension with the spontaneity and freedom generally associated with love and the desires of the heart. Even if spontaneity does not die of its own accord in our love relations, has not Christianity set itself against spontaneous love in such a way as to substitute duty for feeling and inclination?

On the contrary, in Kierkegaard's view, duty and inclination, law and love coincide in Christian love in such a way as to enable us to preserve or to regain the spontaneity of love and keep it from becoming subject to "the lukewarmness and indifference of habit" (WL, 50). Unlike Kant, who would control and repress inclination for the sake of duty, Kierkegaard envisions in the transformation of love a change of heart that makes it one with duty so that what the law requires, love freely gives. A corresponding viewpoint can be found in *Either/Or*, where Judge William defines duty as "to love truly with the inward movement of the heart" (EO, II: 151). Although love is changed by having become duty, it remains a passion, that is, a form of immediacy. But by virtue of being consciously related to the eternal, it becomes a new form of immediacy, a "second immediacy" or "spontaneity after reflection."

These expressions are not used by Kierkegaard in *Works of Love* nor do they receive much explicit mention elsewhere in his writings and journals, yet the notion of a second immediacy underlies the understanding of love, and faith as well, in several of his major works. In *Either/Or*, for example, Judge William argues that love does not lose its immediacy in marriage, and he defines that state as an "immediacy which has mediacy in itself" (EO, II: 96). Similarly, in *Stages on Life's Way* Quidam maintains that married love is a "later immediacy" and that "whereas in all other cases the destroying angel of reflection goes about shouting death to immediacy, there is yet one immediacy it suffers to stand, that of love, which is a miracle" (SLW, 147, 155). Moreover, he goes on to claim that "religion is a new immediacy, it has reflection betwixt it and the first immediacy" (SLW, 159; see also 364). Immediacy, he contends, is not devoid of reflection but precisely through "infinite reflection" relates itself to itself in the idea or God-relationship (SLW, 376).

So, too, in *Works of Love* we have seen that Christian love is viewed as love that is consciously based on the eternal and has undergone the transformation of the eternal. For that very reason it is able to preserve the spontaneity of love. Love that has *not* undergone this transformation is subject to another kind of change: it can become habit and lose "its ardour, its joy, its desire, its originative power, its freshness," in other words, its spontaneity (WL, 50). In a graphic description of how habit overtakes us, Kierkegaard likens it to a preying vampire that cunningly sneaks up on a person unawares, lulls him to sleep, and then drinks the blood out of his life. When at last he awakens and becomes aware of the change that has taken place in his life, it may be too late. Kierkegaard writes:

> [H]e wants to make up for it, but he does not know where he can go to buy new oil to rekindle his love. Then he becomes despondent, annoyed, weary of himself, weary of his love, weary of its being as paltry as it is, weary of not being able to get it transformed—alas, for he had not heeded the transformation of the eternal in time, and now he has lost the capacity to endure the cure. (WL, 51)

However fixed and seemingly intransigent habit is, it is never the unchangeable but is precisely that which should and can be changed. In Kierkegaard's view, however, only the "You shall" of duty can bring this about, for it introduces into love that which is the truly unchangeable, namely the eternal, which "never becomes old and never becomes habit" (WL, 52).

Kierkegaard does not elaborate on exactly how the eternal enables us to avoid or overcome habit in love. But we may find an important clue, I think, in the conclusion of *Works of Love* where Kierkegaard, speaking in the guise of the beloved apostle, makes the following statement:

> [T]he commandment is that you *shall* love, but when you understand life and yourself, then it is as if you should not need to be commanded, because to love human beings is still the only thing worth living for; without this love you really do not live; to love human beings is also the only salutary consolation for both time and eternity, and to love human beings is the only true sign that you are a Christian—truly, a profession of faith is not enough. (WL, 344)

Here we have, I believe, the apotheosis of Kierkegaard's thought, the final insight that unites duty and inclination, passion and reflection, law and love in his understanding of the Christian life. Nothing brings home to us more clearly the rationale for love than the reminder that it is, after all, the only thing worth living for. In the many responsibilities, busyness, and distractions that crowd our everyday life, it is very easy to lose or never attain the insight that love is the ultimate value of life. Too often we realize or remember that too late, like the pathetic person who awakens to find himself overtaken by habit. But if we keep that insight uppermost in our minds and hearts and center our lives in it, then love can never become a habit. It will remain fresh, joyful, vital, and spontaneous, as in the days of our youth, by virtue of having become a second immediacy, seasoned with the wisdom that comes with reflection and self-understanding in life.

Indirect and Inverse

For all its fine features, there is, Kierkegaard claims, an indirectness and a "strange, chilling upside-downness" about Christian love which requires a "prior transformation of mind and thought" corresponding to the transformation of love in order to be able to perceive its logic, its inner coherence (WL, 141, 173). This indirect and inverse character of Christian love is manifested in a number of ways. Love itself is hidden and must reveal itself "in another form," that is, in an outwardness that reduplicates its hidden inner form. Just as thought is hidden and speech is its manifestation, so love that is hidden reveals itself in words and works of love. It differs, therefore, from other forms of "hidden inwardness" in that it is made recognizable by these fruits. Yet there is always an uncertain and ambiguous character about them. No declaration or act is ever unconditionally a demonstration of love, even those deeds and statements that are commonly recognized as demonstrations, such as charitable acts or the oft spoken words "I love you." In the grammar of love, everything depends on *how* a thing is said and done and meant rather than the *what* of a declaration or act or intent. And even then, Kierkegaard points out, we must continue to believe in love, for nothing can finally prove the existence of love. Thus no one has the right to claim to know love or to judge others. Only in abiding in love ourselves do we recognize it in another, for epistemologically the principle holds in relation to love as in other matters that "like is known only by like" (WL, 33).

In Kierkegaard's perspective, the ambiguity of love is intensified in Christian love by the fact that love is understood in an opposite manner from the way it is generally understood in the world (WL, 62, 115, 118, 310–11). What the world regards as love is, from a Christian standpoint, self-love, and conversely, what Christianity calls love is self-love from a merely human standpoint. In their natural forms, erotic love and friendship are really expressions of selfishness, for in them we love others on the basis of personal preference and seek reciprocity and exclusivity in love. Conversely, Christian love may appear to be a form of self-love, even hate, when the one who expresses it is unwilling to understand and practice love as others do. A collision is thus provoked between the two conceptions of love, bringing about the "double danger" of eliciting the possibility of offense from others as well as from within oneself (WL, 83, 86, 90–91, 185–89). So essential is the mark of double danger to Christian love and self-renunciation that Kierkegaard claims: "as soon as the double-mark is missing the self-renunciation is not Christian self-renunciation" (WL, 189).

What is the double danger in the grammar of Christian love described here? Is Christian love really so different from our ordinary conceptions of love? And are our natural expressions of love as narcissistic and self-serving as Kierkegaard suggests? Kierkegaard seems to have caught us coming and going here, for if we disagree with the conception of Christian love which he presents, that may only reflect a merely human mentality that wishes to define Christian love in worldly terms. Our disagreements would then be a form of offense and serve only to confirm, rather than to deny, the validity of his conception. But if we agree that his view is essentially correct, yet decline to embrace it, that too is offense. And if we do embrace it, then we are faced with the difficulty of reduplicating this ideal in our lives. Taking these risks in stride, let us pause here for some assessment of Kierkegaard's understanding of the grammar of love beyond what has already been made. What insights does he offer that provide a base from which reflection on love may be carried forward? And what aspects of his thought need to be more adequately addressed?

Beginning with the latter question first, we can detect several weaknesses in his conception of the grammar of love. First of all, there appears to be a certain ambivalence toward natural love in Kierkegaard's thought. He says that Christianity is not opposed to natural inclination as such, only to the selfishness in it, yet he does not seem to recognize any ability on the part of natural love to love unselfishly. But if all love is rooted in the divine, there must be some natural tendency or desire within us to love others in an unselfish manner. Indeed, our lived experience, I believe, bears this out in many instances. Second, while Kierkegaard presupposes love in others and would seek to elicit love from others in response, he also manifests an ambivalence toward reciprocity in love. Yet surely reciprocity would be the ideal in Christian love, even if it cannot be demanded. Related to this is a third dimension which I think is not adequately addressed by Kierkegaard, namely our human need to *be* loved as well as to love. Although Kierkegaard recognizes that we have such a need and that it is deeply rooted and God-given, Christian love for him is essentially sacrificial. He acknowledges that Christ, who made the ultimate sacrifice in love, felt the need to be loved (WL, 154), but this theme is not developed in his thought.

The positive contributions and potential of Kierkegaard's thought for further development, however, far outweigh its limitations. By interpreting Christian love as a spiritual quality that is brought to our normal love relations rather than as a separate form of love, Kierkegaard shows us a way of affirming the unity of love and of overcoming the dichotomy between *eros* and *agape*, human and divine love, sensuous and spiritual love, that has been fostered by much of classical thought as well as by such recent thinkers as Anders Nygren. Kierkegaard thus provides a perspective that avoids or points beyond the untenable oppositions to which previous thinkers were led. In calling for the grounding of love relations in God and assigning them an ethical task, he shows us also how we may give deeper meaning to love than romantic admiration of others and personal satisfaction for ourselves. His interpretation of love or God as the object of love is one that gives Christian love a concrete, personal focus that is lacking in other views of love.[9] Indeed, Kierkegaard makes sense of this notion in a way that is potentially quite meaningful for contemporary thought. For he takes seriously the identity of God as the transcendent ground of love, thus opening up the way for the working out of a relational rather than a substantive understanding of the divine.

Although Kierkegaard does not altogether solve the problem of personal preference in special relations, he shows us a way also of affirming

[9] See Singer, *The Nature of Love*, and Gilbert C. Meilander, *Friendship: A Study in Theological Ethics* (Notre Dame: University of Notre Dame Press, 1981) for treatments of this issue in Plato, Augustine, and other Christian thinkers.

both universal love and special relations in love of the neighbor. In addition, his view of the neighbor as a true other opens up a path for going beyond a Sartrean conflict model of human relations, allowing the other to appear not as a stranger standing in opposition and fundamental hostility to the self but as a co-lover in the exercise of freedom in love. In particular, Kierkegaard's emphasis on our common humanity and equality of being as neighbors provides an essential theological standpoint for moving beyond a patriarchal as well as Sartrean framework of relations between the sexes. For as a neighbor, woman can no longer be viewed as an other or object over against man but must be regarded as his friend and beloved companion. Likewise, man may not be identified by her as being essentially and intransigently willful in his domination over her but capable of undergoing the transformation of love in relation to her. While Kierkegaard leaves much to be desired in terms of envisioning an outward change of male-female relations, that may be seen as an inconsistency in his doctrine of equality as well as with his emphasis on the "outward direction" that love takes in reduplicating itself in the works of love. Toward the end of his life, Kierkegaard became more cognizant of and sensitive to the external dimensions of the Christian life and reluctantly assumed the mantle for initiating social change. To us is passed on the responsibility for seeing it through, even in some ways he perhaps would not approve.

These are but a few of the ways Kierkegaard's thought sets an agenda for contemporary reflection on love. Clearly, there is much to be done. There is one other aspect to which I would call attention as well, namely, the language of love, which may also be illumined through a consideration of Kierkegaard's views on it in *Works of Love*. From the grammar of love, therefore, let us turn to the language of love.

THE LANGUAGE OF LOVE

Lovers versed in the grammar of love speak the language of love. Spoken in the context of special relations, the language of love is not discourse about love but the communication of love in "heart to heart" talk between lovers. In this section we shall consider two forms of language through which love may be communicated: ordinary language and poetic language. From a Kierkegaardian standpoint, both of these may be regarded as metaphorical language when used in the communication of love. In *Works of Love*, Kierkegaard states that "all human language about the spiritual, yes, even the divine language of Holy Scriptures, is essentially transferred or metaphorical language" (WL, 199). As he sees it, however, religious language is not a special language but rather is the same as ordinary language or what he calls "the language already at hand" (WL, 199). Yet there is an infinite difference between the two. The spiritual person uses the same words as those who live solely within sensuous-psychic categories of being but means something entirely different by them. Like the "twilight language" of Buddhist and Hindu tantras, the language of the spirit is secret in character. Its secrecy consists in the fact that it uses ordinary language in a transferred manner, so that the difference between them is never directly apparent. The indirect character of religious language is thus commensurate with the inward, invisible, and transformed character of the life of love. Just as love itself is made new but retains the outward forms of erotic love and friendship, so the religious or spiritual language of love uses the sensuous-psychic language of natural love.

In *Works of Love* Kierkegaard applies this understanding of spiritual language to the biblical expression "to edify" or "to build up." In its ordinary meaning "to build up" means "to construct something from the ground up" but in its transferred usage it refers to anything that gives expression to love, for "spiritually understood love is the deepest ground of the life of the spirit" (WL, 201).[10] "Building up," Kierkegaard claims, "is exclusively characteristic of love" because it is self-giving (WL: 202). Just as there is no word or work that unambiguously expresses love, so there is none that cannot be edifying. Even opposite words and actions, when spoken or done out of love, may be equally upbuilding in different persons. "Wherever there is building up, love is present, and wherever love is, there is building up" (WL, 204). The two correspond perfectly.

[10] It is interesting to note that Martin Heidegger, in *Poetry, Language, Thought*, tr. Albert Hofstadter (New York: Harper & Row, 1971), also employs the notion of building in his analysis of human Being in the world, and like Kierkegaard he goes back to the etymology of the word to reveal its fundamental meaning. But whereas Heidegger defines building in terms of the cultivation and construction of things for dwelling in the world, Kierkegaard makes a distinction between building and building up: "Everyone who *builds up* also *builds*, but not everyone *builds up* who *builds*" (WL, 200).

In fact, one might even say that they are the epistemological criterion of one another.[11]

If we now extend these insights about the language of love and apply them to our special love relations, new yet old modes of expression may be opened to us. Just as Regina loved forth love in Søren and elicited from him passionate expressions of love both spoken and written to her, the language of lovers everywhere may be seen as the reciprocal response of love brought forth by love and used in a transferred manner to express the spiritual quality of their love. Although love is never adequately "said" through word, lovers are ever searching for new means of saying their love to one another. Oral declarations of love, love letters, love poems, love notes—these are the conventional forms of verbal communication in erotic love, at least for a time. As lovers settle into marriage, domesticity, extended presence, and the passing of the years, the language of love, like the spontaneity of love, tapers off and frequently disappears altogether as relations degenerate into conflict and end in boredom or divorce. Is there a way, we ask almost in desperation, of giving continuity to love through language? Continuity, to recall Kierkegaard's conception of it, is not merely the continuance of a love relation but the assurance that love, secured in the duty to love through having undergone the transformation of the eternal, will endure and remain unchanged amid change. If love is to remain fresh, vital, and spontaneous as in the days of its youth, it is part of the duty to love, I would suggest, to sustain the language of love and to find and exploit new as well as old figures in trying to say that love. For that task, we need to generate what I shall call, to borrow a phrase from Wittgenstein, "language games" of love, that is, verbal forms for expressing and celebrating the reality of love in our lives, in much the same way as sex and other acts of love give expression to that passion. In love games, ordinary language, even the explicit language of sex, can be used in a transferred or metaphorical manner to allude to the spiritual character of love. Bawdy lines on the lips of devoted lovers may be just as

---

[11] On this point I am indebted to Robert L. Perkins, "Kierkegaard: A Kind of Epistemologist," a paper presented at the conference on "Kierkegaard and Contemporary Philosophy" at St. Olaf College in 1985, published in *History of European Ideas* 12 (1990), 7–18, and reprinted in *Søren Kierkegaard: Critical Assessments of Leading Philosophers,* ed. Daniel Conway and K. E. Glover (London and New York: Routledge, 2002), 224–36.

indicative of the purity of their love as words reflecting sexual reserve and moral propriety. Lovers possessing wit and ingenuity may bring added enjoyment and spontaneity to their love by inventing and playing word games with puns, alliteration, rhyme, or inversions of ordinary language to celebrate and perpetuate the vitality of their love.

Along with the playfulness of love, we need to preserve also in the language of love the upbuilding features of memory and hope, gratitude and appreciation, confession and forgiveness, mutual support and acceptance, honesty and trust. Even silence may be cultivated as an unspoken language of love between lovers as long as it is consciously used in a transferred manner as a means of quietly being together or of allowing the other some privacy rather than signifying separation or alienation between them. Finally, if love is grounded in a third, which is love of God, then the language of love needs to refer consciously as well as implicitly to God and the neighbor as the object of love. In giving voice to that which respects the fundamental humanity and not merely the special features of the beloved, the neighbor is included in the language of love to one another, but if lovers are to avoid being egotistically and exclusively turned in upon themselves, they must extend words of love to others as well. Those words will not be erotic in form, as that is appropriate only in special relations, but they will be metaphorical in the sense of being upbuilding of others.

Besides ordinary language, poetry is another form of metaphorical language that may be used as the language of love. In the romantic tradition love is regarded as the absolute subject of poetry, and the poet is the priest of love. In *Works of Love,* however, there is a running diatribe against the poet. "Christianity knows far better than any poet what love is and what it is to love," Kierkegaard claims; in fact, he thinks they explain things in opposite ways (WL, 36, 63). The poet *celebrates* love and makes the friend or beloved the subject of love; Christianity *commands* love and directs it toward the neighbor. The poet sings of loving the beloved above all others; Christianity teaches us to love all humankind. The poet tries to secure love through pledging and swearing by love itself; in Christianity God is the one by whom lovers swear and secure their love. The poet understands love and friendship as good fortune for which one is grateful, while Christianity understands them as containing an ethical task.

These are but a few of the ways, in Kierkegaard's view, Christianity and the poet differ in the understanding of love. If one were to read only *Works of Love*, one would surely conclude that Kierkegaard takes a negative attitude toward poetry and does not regard it as an appropriate medium for the communication of spiritual love. But there is a positive conception of poetry and the poet to be found in his authorship.[12] Kierkegaard regarded himself as a poet of the religious and his specifically religious writings as a form of "poet-communication" in the service of Christianity. His task, as he understood it, was to portray, like an artist, the "ideal picture" of a Christian. There is, then, a legitimate kind of poet and appropriate place for poetry in the Christian life. Even in *Works of Love*, if we read it carefully enough, we can see that Kierkegaard makes a distinction between the godly or religious poet and the ordinary secular poet (WL, 60). Of godly poets he writes:

> These do not celebrate erotic love and friendship; their songs are to the glory of God, songs of faith and hope and love. Nor do these poets sing of love in the sense a poet sings of erotic love, for love to one's neighbor is not to be sung about—it is to be fulfilled in reality. Even if there were nothing else to hinder the poet from artistically celebrating love to one's neighbor in song, it is quite enough that with invisible letters behind every word in Holy Scriptures a disturbing notice confronts him—for there it reads: go and do likewise. Does this sound like an artistic challenge, inviting him to sing? (WL, 60)

Qua poet, the religious poet, like the secular poet, stands in tension with the ethical task of love but is distinguished from the secular poet by the fact that he or she is related to the Christian ideal of love as one who is striving toward it. This seems to be the decisive factor distinguishing the two kinds of poets as Kierkegaard reflects on them in his journals (cf. JP, 6: 6528).

What then of the ordinary poet and of poetic celebrations of love? Shall the poets, as Plato would have it, be banished and erotic poems of love no longer recited? Kierkegaard concludes in *Works of Love* that it

---

[12] See my essays "Don Juan and the Representation of Spiritual Sensuousness," noted above, and "The Subjective Thinker as Artist," *History of European Ideas* 12/1 (1990): 19–29.

would do little good to rid the world of poets as long as people continue to understand existence as they do. Neither does he admonish Christians to shun poetry. A good poet may be read and admired, but one must know how to relate oneself properly to the poet, that is, be aware of the differences between the Christian and poetic life-views. It would seem, too, that the poetry of erotic love might well be employed metaphorically by lovers as a means of expressing and communicating the "deeper erotic" or spiritual quality of their love. For if erotic love has undergone the transformation of the eternal in such a way as to preserve and sanctify the erotic element, then it ought to be possible to retain and affirm that element in the poetry of love too. Thus the poetry of love may become the language of love and give powerful expression to it. It may be, however, that new, more explicitly religious love poems will need to be composed by lovers to express the specifically Christian qualities of their love. But such poetry should come *out of* and *in the midst of* the life of love as a mode of expressing and celebrating the actuality of that love. In an early, undated letter to Regina, Kierkegaard observes that "the poetical precedes the actual, which is not to say that the poetical ceases where the actual begins, but that the former is older than the latter and delimits the latter as the eternal always delimits the temporal."[13] What I am suggesting here is that the poetical may and should continue in the actual, that in becoming true or genuine lovers we may also become poets of love, giving verbal expression to the ideality as well as to the suffering of Christian love in our lives. That does not mean that we should all "try our hands" at poetry writing. The ideality of love can be expressed poetically in many ways, and best of all by living it. Nor will such poetry as is written need to qualify as "great poetry" as measured by the standards of literary critics. What is requisite for the poetry of love is the passion of love. As one of Kierkegaard's pseudonyms puts it: "without passion, no poet" (SLW, 369). Those of us who are more gifted in writing may give poetic expression to that passion for the rest of us, as the great poets have always done. Although the poetry of love, like other forms of speaking in the language of love, is never a sure mark of love, we should not for that reason refrain from writing and saying it. For as Kierkegaard eloquently reminds us in *Works of Love*:

[13] *Kierkegaard: Letters and Documents*, tr. Henrik Rosenmeier (Princeton: Princeton University Press, 1978), 74, no. 28.

> Your friend, your beloved, your child, or whoever is the object of your love, has a claim upon its expression also in words when it really moves you inwardly. The emotion is not your possession but the other's. The expression of it is his due, since in the emotion you belong to him who moves you and makes you conscious of belonging to him. When the heart is full you should not grudgingly and loftily, shortchanging the other, injure him by pressing your lips together in silence; you should let the mouth speak out of the abundance of the heart. (WL, 29)

The heart formed by love thus will speak out in the language of love and offer that, along with its works of love, as the fruit of love by which it may be recognized, received, and returned by the beloved in reciprocal gestures of love.

11

FEMININE DEVOTION AND SELF-ABANDONMENT: SIMONE DE BEAUVOIR AND SØREN KIERKEGAARD ON THE WOMAN IN LOVE*

In spite of the fact that Kierkegaard, more than any other philosopher of the modern age, addressed questions of gender, sexual differences, self-identity, and sexual relations between men and women in his writings, he is rarely mentioned in Simone de Beauvoir's classic study of woman, *The Second Sex*, and on the few occasions when he is referred to in this work, it is generally unfavorably.[1] Yet Beauvoir's phenomenological description and critique of feminine devotion and self-abandonment in this text, especially in the chapter on "The Woman in Love," bears a close affinity with Kierkegaard's treatment of these qualities in two of his most important writings, *The Sickness unto Death* and *Works of Love*.[2] Three

---

* Reprinted by permission from *Philosophy Today*, Vol. 42, Supplement, ed. Linda Martin Alcoff and Merold Westphal (Chicago: DePaul University, 1998), 35–40.

[1] See Simone de Beauvoir, *The Second Sex*, trans. and ed. H.M. Parshley (Random House Vintage Books, 1989), 143, 186, 256, 438, 720. All of these citations refer either directly or indirectly to one book by Kierkegaard, *Stages on Life's Way*, which was published under the auspices of a pseudonym so as to distance himself from the viewpoints represented in it. Beauvoir, however, does not distinguish between Kierkegaard and his pseudonym or the spokespersons representing different stages of life in the book, indiscriminately attributing to him their views of woman. Hereafter references to *The Second Sex* will be indicated in the text in parentheses under the siglum SS, followed by page number.

[2] Søren Kierkegaard, *The Sickness unto Death*, ed. and tr. Howard V. Hong and Edna H. Hong (Princeton: Princeton University Press, 1980), and *Works of Love*, ed. and tr. Howard V. Hong and Edna H. Hong (Princeton: Princeton University Press, 1995). Hereafter references to these works will be given in the

points of similarity in particular will be explored in the present essay, together with some significant differences that serve to distinguish their individual approaches to this topic.

I.

The first similarity to be noticed between Kierkegaard and Beauvoir is that both philosophers see love as signifying something different for woman than for man. According to Beauvoir, woman understands love as involving not only devotion but also total self-abandonment to the other, whereas man remains a sovereign subject who never abdicates himself completely in love (SS, 642). Instead of squandering his existence entirely on woman, as she does on him, man seeks to integrate woman into his existence as one value among others and thus as a being of only relative worth to him (SS, 642). By contrast, man represents for woman the absolute, the essential, for whom she is willing to relinquish everything in order to obtain a master (SS, 642). Denied the opportunity to establish herself as a sovereign subject through freely chosen, self-transcending projects as man is privileged to do, woman is confined to the realm of immanence or the given conditions of existence as determined by her biological function and social situation (SS, xxxv). Thus she has no other way out, it would seem, than complicitly to accept her enslavement, resigning herself to live vicariously through man's self-transcendence and self-realization in projects and acts (SS, 643–44). In this way she hopes to share in his masculinity and male superiority and to recover the experience of childhood security under adult protection and authority, thereby preventing the feeling of existential abandonment in the world and avoiding the agonizing task of assuming responsibility for her own life (SS, 644–45).

Kierkegaard also finds devotedness (*Hengivenhed*) and giving of oneself (*Hengivelse*) to the other to be characteristic of woman in contrast to man, who gives as well but unlike her gains and retains his self apart from giving to others (SUD, 50n). As Kierkegaard sees it, devotedness constitutes woman's nature; it is "the one unique quality" woman possesses and thus is fundamental to establishing her substantive identity as

---

text in parentheses under the sigla SUD and WL respectively, followed by page number.

a woman (SUD, 50n). Woman becomes herself through a metamorphosis of boundless youthful coyness into feminine devotedness, paradoxically gaining herself by losing herself (*tabt sig selv*) or abandoning herself in (*styrter sig i*) the object of her devotion (SUD, 50n). In contrast to Beauvoir, who rejects the notion of "the eternal feminine" or a female essence, viewing feminine devotion and self-abandonment as a consequence of woman's situation or the existential conditions imposed on her by society (SS, xx; 643), Kierkegaard clearly holds an essentialist conception of woman's being. Yet, in consonance with Beauvoir, he recognizes that social experience and development play an important role in shaping the life of woman and the possibility of realizing or not realizing herself authentically as a woman and as a self or fully actualized human being.[3]

II.

Both Beauvoir and Kierkegaard are critical of feminine devotion and self-abandonment insofar as the social cultivation of these qualities in woman results in idol worship, loss of self, and masochism in Beauvoir's account, or becomes a mode of despair, self-love, and false devotion as analyzed by Kierkegaard. Let us examine Beauvoir's critique first. Denied the possibility of transcendence, or the freedom of realizing herself by forming and carrying out meaningful projects of her own, woman seeks to justify herself vicariously, Beauvoir claims, through worship of and abject service to man, who represents the absolute for her, with the result that love becomes a religion for woman (SS, 643). In giving herself completely to her god or idol, woman hopes to gain possession of herself and thus to save herself. Ironically, however, she ends up denying herself through ecstatic union and identification with him. "She wants to merge with him, to forget herself in his arms" in "a complete destruction of the self, abolishing the boundaries that separate her from the beloved," Beauvoir claims (SS, 646, 650). Female sexual pleasure in particular demands complete abandon on the part of woman; in sex

---

[3] On the influence of the social environment in forming woman's existence—an issue that Kierkegaard specifically addresses in *Two Ages*—see my essay, "Issues That Divide: Interpreting Kierkegaard on Woman and Gender" in the present collection.

> [s]he would abolish all surroundings, abolish the singularity of the moment, of herself, and of her lover, she would fain be lost in a carnal night as shadowy as the maternal womb....Being more profoundly beside herself than is man because her whole body is moved by desire and excitement, she retains her subjectivity only through union with her partner. (SS, 396–97)

Ecstatic union and identification with the other are also sought by the woman in love. Believing that "the supreme goal of human love is identification with the loved one," the woman in love is not content with merely serving the man; she must "see with his eyes," enjoy the same books, pictures, expressions, idiosyncracies, etc. (SS, 653). Catherine's assertion in *Wuthering Heights,* "I am Heathcliffe," sums up for Beauvoir the complete identification with man that the woman in love desires: "It is the cry of every woman in love; she is another incarnation of her loved one, his reflection, his double: she is *he.* She lets her own world collapse in contingence, for she really lives in his" (SS, 653).

A further negative consequence of identification with the beloved for woman, as Beauvoir sees it, is that "the love that at the start seemed a narcissistic apotheosis is fulfilled in the bitter joys of a devotion that often leads to self-mutilation" or masochism (SS, 651). Beauvoir does not view masochism as an inevitable outcome of female devotion and self-abandonment, inasmuch as it is not a natural tendency of woman or of resignation and self-forgetfulness (SS, 398, 652). But women are more prone to it than men, she thinks, and it is a "bypath" that is frequently taken by the unsatisfied woman if the gift of herself is not wholeheartedly accepted and / or reciprocated by the beloved (SS, 400, 651–52, 659). Young girls in particular are inclined towards masochism because they are often narcissistic or alienated from themselves in an alter ego that is dependent on the will of others (SS, 399). "Masochism exists," Beauvoir explains, "when the individual chooses to be made merely a thing under the conscious will of others, to see herself as a thing, to play at being a thing" (SS, 399). Blaming herself for submitting her ego to others, the young girl feels guilty and punishes herself by "voluntarily redoubling her humiliation and slavishness" in a "sham abandon" or masochistic play-acting that is "no true solution of the conflict created by woman's sexual destiny, but a mode of escaping from it by wallowing in it" (SS, 400, 401).

For Kierkegaard, too, feminine devotion and self-abandonment are potentially problematic for woman in that her natural tendency to give herself in devotion to others may result in negative consequences with both personal and religious implications. Although devotedness constitutes woman's nature or substantive identity as a woman, it may also function as a mode of despair for her. Abandoning herself "with genuine femininity" to the other, woman instinctively seeks to become herself by losing herself in the object of her devotion, so that she tends to have a sense of self only in and through that object (SUD, 50n). If the object of her devotion is lost or taken away, then her self is also lost and she is in despair at not willing to be herself, or what Kierkegaard calls despair in weakness or "feminine despair" in contrast to despair in defiance or "masculine despair," which is willing to become oneself through an unwarranted self-assertion or self-creation (SUD, 49).[4] While Kierkegaard recognizes that feminine despair is not limited to women, nor masculine despair to men, women are undoubtedly more prone to feminine despair than men since, in his view, devotedness is their nature. It is important to note, however, that devotedness does not, in itself, constitute despair for Kierkegaard; rather, despair results from the loss of oneself in, or identification with, the object of one's devotion in such a way as to lose oneself or have no independent self. Like Beauvoir, therefore, Kierkegaard regards women's self-abandonment in or identification with the other as resulting in a loss of self that is, for him, equivalent to despair, or more precisely, a particular form of despair that is typical of, though not peculiar to, women. While despair is not a necessity in women any more than it is in men, it is a universal phenomenon with which every human being must contend in one form or another.

A second criticism of feminine devotion and self-abandonment in erotic love made by Kierkegaard is that they are really expressions of self-love and thus not true devotion and self-giving (WL, 53–55). Although erotic love entails a passionate, unlimited giving of oneself to the other, the "other self" in erotic relations is really an "other I" inasmuch as erotic love is based on reciprocity, or the expectation of being made the sole

---

[4] For a more extensive analysis of these forms of despair as elaborated in *The Sickness unto Death*, see my essay "On 'Feminine' and 'Masculine' Forms of Despair" in the present collection.

object of the beloved's love in return. "When the lover…is able to love only this one single person in the whole world…there is an enormous self-willfulness in this enormous devotion, and in his impetuous, unlimited devotion the lover is actually relating himself to himself in self-love," Kierkegaard observes (WL, 55).

Such "devoted self-love" or "self-deification" on the part of the woman in love is further exposed by Kierkegaard as false devotion, and thus as something that ought to be given up, inasmuch as it constitutes idol-worship and results in masochism—as Beauvoir also contends (WL, 55,57,107, 125). Kierkegaard exclaims:

> A person dare not belong to another as if that person were everything to him; a person dare not allow another to belong to him as if he were everything to that other….Whether a person is a man or woman, poorly or richly endowed, master or slave, beggar or plutocrat, the relationships among human beings ought and may never be such that the one worships and the other is the one worshiped….To love another person as God is to deceive oneself, and to allow another person to love one as God is to deceive this other person. (WL, 108, 125)

Anticipating Beauvoir's analysis of masochism, Kierkegaard notes that while such an abomination may have its origin in the misuse of power by the superior person over the powerless, it may also originate in the powerless, who "know of no other expression for the relation than to abase themselves and to throw themselves away" (WL, 125). Like Beauvoir, he cites as an example of such masochistic behavior the young girl, who "would rather inhumanly throw herself away and worship the idolized one, craving only one thing of him, that he inhumanly should demand everything of her" (WL, 125). But whereas Beauvoir locates the source of masochism in self-alienation and narcissism, Kierkegaard attributes it to a forgetfulness of God, who is or should be the true object of love and devotion for human beings (WL, 107, 112, 126). As Kierkegaard sees it, devotion to God is what constitutes woman's (as well as man's) spiritual identity as a self before God (SUD, 50n). For him, therefore, true love, devotion and self-abandonment come to expression only in loving God, which is to say "the neighbor"—a category that includes all human beings, not just one other person. Since love is God, God or love constitutes "the middle term" in every love relation (WL,

107, 265). The true idea of what it means to love another person is to help that individual love God, which is to love others first and foremost on the basis of their eternal equality as human beings or neighbors, not out of personal preference or a desire to be loved in return (WL, 57–58, 113).

III.

A third point of similarity between Kierkegaard and Beauvoir may be observed in their agreement that genuine love requires a mutual independence of woman and man as selves. For Beauvoir this implies both self-transcendence and economic independence for woman as well as an erotic specificity and reciprocity in personal relations with men. For Kierkegaard it implies a spiritual, but not necessarily social, equality of woman with man before God. In the realm of spirit, Kierkegaard claims in *Works of Love*, the highest achievement is to become one's own master; thus the greatest beneficence one human being can do for another is to help that person stand alone, to become free and independent as an individual or self (WL, 274–78, cf. 56).[5] In the social realm, however, man remains woman's master, and she is to be subservient to him (WL, 138). Envisioning a fundamental transformation of love in inwardness but not in outwardness, Kierkegaard opts for maintaining the social status quo in the recognition that the establishment of "worldly similarity"—even if that were possible, which it is not—is not the same as Christian equality, which has to do with our fundamental spiritual equality or similarity as human beings before God (WL, 72, 138). Yet he does acknowledge that

---

[5] Whether it is actually possible for woman to gain the kind of independence of selfhood that Kierkegaard envisions in *Works of Love* remains highly questionable in light of other works in the Kierkegaardian corpus, e. g. *The Concept of Anxiety*, ed. and trans. Reidar Thomte (Princeton: Princeton University Press, 1980), where it is suggested that man "is more qualified as spirit" than woman, presumably because her being culminates in procreation, which precludes her from being truly independent (CA, 67; cf. also 189). On this issue see my book, *Living Poetically* (University Park: The Pennsylvania State University Press, 1994), 155–57. See also Leslie A. Howe, "Kierkegaard and the Feminine Self," in *Feminist Interpretations of Søren Kierkegaard*, ed. Céline Léon and Sylvia Walsh (University Park: The Pennsylvania State University Press, 1997), 217–47.

Christianity has brought about important social change in the past, such as the end of slavery, and that the oppressed may devise various strategies, such as "crafty defiance," hidden reluctance, and outright refusal as ways of saying "no" to those who wield power over them (WL, 74, 80). Moreover, since "love in all its expressions turns outward towards people" and the expression of neighbor love in the world inevitably exposes one to "double danger," or the possibility of external attacks from others in addition to inward trials before God, it would seem that some external consequences should ensue and are likely to occur from an inward transformation of love (WL, 189, 72–73, 76, 82). If one has been genuinely changed inwardly, then there ought to be a corresponding outward change in the way one relates to others.

In contrast to Kierkegaard's reluctance to embrace equal rights for women in the social realm, Beauvoir sees a need for both ideological and social change. On the ideological front, Beauvoir thinks it is possible to rise above hostile, dualistic, and imperialistic ontology of human relations, but this can happen only when man and woman come to recognize each other simultaneously as subject and object, as an independent self and other, in a reciprocal manner (SS, 140). "Genuine love," she claims, "ought to be founded on the mutual recognition of two liberties; the lovers would then experience themselves both as self and as other: neither would give up transcendence, neither would be mutilated; together they would manifest values and aims in the world. For the one and the other, love would be revelation of self by the gift of self and enrichment of the world" (SS, 667). Beauvoir also envisions a new form of female eroticism emerging from this change, one in which woman seeks her own sex pleasure, thus upholding her own subjectivity as well as that of her lover, and in which ecstatic union with the other represents a transcendence, not an abdication, of her being in self-giving to the other (SS, 263, 399, 726–27, 731). "On the day when it will be possible for woman to love not in her weakness but in her strength, not to escape herself but to find herself, not to abase herself but to assert herself—on that day love will become for her, as for man, a source of life and not of mortal danger," Beauvoir observes (SS, 669). But until social and economic changes also take place, including the achievement of economic independence by woman, this "new woman" cannot and will not appear (SS, 725). "It is through gainful employment that woman has traversed most of that distance that separated her from the male; and nothing else can guarantee her liberty in practice," Beauvoir claims (SS, 679).

IV.

From the foregoing brief comparison of Beauvoir and Kierkegaard on feminine devotion and self-abandonment, it is apparent that there are several areas of agreement as well as significant disagreement in their respective analyses. Perhaps the most interesting similarity to emerge is the degree to which both, in spite of their strong and similar critiques of feminine devotedness and self-abandonment, reaffirm the validity and importance of these qualities when given expression in appropriate form and in the proper social and / or spiritual context. By the same token, perhaps the most significant dissimilarity that emerges between them is their diverging attitudes toward the importance of reciprocity in bringing about a proper expression of those qualities in women and men. For Beauvoir, a real relation requires reciprocity, while for Kierkegaard true love does not; it abides whether reciprocated or not (SS, 253; WL, 100, 237, 241–42, 349–51). The demand for reciprocity is an expression of self-love or selfishness that needs to be rooted out in the transformation of erotic love into unselfish, unconditional love of the other as a neighbor. The most completely unselfish work of love one person can perform in relation to another, Kierkegaard claims, is one in which every possibility of repayment is removed, as in, for example, recollecting a loved one who is dead (WL, 349). Yet, "in the love-relationship between living persons there usually is still the hope and the prospect of repayment, at least the repayment of reciprocal love, and ordinarily this repayment does come" (WL, 351). But true love is not dependent on it, nor is true devotion and self-abandonment in love. On the contrary, the life of one who truly loves is "completely squandered on...the existence of others. Unwilling to waste any time or energy on asserting himself [or herself], on being something for himself [or herself], in his [or her] self-sacrifice he [or she] is willing to perish, that is, he [or she] is completely and wholly transformed into simply being an active power in the hands of God" (WL, 279). The paradox of this transformation for Kierkegaard is that one most truly becomes oneself in devotion and self-abandonment to others out of love for God and / or the neighbor. Consequently, Kierkegaard embraces a far more radical reaffirmation of devotion and self-abandonment in love than does Beauvoir. From his perspective, in advocating an ontology of reciprocity, Beauvoir does not secure for woman the possibility of true selfhood, nor of true devotion and self-abandonment in love, but rather perpetuates in a subtler form the narcissism and loss of self in erotic love that she criticizes and hopes to reform. In calling for social equality and economic independence for woman, however, Beauvoir surely corrects a major shortcoming or ambiguity in Kierkegaard's philosophy of love.

12

SUBJECTIVITY VERSUS OBJECTIVITY: KIERKEGAARD'S *POSTSCRIPT* AND FEMINIST EPISTEMOLOGY*

The Western philosophic / scientific epistemological tradition has been widely criticized by feminists for its objectivist emphasis on dispassionate inquiry in the search for value-free, universalizable truths. In this essay I shall argue that feminists may find in Kierkegaard's *Concluding Unscientific Postscript* (1846) both a philosophical precursor of and ally in this critique as well as an important resource for re-visioning the concept of subjectivity in a manner that does not collapse into an isolated subjectivity, on the one hand, or into a "chummy" form of inter-subjectivity that compromises the integrity of the individual, on the other.

This is not to say that the position of Johannes Climacus, the pseudonymous "author" of this text, is not subject to feminist criticism on various aspects of his understanding of objectivity and subjectivity.[1] On the contrary, as I shall point out, from a feminist perspective there are

---

* Reprinted by permission from *International Kierkegaard Commentary: Concluding Unscientific Postscript to "Philosophical Fragments,"* Vol. 12, ed. Robert L. Perkins (Macon: Mercer University Press, 1997), 11–31, and *Feminist Interpretations of Søren Kierkegaard*, ed. Céline Léon and Sylvia Walsh (University Park: The Pennsylvania State University Press, 1997), 267–85.

[1] In "A First and Last Explanation" appended to the text of *Concluding Unscientific Postscript*, to which Kierkegaard affixed his name only as "editor" of the published version, the claim is put forth that in his pseudonymous works "there is not a single word by me" and that he is responsible for these works only "in a legal and in a literary sense" (CUP, 626–27). Therefore, one cannot unequivocally equate the views expressed here with those of Kierkegaard himself; however, inasmuch as it constitutes the central philosophical statement of his authorship, this work undoubtedly contains much with which Kierkegaard is in agreement. On the purpose and role of pseudonymity in Kierkegaard's writings, see Walsh (1994), 10–15; Evans (1983), 6–16, and Hartshorne (1990).

some serious deficiencies in Climacus' thought. It should be noted at the outset, however, that feminist philosophy is not monolithic in its critique and rethinking of the concepts of objectivity and subjectivity. Before turning to a consideration of the *Postscript*, therefore, I shall briefly characterize the conventional understanding of objectivity and the knowing subject that has provoked feminist critique, indicate the main objections feminists have raised to it, and sketch several feminist approaches that have emerged in the process of assessing and reformulating these concepts from a feminist perspective.

Feminist Criticisms of and Responses to the Conventional Understanding of Objectivity and the Knowing Subject

The conventional understanding of objectivity in Western philosophy is variously analyzed by feminist philosophers as having its inception in Plato (Duran 1991, 5–8; Keller 1985, 30–32; Irigaray 1985), Descartes (Bordo 1987; Hodge 1988, 152–68), and the empiricist as well as rationalist epistemologies of the Enlightenment that gave birth to modern science (Code 1991, 51; Hekman 1990, 1–10; Harding 1986, 36–57).[2] This concept is typically characterized by feminists as one that assumes a separation between subject and object, fact and value, and requires the rendering of an impartial, dispassionate, value-free, empirically verifiable, and rationally coherent account of the objective world. The concept of the knowing subject corresponding to this view of objectivity is that of an autonomous, dispassionate, detached individual who has the capacity to adopt the stance of an independent, neutral observer in relation to the external world and to suppress or eliminate personal or merely subjective feelings, interests, and values in coming to know and describe that world (Hodge 1988, 154–66; Code 1991, 46–52; Hawkesworth 1989, 533–57).

According to some feminists, such a view of objectivity and the knowing subject, exemplified in the modern scientific method, with

[2] For a concise differentiation between four senses of objectivity (absolute, disciplinary, dialectical, and procedural) in current discussions, see Megill (1994), 1–20. It is primarily the absolute sense of objectivity that corresponds to the concept of objectivity attacked by feminist epistemologists, although the disciplinary and procedural senses of the term also involve elements of the absolute sense.

physics serving as its paradigm,[3] reflects a typically masculine way of relating to the world and thus actually represents an androcentric, male-biased, and male-constructed perspective rather than a gender-neutral stance toward reality (Gergen 1988, 27–48; Code 1991, 35, 117–19; Duran 1991, 5–14, 44; Harding 1991, 39–50; Nelson 1990, 189–90; MacKinnon 1987, 50, 54–55). This means that the so-called value-free descriptions of modern science and epistemology are not value-free but rather reflect the social values and interests of a specific gender. A particularly objectionable feature of this androcentric viewpoint for many feminists is that it is predicated on and perpetuates a fundamentally dichotomous form of thought in which one term is privileged, the other negated or suppressed, in the affirmation of reason against passion, mind over body, objectivity over subjective interests and values (Code 1991, 27–55; Hekman 1990, 9, 16; Ring 1991, 17–25). Since women traditionally have been associated with the devalued terms of these dichotomies, the effect has been an exclusion of women from participation in philosophic and scientific endeavors or else a denial of their female nature (assuming there is one) in the requirement that they become more like men by developing the kind of detached subjectivity or objective stance necessary for acquiring a true knowledge of the world. Another objection voiced by some feminists is that the "male gaze" or indifferent, disinterested, and nonreciprocal objective stance associated with conventional objectivity results in the objectification or reification and dehumanization of women (MacKinnon 1987; Haslanger 1993, 85–125; Hawkesworth 1994, 151–77).

Feminist responses to this understanding of objectivity and the knowing subject are varied but may be grouped into four major approaches: feminist empiricism, feminist standpoint theory, postmodern

[3] For a critique of physics as a paradigm of scientific knowledge-seeking, see Harding (1996), 43–48, and (1991), 77–102. In place of physics, which in her view is atypical of scientific inquiry and anachronistic in its exclusion of values or social influences in explaining reality, Harding recommends that the social sciences be regarded as the model of all science. See also Code (1991), 40–41, and Hubbard (1988), 1–15, who concur with Harding's recommendation. Hubbard points out, however, that even physicists recognized early in this century that experimenters influence the outcome of their experiments, an insight expressed in Heisenberg's "uncertainty principle" (11).

feminism, and a mediating, integrationist understanding of objectivity and subjectivity.[4]

Feminist Empiricism

Orienting their positions in the naturalized, contextualized epistemology of Kuhn, Quine, and other contemporary theorists in the philosophy of science, linguistics, and analytic philosophy, feminist empiricists argue that there is no need to abandon an empirical and scientific approach to knowledge (Nelson 1990, 5–7; Duran 1991, 3–5, 19–69, 105–10; Antony 1993, 185–225). Rather, what is needed, in their view, is a new empirical science that is anti- or post-individualist in its recognition of the communal, contextual, socially constructed, non-foundational character of knowledge and that incorporates, rather than excludes, social, political, moral, and gender values in a self-conscious and self-critical fashion in its understanding of objectivity (Nelson 1990, 5, 7, 14; Duran 1991, 3–5, 13–14, 43–69, 110–15; Antony 1993, 213; Longino 1990, 62–85, 215–25). By becoming more inclusive of the experiences and participation of women in the scientific enterprise, it is believed that empirical science will be able to give a less androcentric, more complete, and therefore more objective account of the world.

Feminist-Standpoint Theory

Feminist-standpoint theorists, like feminist empiricists, acknowledge the social situatedness of knowledge and advocate the use of women's experience as a basis for scientific research in the belief that it will yield a greater objectivity, or "strong objectivity," in contrast to the "weak objectivity" of objectivism or the conventional perspective (Harding 1991, 138–63).[5]

---

[4] For more extended discussions of the first three approaches, see Harding (1991), 111–87, and (1986), 136–62; Hekman (1990), 128–35.

[5] While objectivists advocate the elimination of all social values and interests in the pursuit of objective knowledge, Harding claims they fail to recognize and critically examine the historical, social position of their own background assumptions and beliefs, thus providing only a limited, partial, distorted view of reality. Strong objectivity, by contrast, "requires causal analyses not just of the micro processes in the laboratory but also of the macro tendencies in the social order, which shape scientific practices" (Harding 1991, 144, 147).

Having its theoretical basis in post-Freudian object-relations theory and in a post-Marxist historical-materialist analysis of female oppression as resulting from the sexual division of labor, this position claims that "women's lives differ structurally from those of men" and provide "a particular and privileged vantage point" that is less partial and distorted than that of men (Hartsock 1983, 284; Harding 1983, 321).[6] In other words, the feminist standpoint, oriented as it is in the historical development of personality structures and modes of reasoning that foster contextual understanding, psychosomatic unity, and a sense of connectedness with other persons and nature, not only provides *greater* objectivity but also a *better* objective basis for making observations about nature, social relations, and the social order (Harding 1991, 124–33; Hartsock 1983, 298–304; Rose 1983, 73–90). Because women are "strangers" or "outsiders" both to and within the established order, their experiences provide a fresh, more distant perspective from which to test and evaluate conventional knowledge claims (Harding 1991, 124–26, 128–32).

Postmodern Feminist Epistemology

Rejecting the notion of a univocal and universal feminist standpoint, or a "women's way of knowing," as well as the masculine, unitary conception of truth fostered by the Enlightenment tradition, postmodern feminists recognize a plurality of women's voices and interpretations of truth, none of which, in their view, is epistemologically privileged. Thus they seek to abandon the conventional categories of objectivity and subjectivity altogether, finding them to be a perpetuation of the masculinist, dichotomous thinking inherent in Enlightenment epistemology (Hekman 1990,

---

[6] As Harding points out elsewhere, this position is not based on biological differences between men and women or upon essentialist claims of a distinctive "female nature," although it is often misunderstood as doing so. Rather, it is based on gender differences, or differences rooted in women's social situation and experiences, which provide an objective location from which to conduct feminist research and to criticize knowledge claims—although not an epistemological foundation for grounding knowledge claims as such, since "experience itself is shaped by social relations" (Harding, 1991, 120–21 and n. 19; 123, 132–34, 137, n. 39). On object-relations theory, which accounts for the development of gender differences between males and females on the basis of how their Oedipal relation to the mother is resolved, see Chodorow (1978).

16).[7] In their view, both knowledge and the knowing subject are socially constituted through language or forms of discourse. The focus of their attack thus falls upon the humanist ideal of the autonomous, self-constituting subject—an ideal they find to be inherently masculine, and thus hopelessly phallocentric, in spite of the fact that feminism historically has appealed to humanist values such as natural rights, dignity, and autonomy in its fight against female oppression (Hekman 1990, 63, 79; Jardine 1985, 44). From the viewpoint of postmodern feminists, therefore, it will not do to argue, as Simone de Beauvoir does in *The Second Sex* (1989), for example, that women should become independent subjects like men in order to realize their self-identity; all the qualities that characterize the humanist / existentialist subject are associated with the masculine (Hekman 1990, 77). Postmodern feminists opt instead to view woman as a process whose self-identity is multiple, de-centered, non-personal, and / or constantly deferred.[8] Although the female subject is a construct of discourse, and thus socially determined rather than self-constituting, she nevertheless has the power, they claim, to resist those modes of discourse that historically have constituted her in oppressive ways (Hekman 1990, 68, 73, 87, 189).[9] Accordingly, the possibility of fashioning new modes of female subjectivity that transgress the traditionally sharp boundaries between subject and object, self and other, is opened up.

---

[7] Hekman thus opposes a feminist epistemology that would privilege the feminine over against the masculine. As Gergen (1988) points out, the problem with the feminist standpoint theory is that it is difficult, if not impossible, to locate a common perspective on knowledge among women, as there is a variety of schools of feminist interpretation. Which among these, he asks [(32)], should be granted epistemological privilege as the feminist standpoint, and on what grounds? On the abandonment of the concept of objectivity, see also MacKinnon (1987), although her critique of objectivity proceeds from a Marxist rather than postmodernist perspective.

[8] For a discussion of French postmodern feminist concepts of self-identity, see the next essay in the present collection and other works cited therein.

[9] Hekman (1990) appeals to Foucault's view of the constituted subject as "the subject that resists" and to Julia Kristeva's claim that the subject in process is one that has revolutionary potential, although it is not clear from either of these analyses how the subject who is constituted by discourse has the power to resist that constitution.

Integrationist Approach

Many feminist thinkers, however, are unwilling to embrace postmodernism as well as some forms of feminist standpoint theory because, in their interpretation, these positions not only endorse cultural relativism but also an epistemological relativism that lapses into subjectivism or a denial of objective knowledge altogether.[10] As Sandra Harding succinctly states their objection: "One cannot afford to 'just say no' to objectivity" (Harding 1991, 160). Along with postmodern feminists and feminist theorists from the other feminist approaches, this group recognizes the fundamentally communal or contextual character of knowledge and thus denies the possibility of a pure or value-free objectivity, but not the "independent integrity" of the objective world and the possibility of gaining an objective knowledge of it (Keller 1985, 117; see also Longino 1990). Consequently, these feminist epistemologists seek to articulate a mediating position that involves an integration, interpenetration, or dialectical interplay of objectivity and subjectivity rather than a negation of them.[11] In line with the postmodernist critique of dichotomizing forms of thought, this approach envisions at least a momentary dissolution of the boundaries between subjectivity and objectivity in a mutuality of influence or inter-subjectivity that affirms both separation and unity, a merging and differentiation of subject from object.[12] What is needed, then, in

---

[10] For an example of feminist standpoint theory that advocates subjectivism, see Belensky et. al. (1986), 10, 52–75. For a critique of this position, see Code (1991), 253–64. Harding (1991) argues that feminist standpoint theory advocates cultural or historical relativism but not an epistemological or judgmental relativism, as critical evaluation based on a scientific account is required "to determine which social situations tend to generate the most objective knowledge claims" (142). Hekman (1990) counters the charge of relativism in postmodernist thought by arguing that "all knowledge is contextual and historical, thus rendering the opposition between absolute and relative obsolete" (153).

[11] See Ring (1991) who espouses a "minimalist dialectics" in line with the positions of Harding and Keller but places greater emphasis on the element of conflict than they do (27). On dialectical objectivity generally, see Megill (1994), 7–10. See also Code (1991), who advocates a "mitigated relativism" that is constrained by objectivity but takes subjectivity into account (251).

[12] For an account of scientific practice involving such an interaction, see Keller (1983). See also Code (1991), who argues with regard to knowing sub-

such a context, is a recasting or re-conceptualization of objectivity and subjectivity in a non-dichotomous, more harmonious relationship.[13]

Objectivity and Subjectivity in Kierkegaard's *Concluding Unscientific Postscript*

In light of these developments in feminist epistemology, let us now examine the critique of objectivity and the concept of subjectivity offered by Kierkegaard's *Concluding Unscientific Postscript.* Although the central problem for the pseudonymous author, Johannes Climacus, is a religious one concerning the individual's relation to Christianity, the text addresses this issue in the context of a wide-ranging discussion of historical, scientific, and speculative modes of inquiry as ways of determining objective truth and knowledge. Climacus' critique of objectivity primarily revolves around an analysis of two issues: (1) the presumed certainty of objective knowledge and (2) the indifferent or disinterested stance of the objective knower. He begins by making a fundamental distinction between two kinds of truth and, in correspondence with these, two modes of knowing: (1) objective truth, which is reached through a rational and / or empirical mode of inquiry; and (2) subjective truth, the truth of appropriating or making something one's own (*Tilegnelse*), attained by existing in a particular state (CUP, I: 21, 53–54; II: 185 n. 2). Objective truth is further subdivided by Climacus into two forms, historical and philosophical. The former, he states, is determined empirically by the historical-critical method of examining and assessing various historical reports, while the latter is established rationally by showing how doctrines that have been

---

jects "that there is no stark dichotomy between interdependence and autonomy, that they are neither oppositional nor mutually exclusive" (74).

[13] Feminists taking this approach do not entirely agree, however, in their re-inscription of these terms. While Keller, for example, calls for a "dynamic objectivity" that includes a sense of connectedness to the objective world, thus redefining objectivity in a feminine manner that downplays (masculine) separation or autonomy (Keller 1985, 115–26), Ring (1991) retains the traditional association of objectivity with distance, detachment, and isolation, but is unwilling to concede that these characteristics are specifically male or entirely bad (54). Indeed, feminist-standpoint epistemologists appeal precisely to women's outsider or isolated status in relation to the established order as that which enables them to give a better and more objective account of the world.

"historically given and verified" are related to eternal truth (Climacus does not address here the status of non-historical objective truths such as logic and mathematics). From Climacus' perspective, both forms of objective truth may be regarded as "scientific," in the broad sense in which that term was understood in the nineteenth century, inasmuch as they are purported to provide an absolute certainty of knowledge.

Far from yielding such absolute certainty, however, all objective knowledge relating to history or actuality is really uncertain and only an approximation, Climacus claims (CUP, I: 38). Historical knowledge in particular, he points out, is incomplete and always subject to doubt and revision on the basis of further observation and research (CUP, I: 30, 42, 150), but the charge is expanded to include sense-certainty and speculative philosophical truths as well in the claim that "objectively there is no truth for existing beings, only approximations" (CUP, I: 38, 44, 218). All "positive" knowledge is therefore declared to be untrue by Climacus, and sense-certainty, historical knowledge, and speculative results are branded a delusion, illusion, and phantom respectively (CUP, I: 31, 314, 316).[14]

As Climacus sees it, the only certainty lies in the infinite and the eternal, which speculative thought in particular claims to have grasped

[14] Cf. PF, 79–84 and n. 53, where Climacus shows that, in a very fundamental way, every historical event requires an element of belief in its having come into existence, as events are always known after the fact; that is, after they have come into existence. The illusive quality of every historical event, to which we are not privy through immediate sensation and cognition, is the transition moment of coming into existence, by which the occurrence of that event is rendered uncertain. Climacus also points out—in conformity, he claims, with Greek skepticism as well as with Plato and Aristotle—that immediate sensation and cognition are not in themselves deceptive; rather, the possibility of deception arises in the conclusions one draws on the basis of immediate sensation and cognition. But, whereas the Greek skeptics engaged in a suspension of judgment in order to avoid error, Climacus calls for a decision or resolution (*Beslutning)* in the form of belief that involves risk or the possibility of error in contrast to a conclusion (*Slutning*), whose claims are those of a positive or certain knowledge. Belief, like doubt, he further points out, is not a cognitive act or form of knowledge. Rather, these existential modes are opposite passions, belief constituting "a sense for coming into existence," while "doubt is a protest against any conclusion that wants to go beyond immediate sensation and immediate knowledge" (84).

but has not, since the knowing subject does not exist *sub specie aeterni* but is continually in the process of arriving at truth (CUP, I: 82). "Whatever is known is known in the mode of the knower"—an old saying to which Climacus appeals in his discussion—may be taken as stating a fundamental principle of his epistemology (CUP, I: 52). Thus the fact that the knowing subject is an existing subject, for whom everything historical (except one's own existence, which we shall consider in a moment) is uncertain, must be expressed in all of our knowing. Otherwise, Climacus maintains, that knowledge does not pertain to the state of the knowing subject in *existence* but to a fictive "objective subject" who does not exist (CUP, I: 81).

Climacus further points out that all objective knowledge is an abstraction from existence that gives a false rendition of actuality, which must be annulled or transposed into possibility in order to be grasped conceptually (CUP, I: 314–18). The only actuality to which one has more than a cognitive relation, or "knowledge about," Climacus claims, is one's own existence; every other actuality is known only in the form of possibility (CUP, I: 316–17). This means that the only certain historical knowledge to be had by an existing individual is self-knowledge or subjective truth—not in the Cartesian sense of being certain of one's own existence on the basis of thought, which in Climacus' view is an abstraction from existence rather than a demonstration of it, but in the Socratic sense of being infinitely interested in relating oneself to the truth, so as to exist in it (CUP, I: 37, 82, 152, 153–54, 204–05, 316–17).

It is this relation of the knowing subject to the truth that constitutes the chief concern and "knotty difficulty" for Climacus (CUP, I: 37). Like feminists, Climacus describes the posture of the inquiring, knowing subject in objective modes of knowledge as that of a disinterested observer: "Let the scientific researcher labor with restless zeal, let him even shorten his life in the enthusiastic service of science and scholarship; let the speculative thinker spare neither time nor effort—they are nevertheless not infinitely, personally, impassionedly interested" (CUP, I: 21–22). Nor should they be, Climacus thinks, for in objective modes of knowledge it is the truth itself that is important, not the individual's relation to the truth, which in this context must be placed in parentheses (CUP, I: 27–29, 38, 47). Thus, whereas feminists fault objective modes of knowledge for failing to recognize the masculine subjective agendas that currently drive them and for neglecting to incorporate the subjective interests and values of women as well as men, Climacus accepts the essentially disinterested character of objective modes of inquiry, although he admits that in those endeavors "where one should be objective, in strict scholarship, objectivity is rare" (CUP, I: 43, 76n).

But Climacus also proceeds to fault objective modes of knowledge, in company with feminists, precisely because one is required to move away from and abandon oneself in objectivity, thereby becoming indifferent to one's own existence and relation to the truth and ultimately disappearing from oneself altogether in becoming the "gazing power of speculative thought" (CUP, I: 56,75, 116).[15] In Climacus' view, every human being has, or should have, an infinite interest or passionate concern about his or her own existence and eternal happiness. This passionate self-interest is understood in an ethical, not an egotistical, sense by Climacus; that is, it has to do with the cultivation of subjectivity and inwardness in the human personality—the highest ethical task assigned to every human being (CUP, I: 134, 151, 158, 163, 346). The adoption of an objective posture, especially in relation to ethical or existential matters, is not only incongruous with this self-interest but also renders the individual *comic* inasmuch as it requires one to move away from, rather than toward, oneself in infinite interest (CUP, I: 43, 54–56, 120, 124, 353). Thus, while Climacus recognizes that there are legitimate objective disciplines, such as logic and mathematics, that bear no relation to existence or else require one to abstract from existence, in general he regards the objective tendency as "a venture in the comic" that encourages human beings to forget what they are, what it means to exist, and what inwardness is (CUP, I: 110–11, 124; cf. also 249, 259, 263, 269, 275 n. 287, 289). "Even if a man his whole life through occupies himself exclusively with logic, he still does not become logic; he himself therefore exists in other categories," Climacus points out (CUP, I: 93), and if that fact is ignored or neglected, "existence mocks the one who keeps on wanting to become purely objective" (CUP, I: 93). Over against a disinterested pursuit of objective truth, therefore, Climacus recommends striving for subjective

[15] See also Perkins (1973), where it is pointed out that "the ultimate limit of the objective way of knowing is to forget the subjective aspect, the knower, entirely and arrive at some type of fantastic knowledge without a knower....Objective knowledge can and does with profit exclude the subjective, but it cannot exclude the knower" (213).

truth and propounds the thesis that "[the] subjectivity, [the] inwardness, is [the] truth" (*Subjektiviteten, Inderligheden er Sandheden*) as the central tenet of his thought (CUP, I: 278).[16]

From a feminist perspective, however, it is imperative to determine exactly what subjectivity is and is not for Climacus. Subjectivity is defined as inwardness and passion—maximally a passion for eternal happiness—by Kierkegaard's pseudonym, but he does not consider it equivalent to any and every form of inwardness and passion (CUP, I: 33, 131, 203). In fact, Climacus takes pains to distinguish true inwardness or subjectivity from two forms of inwardness in particular: (1) "feminine inwardness" or the momentary inwardness of a "woman's infatuation" that corresponds, in his view, to the "feminine nature" and "to what is ordinarily understood by inwardness" (CUP, I: 236); and (2) the "chummy inwardness" of friends (CUP, I: 249). Let us examine each of these a bit more closely.

Associating "the feminine" in stereotypical fashion with the expression of momentary, emotional outbursts of feeling, which he characterizes elsewhere in the text as "feminine screaming," "blather," and "momentary feminine squealing" (CUP, I: 266, 430, 443), Climacus rejects feminine inwardness as an expression of true inwardness because in his opinion the latter is hidden and cannot be given expression in any direct or external form (CUP, I: 36–37, 260). Eternally, the person who possesses true inwardness relates to it as a dead person: "He does not gesticulate, he does not protest, he does not flare up in a moment of inwardness, but, silent as the grave and quiet as a dead person, he maintains his inwardness and stands by his word" (CUP, I: 236). It is not out of mere conformity to grammatical convention that Climacus uses the third-person masculine pronoun to describe such a person, for he explicitly states that "such a person is a man (*en Mand*)" (CUP, I: 236). It

[16] Although the definite article may be used enclitically to form abstract nouns in Danish, I have amended the Hong translation of this passage to emphasize its reference to the truth of subjectivity in the concrete individual rather than to the subjective nature of truth. The construal of Climacus' statement in terms of the latter meaning leaves him open to the charge of subjectivism, which is entirely unjustified. For the Danish phrase see SV, 7: 237. On the need for amending the standard translation of this phrase, see Perkins (1973), 211. For an interpretation of Kierkegaard's understanding of subjectivity in terms of the concept of upbuilding, see also Perkins (1990), 7–18.

would seem, then, that only men are capable of manifesting true inwardness, while women are given to momentary excitement and external outbursts of feeling which, although "not unlovely" in them, are "always dangerous" because they frequently result in lethargy (CUP, I: 236, 239–40). Even more enduring expressions of feminine inwardness in the form of devotedness to others are relegated to the level of "less inwardness" by Climacus, because "the direction is obviously outward," whereas true inwardness is directed inward to the contrast or comic discrepancy between the individual's existence and the eternal (CUP, I: 291).

It is unfortunate that Climacus' negative opinion of women leads him here to compromise universal human claims made elsewhere in the text, such as his statement that "every human being is by nature designed to become a thinker" (CUP, I: 47) and the oft-repeated claim that the ethical, or the task of becoming subjective, "is the highest task assigned to every human being" (CUP, I: 151, 158, 163; cf. also 134). On the basis of his derogatory remarks about women and "the feminine nature" in relation to the expression of true inwardness, one must conclude either that women are excluded from the category of "human being" or else that they are constitutionally incapable of assuming the highest task assigned to them as human beings. Consequently, they must be regarded as unethical creatures who, ironically, lack subjectivity—the very quality with which they traditionally have been associated, although that quality is understood here quite differently from its conventional conception.

Climacus' relegation of feminine devotedness to the status of "less inwardness" is particularly problematic when considered in relation to *Works of Love*, a collection of deliberations published only a year after the *Postscript* under Kierkegaard's own name and therefore unequivocally reflecting the philosopher's own views as opposed to those of a pseudonym. While recognizing that there are forms of devotion that are really expressions of self-love, or a "devoted self-love," in the "enormous self-willfulness" with which one other person is loved exclusively in an "unlimited devotion" that ought to be given up (WL, 55), Kierkegaard sets forth in this book a Christian understanding of love based on the biblical commandment to love the neighbor, or all human beings, as oneself.[17]

[17] For more extended treatments of this work see Walsh (1988), 234–56, and (1995), 167–79. See also SUD, where Kierkegaard's pseudonymous Christian author, Anti-Climacus, also associates the feminine nature with devoted-

Although hidden in its inmost depths, having its ground in the mysterious love of God, neighbor love seeks outward expression and is made known or recognizable by its "fruits" or works of love for others (WL, 8–16). Optimally the Christian view of love, as Kierkegaard understands it, is one in which one's life is "completely squandered . . . on the existence of others" (WL, 279). Such a view of love, however, does not square with the "hidden inwardness" of Johannes Climacus, who can find no satisfactory external expression for subjectivity or inwardness and thus cloaks it in humor as the incognito for the incongruity between the internal and the external in the religious individual's life (CUP, I: 461–2, 472–75, 492, 499–500).[18] In equating true inwardness with hidden inwardness, therefore, Climacus does not reflect Kierkegaard's own viewpoint, or at least not his view of inwardness as given expression in Christianity, which for him constitutes the highest form of subjectivity.

The second form of inwardness from which Climacus seeks to distinguish true inwardness is "chummy inwardness," or what I take to be a form of inter-subjectivity that compromises the integrity of the individual. In contrast to the anti-individualist stance of some feminist epistemologists, Climacus emphasizes the distinctiveness and importance of the single individual or the individual subject, which every human being

---

ness and, like Climacus, regards femininity as constituting a "lower synthesis" than does masculinity, which he thinks "essentially belongs within the qualification of spirit" (SUD 50n; 67). But Anti-Climacus nevertheless claims that in relation to God it holds for both men and women that "devotion is the self" and that "in the giving of oneself the self is gained" (50n). This suggests that while devotedness in woman is a natural phenomenon that may serve as a mode of despair, or failure to become a self, because of a misplaced identification of the self with the object of her devotion, it is essential to the definition of a self and to becoming such in relation to God. For a more detailed discussion of devotedness as a mode of despair, see Walsh (1987), 121–34, or its revised version in the present volume.

[18] For a more extended discussion of the role of humor in CUP, see Walsh (1994), 212–17. On hidden inwardness see also PC, 212–20, where Kierkegaard, in the persona of his Christian pseudonym, Anti-Climacus, explicitly rejects the notion of hidden inwardness because it too easily may serve in established Christendom as a ploy for claiming that all are true Christians. Instead, Anti-Climacus insists upon an "inverted recognizability" of the Christian life in voluntary suffering as a result of opposition from the world.

is and has as his or her task to become (CUP, I: 49, 131,149, 355). In his view, "subjective individuals must be held devoutly apart from one another and must not run coagulatingly together in objectivity" (CUP, I: 79). We have already seen that, from Climacus' perspective, every actuality outside oneself can be grasped only through thought or in the form of possibility. To know another person as an actuality would require one to make oneself into the other, or vice versa, to make the actuality of the other into one's own personal actuality, which in Climacus' view is clearly impossible (CUP, I: 321). Even if one were able to do that, he says, the new actuality would belong to oneself as distinct from the other (CUP, I: 321). Ethically considered, then, "there is no direct relation between subject and object" (CUP, I: 321).

This does not mean, however, that there is no communication or commonality between subjects. Like Socrates and Lessing, who closed themselves off in the isolation of subjectivity, or what Climacus calls "inclosed reserve," the subjective individual is solitary in relation to God, where "the meddling busyness of a third person" signifies "a lack of inwardness" (CUP, I: 65, 69, 77, 80).[19] But the subjective individual does sustain, like Socrates, a maieutic relation to others, seeking to help them acquire the same understanding he (or she) possesses through the practice of indirect communication, or the communication of subjective truth in such a way as to leave the other free to appropriate that which constitutes the essentially human (CUP, I: 73–79). As Climacus sees it, "[e]very human being must be assumed to possess essentially what belongs essentially to being a human being. The subjective thinker's task is to transform himself [or herself] into an instrument that clearly and definitely expresses in existence the essentially human" (CUP, I: 356). But Climacus goes on to point out that "to depend upon differences in this regard is a misunderstanding," for "to will to be an individual human be-

---

[19] Although the phenomenon of inclosing reserve is analyzed in CA as a demonic attempt to close oneself off from others in anxiety about the good or the possibility of freedom, Vigilius Haufniensis, the pseudonymous author of this book, also identifies a "lofty inclosing reserve," exemplified by Socrates, which he associates with earnestness and true (as opposed to spurious) religious inwardness. For a discussion of this form of inclosed reserve, which is what Johannes Climacus has in mind when he uses these terms in CUP, see Walsh (1994), 159–63.

ing (which one unquestionably is) with the help of and by virtue of one's difference is flabbiness; but to will to be an individual existing human being (which one unquestionably is) in the same sense as everyone else is capable of being—that is the ethical victory over life and over every mirage" (CUP, I: 356). For Climacus, therefore, the art of subjectivity is to become what one essentially is, an individual human being or subject in common with others, not merely a "subject of sorts," in whom "the accidental, the angular, the selfish, the eccentric, etc." is accentuated in distinction form others. True subjectivity is rooted in our commonality as human beings, not in our individual differences, although paradoxically individuality is affirmed and cultivated precisely in and through a recognition of our common humanity in striving personally to appreciate that which constitutes the essentially human and to communicate it indirectly to others. At the most fundamental level, then, all essential knowledge, or that knowledge which pertains essentially to human existence (CUP, I:197–98), is communally shared in the sense that it belongs essentially to every human being, but it is known and appropriated subjectively by each individual.

Conclusions

From this brief account of Johannes Climacus' views on objectivity and subjectivity, several conclusions vis-à-vis recent developments in feminist epistemology may be proposed.

First of all, Climacan subjectivity clearly is not subjectivism, as Climacus does not deny the reality of objective truth or our ability to acquire a limited or approximate knowledge of that truth by objective means. Although he shares the postmodernist suspicion of the positivity or certainty of objective knowledge, he avoids epistemological relativism by recognizing that objective knowledge is approximate and for that reason, none other, is uncertain.

Second, we have seen that, while feminists fault the conventional view of objectivity because of its androcentric orientation, which purports to be disinterested but is not, Climacus accepts the essentially disinterested character of objective knowledge but faults it precisely because subjectivity is abandoned in objective modes of inquiry. Whereas feminist epistemologists view objectivity itself as including subjective factors, either surreptitiously (as in the masculinist concept of objectivity) or self-consciously (as in a feminist perspective), Climacus clearly separates the objective and subjective spheres. However, some forms of knowledge that currently fall under the sphere of subjectivity, such as the social sciences, might qualify as essential knowledge for him if one is able to detect and appropriate an existential significance behind the numerical, quantitative analysis to which such knowledge is subjected.

Third, while Climacus would reject the anti-individualist stance of feminist epistemologists in emphasizing the single individual whose task first and foremost is to develop subjectivity or inwardness, he nevertheless affirms the concrete, contextual, and communal character of subjective truth or essential knowledge inasmuch as it pertains equally to all human beings with respect to the existential task of realizing in oneself and communicating to others that which constitutes the essentially human. Climacus would deny the communal character of such knowledge, however, if that means we learn and communicate truth through a form of inter-subjectivity that blurs the distinction between self and others, as in some postmodernist and integrationist feminist epistemologies. He does not deny that individual subjects are socially constituted through relations to others, but in his view they are able to transcend human relations in the relation to God. Part of the task of subjectivity, therefore, is to assert oneself as an individual over against the determining forces of society such as family, church, and state. In this feminists may find an emancipatory pulse in Climacan subjectivity that, unlike the social determinism of some feminist positions, is able to explain why and how women are capable of resisting the social forces that historically have oppressed them.

Fourth, in emphasizing the cultivation of passion and subjectivity—capacities traditionally associated with women—Climacus can be said to be calling for the incorporation of "the feminine" into epistemology as a way of knowing. But insofar as he associates a particular form of subjectivity—momentary inwardness or emotional enthusiasm—stereotypically with women and distinguishes true inwardness from it, he compromises the feminist thrust of his insights and appears to be anti-women. Essentially, however, existential pathos is non-gendered for him inasmuch as it constitutes "the pathos for everyone" (CUP, I: 394). Stripped of its sexist associations and narrow conception as hidden inwardness, his understanding of subjectivity or pathos could form the basis for a feminist rethinking of subjectivity in a manner that gives greater depth to the concept as it relates to women and serves to distinguish female subjectivity precisely from the stereotyped sexist view of feminine inwardness perpetuated by Climacus.

Fifth, while Climacus agrees with feminism in criticizing the epistemological privileging of objectivity over subjectivity, his failure to recognize the masculinist character of objectivity and his own reverse privileging of subjectivity over against objectivity would lead some feminists to conclude that he was not radical enough in his critique of the speculative-scientific mentality of his time and that his thought continues to reflect and perpetuate the very structures of the dualistic or dichotomous thinking they are intent on displacing. Inasmuch as Climacus does not question the validity of objective thought in itself, however, it would perhaps be more accurate to characterize his understanding of the relation between objectivity and subjectivity, in the manner of some integrationist feminists, as dialectical rather than dualistic or dichotomous, but dialectical in such a way as not to blur the distinction between these terms.

These conclusions suggest that Kierkegaard's *Concluding Unscientific Postscript*, often ignored by the philosophical community because of its emphasis on subjectivity, deserves a sympathetic as well as critical rereading by feminist epistemologists. They may find some viewpoints in it to reject, but also much to support and advance their own attempts to rethink and reformulate the concepts of objectivity and subjectivity in the context of the present age.

References

Antony, Louise M. "Quine as Feminist: The Radical Import of Naturalized Epistemology." In *A Mind of One's Own: Feminist Essays on Reason and Objectivity*, edited by Louise M. Antony and Charlotte Witt, 185–225. Colorado: Westview Press.

Beauvoir, Simone de. *The Second Sex.* Translated and edited by H. M. Parshley. New York: Vintage Books, 1989.

Belenky, Mary Field, Blythe McVicker Clinchy, Nancy Rule Goldberger, and Jill Mattuck Tarule. *Women's Ways of Knowing: The Development of Self, Voice, and Mind.* New York: Basic Books, 1986.

Bordo, Susan. *The Flight to Objectivity: Essays on Cartesianism and Culture.* Albany: State University of New York Press, 1987.

Chodorow, Nancy. 1978. *The Reproduction of Mothering.* Berkeley and Los Angeles: University of California Press.

Code, Lorraine. 1991. *What Can She Know: Feminist Theory and the Construction of Knowledge.* Ithaca: Cornell University Press.

Duran, Jane. 1991. *Toward a Feminist Epistemology*. Savage, Md.: Rowman and Littlefield.

Evans, C. Stephen. 1983. *Kierkegaard's "Fragments" and "Postscript": The Religious Philosophy of Johannes Climacus.* Atlantic Highlands, NJ: Humanities Press.

Gergen, Kenneth. 1988. "Feminist Critique of Science and the Challenge of Social Epistemology." In *Feminist Thought and the Structures of Knowledge*, ed. Mary McCanney Gergen, 27–48. New York: New York University Press.

Harding, Sandra. 1983. "Why Has the Sex / Gender System Become Visible Only Now?" In *Discovering Reality: Feminist Perspectives in Epistemology, Metaphysics, Methodology, and Philosophy of Science*, ed. Sandra Harding and Merill B. Hintikka, 311–24. Dortrecht: Reidel.

_______. 1986. *The Science Question in Feminism.* Ithaca: Cornell University Press.

_______. 1991. *Whose Science? Whose Knowledge?* Ithaca: Cornell University Press.

Hartshorne, M. Holmes. 1990. *Kierkegaard, Godly Deceiver: The Nature and Meaning of His Pseudonymous Writings.* New York: Columbia University Press.

Hartsock, Nancy C. M. 1983. "The Feminist Standpoint: Developing the Ground for a Specifically Feminist Historical Materialism." In *Discovering Reality: Feminist Perspectives in Epistemology, Metaphysics, Methodology, and Philosophy of Science*, ed. Sandra Harding and Merill B. Hintikka, 283–310. Dortrecht: Reidel.

Haslanger, Sally. 1993. "On Being Objective and Being Objectified." In *A Mind of One's Own: Feminist Essays on Reason & Objectivity*, ed. Louise M. Antony and Charlotte Witt, 85–125. Boulder: Westview.

Hawkesworth, Mary E. 1989. "Knowers, Knowing, Known: Feminist Theory and Claims of Truth." *Signs* 14, no. 3:533–57.

__________. 1994. "From Objectivity to Objectification: Feminist Objections." In *Rethinking Objectivity*, ed. Allan Megill, 151–77. Durham: Duke University Press.

Hekman, Susan J. 1990. *Gender and Knowledge: Elements of a Postmodern Feminism.* Boston: Northeastern University Press.

Hodge, Joanna. 1988. "Subject, Body and the Exclusion of Women from Philosophy." In *Feminist Perspectives in Philosophy*, ed. Morwenna Griffiths and Margaret Whitford, 152–68. Bloomington: Indiana University Press.

Hubbard, Ruth. 1988. "Some Thoughts about the Masculinity of Science." In *Feminist Thought and the Structure of Knowledge*, ed. Mary McCanney Gergen, 1–15. New York: New York University Press.

Irigaray, Luce. 1985. *Speculum of the Other Woman*, tr. Gillian C. Gill. Ithaca: Cornell University Press.

Jardine, Alice. 1985. *Gynesis: Configurations of Women and Modernity*. Ithaca: Cornell University Press.

Keller, Evelyn Fox. 1983. *A Feeling for the Organism: The Life and Work of Barbara McClintock*. New York: W. H. Freeman.

_____. 1985. *Reflections on Gender and Science*. New Haven: Yale University Press.

Lloyd, Genevieve. 1984. *The Man of Reason*. London: Methuen.

Longino, Helen. 1990. *Science as Social Knowledge: Values and Objectivity in Scientific Inquiry*. Princeton: Princeton University Press.

MacKinnon, Catherine. 1987. *Feminism Modified*. Cambridge: Harvard University Press.

Megill, Allan. 1994. *Rethinking Objectivity*. Durham: Duke University Press.

Nelson, Lynn Hankinson. 1990. *Who Knows? From Quine to a Feminist Empiricism*. Philadelphia: Temple University Press.

Perkins, Robert L. 1973. "Kierkegaard's Epistemological Preferences." *International Journal of Philosophy of Religion* 4, No. 4: 197–217.

______. 1990. "Kierkegaard, A Kind of Epistemologist." *History of European Ideas* 12, No. 1: 17–18.

Ring, Jennifer. 1991. *Modern Political Theory and Contemporary Feminism: A Dialectical Analysis*. Albany: Albany State University of New York Press.

Rose, Hilary. 1983. "Hand, Brain and Heart: A Feminist Epistemology for the Natural Sciences." *Signs* 9, No. 1: 73–90.

Walsh, Sylvia. 1987. "On 'Feminine' and 'Masculine' Forms of Despair." In *International Kierkegaard Commentary: The Sickness unto Death*, ed. Robert L. Perkins, 121–34. Macon: Mercer University Press.

_____. 1988. "Forming the Heart: The Role of Love in Kierkegaard's Thought." In *The Grammar of the Heart: New Essays in Moral Philosophy and Theology*, ed. Richard H. Bell, 234–56. San Francisco: Harper and Row.

_____. 1994. *Living Poetically: Kierkegaard's Existential Aesthetics*. University Park: The Pennsylvania State University Press.

_____. 1995. "Kierkegaard's Philosophy of Love." In *The Nature and Pursuit of Love: The Philosophy of Irving Singer*, ed. David Goicoechea, 167–79. Amherst, NY: Prometheus Books.

13

THE PHILOSOPHICAL AFFIRMATION OF GENDER DIFFERENCE: KIERKEGAARD VERSUS POSTMODERN NEO-FEMINISM*[1]

Philosophically, the issue of gender may be elucidated through the concepts of identity and difference, self and other, masculinity and femininity. In what follows, I shall try to show how the penchant of recent postmodern, neo-feminist philosophies to privilege difference and alienation between self and other, man and woman, is dialectically countered in the thought of the Danish philosopher Søren Kierkegaard by a recognition of human commonalities as well as differences and by the possibility of reconciliation in love of the other as neighbor.

I. FEMINIST AFFIRMATIONS OF DIFFERENCE

In the resurgence of feminism in the first half of the twentieth century, thinkers such as Simone de Beauvoir, the foremost feminist philosopher of the early post-war period, sought to deny any essential gender difference between women and men. Such differences as existed, Beauvoir believed, were on the whole culturally determined and imposed rather than biologically given in the forms of feminine and masculine essences. Setting out to dethrone "the myth of femininity" in her now classic manifesto *The Second Sex*, Beauvoir analyzed women's situation as one in which they are pressured either to comply with the inessential, inferior, submissive role of "the other" assigned to them by men or to deny their sexual identity as women by adopting the ways of men (Beauvoir: 1952). Over against this unhappy pseudo-choice, Beauvoir urged women, in the spirit of Sartrean radical freedom, to affirm themselves as equal, independent, creative subjects without renouncing their womanliness. Although she

---

[1] *Reprinted with permission of the Christian Association for Psychological Studies, Inc. from *Journal of Psychology and Christianity*, Vol. 74, 1988, pp. 18–26.

rejected the notion of "equality in difference," an equal but separate status for women, she did want to affirm the possibility of "differences in equality," that is, special forms of relation to their own bodies, to each other, and to children (Beauvoir, 1952: 813). Thus Beauvoir was prepared to acknowledge the validity of some gender differences between women and men, but not gender essences defining different natures of male and female being.

Seeking to reaffirm and to preserve a more distinctive character for woman, some feminist thinkers in recent decades have placed greater emphasis on gender differences. In America, for example, the radical feminist philosopher Mary Daly, like Simone de Beauvoir, rejects the traditionally defined stereotype of femininity, but she thinks that by "spinning" threads of connectedness with their sisters, women can develop genuine differences from men that are not male-defined (Day, 1978). Also detecting "a different voice" of women in her studies of women's development, but one more in line with traditional conceptions of the feminine, Harvard psychologist Carol Gilligan emphasizes the importance of intimacy, relationships, and care for others in the formation of female identity (Gilligan,1982). By far the greatest emphasis on female difference, however, has come from a group of French neo-feminist writers, e.g. Julia Kristeva, Hélène Cixous, Catherine Clément, and Luce Irigaray, who are heavily influenced by French post-structuralism. Following the psychoanalytic and deconstructive analyses of such thinkers as Lacan, Derrida, and Foucault, they seek to reclaim a sense of female difference through the non-exclusion and internalization of difference.

Historically, in the analysis of this neo-feminist group, "the problem with Western literature, philosophy, and politics is not that it has asserted the difference of women from men, but rather that it has denied and repressed the specifically feminine" (Sawicki and Young, 1988: 14). At the root of the human psyche there is, according to the Lacanian psychoanalytic perspective of this movement, a traumatic sense of separation of the subject from itself and from others reflecting and veiling the separation of the subject at birth from its mother. Desiring, but forever barred from, a return to primordial unity with her, the subject struggles to become an independent being by differentiating itself from everything other than itself. As this process takes place in man, woman (the mother) is pushed to the margin of his existence and excluded as "the other" (Cixous and Clément, 1986) or "the abject" (Kristeva, 1987) who threatens to engulf and return him to an original, primordial identity with her. Unable to tolerate this otherness, he represses it to the level of the unconscious, reduces woman to sameness with himself by domesticating her into structures of symbolic order or "language" established by him (including psychological, sociological, political, religious and economic codes and systems of signification which form the unconscious matrix out of which consciousness is shaped), and dominates over her. Although uniformity prevails at the conscious and social levels of existence, traces of the excluded and repressed other in the unconscious reveal an underlying metaphysical state of difference rather than identity, alienation rather than reconciliation, endless lack and desire rather than satisfaction and fulfillment in personal relations.

Instead of despairing of their situation, as an earlier generation of existentialists may have done, neo-feminists make it an occasion for affirming, even flaunting, their difference and liminal position in the face of the phallocentric and patriarchal society that has marginalized woman's existence. Catherine Clément, for example, sets forth in one of her writings the figures of the sorceress and the hysteric (metaphors representing most graphically the exclusion of woman in Western culture) as models of female liberation (Cixous and Clément, 1986). As the writer of the introduction to the English translation of her work explains:

> Since the etymological root of the word 'hysteria' is the Greek *hyster*, or womb, the hysteric is, after all, the creature whose wandering, even wondering womb manifests the distinctively female bonding, or bondage, of mind and body, the inescapable female connection between creation and procreation, the destiny that is inexorably determined by anatomy. And the sorceress—the witch, the wisewoman, destroyer and preserver of culture—is she not the *midwife*, the intermediary between life and death, the go-between whose occult yet necessary labors deliver souls and bodies across frightening boundaries? (Cixous and Clément, 1986: xiii)

Similarly, the American feminist philosopher Mary Daly exploits the metaphors of Spinster, Lesbian, Hag, Harpy, Crone, and Fury—all traditionally negative images associated with women—as patterns for women's journey to true selfhood (Daly, 1978). But while Daly encourages women to create / celebrate their own identities and differences in bonds of female friendships (which may or may not involve genital relations), some of the French neo-feminists revel in the expression of a radical bisexuality through which they explore and identify with multiple personalities, both masculine and feminine, seeking in this manner to experience ecstasy or "jouissance" and to construct their identities as women. "Femininity and bisexuality go together," declares Hélène Cixous, for woman more so than man is disposed to venture out of herself, to explore other possibilities of identity, in the expression of a cosmic "libido of the other" that is diffused and infinitely changing (Cixous and Clément, 1986: 85, 88, 92). Whereas man is self-absorbed, engrossed in a mirror economy of narcissistic self-love that seeks to protect and reinforce the traditional image of masculinity and male self-identity, woman seeks without self-interest to love, to love the other, to become the other. Paradoxically, by depropriating, depersonalizing, and diffusing herself, she becomes herself.

For Cixous it is most of all in *writing* that woman becomes herself. There are, she claims, not only physical and psychological differences between women and men but also distinctively feminine and masculine styles of writing, distinguished by differing ways of relating to the other and to the law of return. While woman is disposed to admit in her writing that there is an *other*, man has difficulty in letting the other come through his. And whereas she gives of herself without expectation of returning to herself, he seeks to gain more masculinity (virility, authority, power, money, pleasure) through his giving of himself. "Rare are the men able to venture onto the brink where writing, freed from law, unencumbered by moderation, exceeds phallic authority, and where the subjectivity inscribing its effects becomes feminine," says Cixous (Cixous and Clément, 1986: 86).

It is also in writing that love, in her view, becomes love of the other, for writing, she thinks, is what makes love other. Indeed, she goes even further to proclaim: "It is itself this love. Other-love is writing's first name" (Cixous and Clément, 1986: 99). For the woman who writes, however, this other-love is fleeting and unattached: "She will let nothing intervene in her fight, other than the 'natural' desire for 'a' man, whoever he is, without any preference, for she must not be *attached* to any man. Love for a unique one cannot occur" (Cixous and Clément, 1986: 116). Like Simone de Beauvoir and Mary Daly, Cixous sees the sexes as being at war with one another. "For a free woman," she says, "there can be no relationship with men other than war" (Cixous and Clément, 1986: 116). Just as man has tried to conquer and dominate woman, so she now seeks to capture and dominate him, but with a difference: whereas he seeks to dominate in order to destroy, she dominates in order not to be dominated. Ultimately, Cixous maintains that man and woman "must kill warring power to liberate loving power" in themselves, but she does not tell us how this can be done (Cixous and Clément, 1986: 118).

Although neo-feminist affirmations of female difference support the liberation of women from male domination and the formation of female identities as separate subjects, they do not envision "sorties" (Cixous) or ways out for women that heal the wound of alienation between woman and man or allow for a truly positive view of man as other. For the internalization of masculine otherness through sexual experimentation and imagination in writing does not involve any real or enduring relationship, commitment, and concern for men as actual others. Thus it appears that the other, particularly male alterity, is not really affirmed and respected as an independent other in their perspective but merely appropriated as a possibility and exploited as an object of play in the narcissistic construction of their own identities.

Yet, true to their poststructuralist roots, neo-feminists are hesitant to encode female identity and femininity, purposely leaving them conceptually vague and undefined. Since, in their nominalistic viewpoint, there is no general woman or one typical woman, the concept of female identity must be kept open and fluid to reflect the "infinite richness" of the individual (Cixous in Marks and de Courtivron, 1980: 245–246). Julia Kristeva expresses the same belief in an interview: "I am in favour of a concept of femininity which would take as many forms as there are women" (Moi, 1987: 114). Furthermore, in her view, identity is something that is constantly reborn and remade. Thus there is no continuity of identity or perduring ideal of a self to which women should aspire. In the final analysis, therefore, the neo-feminist assertion of female difference ironically results in a disappearance of the self—a fundamental motif of postmodern thought (Taylor, 1984: 34–51)—rather than an affirmation of it. We may well wonder, then, whether, by following the deconstructionist path of postmodernism, they have been led astray, into self-deception, aestheticism, and despair rather than to self-clarity, ethical seriousness, and genuine *jouissance*.

II. KIERKEGAARD ON GENDER DIFFERENCE

An alternative and, in a number of ways, more satisfactory approach to the issue of gender may be found in the thought of Søren Kierkegaard, whose writings offer a perspective that affirms both the self and the other, woman and man, as independent subjects in the context of concrete human relations. Although postmodern thinkers like to claim Kierkegaard as a precursor of their own philosophies of difference (Inglis, 1981; Taylor, 1987; Agacinski, 1988), his thought constitutes, in many ways, a critique of postmodernism as well as of the Hegelian and romantic philosophies of the modern era. In fact, postmodern deconstructionist and neo-feminist philosophies manifest a close resemblance to romanticism in their ironic negation of the established order and assertion of a boundless freedom of the subject to create him / herself through experimentation and play with a multiplicity of possible identities concocted by the imagination and / or encountered in a variety of sensual experiences. Such similarities suggest that these philosophies are better viewed as the culmination of romanticism rather than the beginning of a new era of thought. Certainly some of the criticisms Kierkegaard leveled against romanticism are just as applicable to postmodern thought, especially neo-feminism.

Kierkegaard's authorship is so extensive and complex that only a couple of texts and themes relating to the issue of gender can be considered here. First, I shall briefly examine the use of gender categories in the analysis of selfhood and despair which Kierkegaard carries out via a pseudonym in *The Sickness unto Death.* Since I have written recently about this in some detail (Walsh, 1987), only a summary account will be given below. Second, I shall examine the concept of the other in *Works of Love*, a book of Christian reflections written at the midpoint of his authorship under his own name as author. From consideration of these texts and concepts, it may be seen that Kierkegaard affirms gender difference, but within a common structure of selfhood and the more fundamental qualification of our common humanity. These elements of commonality, I shall argue, point the way to the overcoming of alienation and opposition between woman and man, self and others, through the transformation of narcissism into love of the other as neighbor.

A. Gender Differences as Modes of Selfhood and Despair

Unlike neo-feminism and the postmodern movement in general, Kierkegaard affirms throughout his writings an essential form of selfhood or personal identity which is the task of every human being to realize in existence. In *The Sickness unto Death* the self is defined in spiritual terms as a conscious and dynamic relating to oneself as a synthesis of the finite and the infinite, the temporal and the eternal, necessity (given limitations) and freedom or possibility (Kierkegaard, 1980: 13). Since no distinction is made between the sexes in this definition and the generic term "human being" is used to refer to the being whose task is to become a self, both woman and man may be assumed to become and be constituted as selves in the same manner. Within this common structure of selfhood, however, substantive differences may be observed in the ways woman and man are oriented toward themselves and falter on the pathway to selfhood by falling into despair.

Woman's nature, Kierkegaard claims, is characterized by devotedness and givingness (Kierkegaard, 1980: 50). She acquires her sexual identity as a woman instinctively by giving herself in devotion to others. Man, by contrast, is more self-contained and intellectual. Although he gives himself to others, he has and retains a sense of self-awareness apart from that giving. In Kierkegaard's view, then, woman and man manifest different modes of acquiring their substantive or sexual identities. Her being is centered in relatedness to others ("the feminine mode") while his is centered in the relation to himself ("the masculine mode"). Neither mode is equivalent to or sufficient in itself to become a spiritually qualified self, although masculine self-consciousness corresponds more closely than feminine devotedness does to the definition of the self as a self-relation. In Kierkegaard's view, however, to become a self it is necessary not only to be related to oneself but also to the power or spirit that constitutes the self, namely God. In relation to God, he maintains, "it holds for men as well as for women that devotion is the self and that in the giving of oneself the self is gained" (Kierkegaard, 1980: 50). Thus the feminine mode as well as the masculine mode is integrally involved in the process of becoming a true self or religious personality. That both modes are needed is explicitly indicated in a late journal entry (1854) by Kierkegaard:

> In a certain sense woman is by nature better suited for essentially religious service, for it is a woman's nature wholly to give herself.—But on the other hand she does not explain anything.—An eminently masculine intellectuality joined to a feminine submissiveness—this is the truly religious. Woman's devotedness is essentially limited to interjections, and if it is more than that it is unfeminine. But on the other hand an eminent masculine intellectuality is directly related to an enormous selfishness which must be slain in submissiveness. (Kierkegaard, 1975: JP 4: 5006)

To become a true self, therefore, woman and man need to develop not only the natural inclinations which constitute their respective sexual identities but also the qualities characteristic of the opposite sex, that is, both the feminine and masculine modes of relating to oneself and to God, in a manner comparable to what modern psychologists identify as "psychological androgyny" (Walsh, 1987: 130).

In *The Sickness unto Death* Kierkegaard distinguishes between unconscious despair, in which there is no awareness of potentially being a self, and conscious despair, which manifests itself in two basic forms: despair in weakness and despair in defiance. Despair in weakness is characterized by an unwillingness on the part of an individual to become a self while despair in defiance is manifested in willing to become the self one wants to be rather than the self one is intended to be by God. Kierkegaard further distinguishes between these forms of despair by identifying the despair of weakness as "feminine despair" and despair in defiance as "masculine despair" (Kierkegaard, 1980: 49). Although either form of despair may appear in both women and men, women are more inclined, he thinks, to manifest despair in weakness or feminine despair, while men are more prone to defiant or masculine despair. Since women tend by nature to lose or abandon themselves in devotion to others, their despair is to lack a sense of self apart from the object of their devotion (the masculine mode). Man's despair, by contrast, is characterized by an unwillingness to lose or submit himself in devotion to God (the feminine mode). His despair thus consists in an unwarranted self-assertion as an autonomous being over against God while hers lies in an unwarranted self-abandonment in something or someone other than God. Her self is lost or misplaced in a finite object outside herself while his is inwardly misplaced in himself.

Although Kierkegaard's characterization of selfhood and despair reflects the traditional types of masculine and feminine natures, the thrust of his analysis is to call into question the adequacy of either as a mode of identity and to show their potentiality as modes of despair. Thus it serves to illumine some of the dangers and limitations of the traditional modes and points to a complementary wholeness of identity as a self toward which both woman and man should strive. Viewed in terms of Kierkegaard's analysis, the feminine abandonment in the other advocated by recent neo-feminism appears to be a manifestation of feminine despair rather than a legitimate mode of forming female identity. Instead of losing themselves in a single object of devotion, however, they lose themselves in a multiplicity of other identities and attempt to construct, in the manner of defiant despair, their own identities in terms of the many possibilities with which they experiment. Although, in Kierkegaard's view, possibility is an integral component in the composition of the self, one may fall into despair by getting lost in possibility and fantasy. What is needed in that event is an antidote of necessity and finitude, that is, the recovery of a sense of one's given essence and limitations as a self. In this respect the neo-feminist movement could benefit from Kierkegaard's analysis.

B. The Neighbor as the True Other

Another way Kierkegaard affirms difference is through the concept of the other. But who or what is the other and how is it related to the self from whom it is differentiated? In *Works of Love*, Kierkegaard ponders the question of the other in the course of a series of reflections on the Christian commandment, "You shall love your neighbor as yourself" (Matt. 22:39). In his view, the other appears in true form only in the person of the neighbor. Establishing a conceptual identity between these two categories, Kierkegaard claims: "Neighbor is what philosophers would call the *other*, that by which the selfishness in self-love is to be tested" (Kierkegaard, 1962: 27). As he sees it, Christianity presupposes self-love in human beings and seeks to bring about a transformation of that love, eradicating the element of narcissism or selfishness in it by requiring us to love others as neighbors. While natural expressions of love in erotic love and friendship may appear to be unselfish love of others, in Kierkegaard's view these modes of love are secretly expressions of self-love. The beloved or friend is really an "other-I" or "other-self" with whom we unite in exclusive relationships to create "a new selfish self" based on our common likenesses and differences from others (Kierkegaard, 1962: 66–69). Erotic love and friendship are formed on the basis of personal preference and require mutuality and reciprocity in love, that is, the satisfaction of our needs and desires in return. Thus they are fundamentally selfish in character and need also to be transformed.

In Kierkegaard's view the transformation of self-love occurs in coming to love others as a neighbor. Etymologically defined, the neighbor is the "near-dweller," one who is or ought to be as near to us as we are to ourselves. Neighbor love thus involves a duplication of the self in the other in such a manner as to place demands upon ourselves rather than upon the other. Only in neighbor love, therefore, do we truly love the other as we love ourselves, that is, want for the other what we would want for ourselves. The neighbor is thus the "first-Thou" or "other-you" (Kierkegaard, 1962: 66, 69). Although one other person is sufficient to test our ability to love the other as a neighbor (and thus erotic love and friendship may become modes of neighbor love), Kierkegaard emphasizes that the concept of neighbor includes all human beings in their absolute equality before God (Kierkegaard, 1962: 37, 72). The category of the neighbor is thus equivalent to the category human being, which is the fundamental qualification of human existence. Elaborating on this point at some length, Kierkegaard writes:

> Every one of us is a human being and at the same time the heterogeneous individual which he is by particularity; but being a human being is the fundamental qualification. No one should mistake his distinctiveness to the degree that he cravenly or presumptuously forgets that he is a human being. No one should be preoccupied with the differences so that he cowardly or presumptuously forgets that he is a human being; no man is an exception to being a human being by virtue of his particularizing differences. He is rather a human being and then a particular human being (Kierkegaard, 1962: 142).

Similarly, in another passage he says: "In being king, beggar, scholar, rich man, poor man, male, female, etc., we do not resemble each other—therein we are all different. But in being a neighbor we are all unconditionally like each other" (Kierkegaard, 1962: 97). To love the other as a neighbor means, then, to love that person first of all as a human being, on the basis of our common humanity rather than personal preference; secondly, it involves the exercise of an "eternal equality" in loving others (Kierkegaard, 1962: 70; Walsh, 1988: 240). Although special relations are still permitted, Kierkegaard maintains that "Christianity has not come into the world to teach this or that modification in how you *in your particularity* should love your wife or friend but to teach you *in your universal humanity* shall love all human beings" (Kierkegaard, 1962: 143, translation slightly altered). He is quick to point out, however, that spouses and friends must not be made exceptions to this requirement but are to be loved first and foremost, like others, as neighbors rather than for their attractive qualities. Certainly they are loved in some ways differently from the way others are loved, but essentially there is no difference in the way persons are to be loved in special relations than others should be loved in general.

How then, are distinctions or differences to be regarded? In one sense, Kierkegaard claims, Christianity disregards all distinctions, requiring us to look away from them or to lift ourselves above them in order to see the essential humanity of the other. Although every person is by virtue of his or her differences a particular individual, essentially each person is something other than that, namely a human being. Because of the differences, which form a disguise, this essential humanity is not seen. The task, therefore, is to allow the differences to "hang loosely" so as to perceive "in every individual that essential other person, that which is common to all men, the eternal likeness, the equality" (Kierkegaard, 1962: 96). In another sense, however, Christianity "makes infinite distinctions in loving the differences" (Kierkegaard, 1962: 252). All persons should be loved according to their own individualities, as the particular persons they are rather than as we might wish them to be. Moreover, the only real benefaction we can give to others, Kierkegaard maintains, is to help them stand on their own as independent persons before God.

From this brief examination of Kierkegaard's concepts of the self and the other, it can be seen that his thought includes a strong affirmation of individuality and gender difference, but within a common structure of selfhood and a fundamental recognition of our universal humanity in love for others as neighbors. It thus provides a philosophical framework for moving beyond narcissism, alienation, and differences between man and woman, self and others, to genuine love, reconciliation, and a shared consciousness that affirms the fundamental humanity and equality of all persons. This possibility is spelled out by Kierkegaard in considerable detail in *Works of Love* and other writings (see Walsh, 1988). Inasmuch as there is much that is resonant with, as well as antithetical to, postmodern neo-feminism in his thought, feminist philosophers and others would do well to take close account of it as they struggle with the issue of gender and related problems in their own thought.

REFERENCES

Agasinski, Sylviane, (1988). *Aparté: Conceptions and Death of Søren Kierkegaard*, trans. Kevin Newmark. Tallahassee: Florida State University.

Alcoff, Linda, (1988). "Cultural Feminism versus Post-Structuralism: The Identity Crisis in Feminist Theory." *Signs*, vol. 13, no. 3 (Spring), 405–436.

Barrett, Michèle, (1987). "The concept of 'Difference,'" *Feminist Review*, no. 26, 28– 41.

Beauvoir, Simone de, (1952). *The Second Sex*, trans. and ed. H.M. Parshley. New York: Vintage Books.

Cixous, Hélène and Catherine Clément, (1986). *The Newly Born Woman*, trans. Betsy Wing and intro. Sandra M. Gilbert. Minneapolis: University of Minnesota Press.

Daly, Mary, (1978). *Gyn/ecology: The Metaethics of Radical Feminism*. Boston: Beacon Press.

Gilligan, Carol, (1982). *In a Different Voice: Psychological Theory and Women's Development*. Cambridge: Harvard University Press.

Inglis, Laura Lyn, (1981). *The Dialogue of Action: Søren Kierkegaard's Dialectical Conception of Ethics*. Ph. D. Dissertation, Princeton Theological Seminary.

Kierkegaard, Søren, (1975). *Søren Kierkegaard's Journals and Papers*, vol. 4, ed. and trans. Howard V. Hong and Edna H. Hong. Bloomington: Indiana University.

Kierkegaard, Søren, (1980). *The Sickness unto Death*, ed. and trans. Howard V. Hong and Edna H. Hong. Princeton: Princeton University Press.

Kierkegaard, Søren, (1962). *Works of Love*, trans. Howard and Edna Hong. New York: Harper & Row Publishers.

Kristeva, Julia, (1987). *Tales of Love*, trans. Leon S. Roudiez. New York: Columbia University Press.

Malantschuk, Gregor, (1980). "Kierkegaard's View of Man and Woman." *The Controversial Kierkegaard*, trans. Howard V. Hong and Edna H. Hong. Waterloo, Ontario: Wilfrid Laurier University.

Marks, Elaine and Isabelle de Courtivron, eds., (1980). *New French Feminisms: An Anthology*. Amherst: University of Massachusetts.

Moi, Toril, ed., (1987). *French Feminist Thought: A Reader*. Oxford: Basil Blackwell.

Sawicki, Jane and Iris Young, (1988). "Issues of Difference in Feminist Philosophy," *Feminism and Philosophy Newsletter*, April, 13–17.

Taylor, Mark C. (1984). *Erring: A Postmodern A/Theology*. Chicago: University of Chicago Press.

Taylor, Mark C. (1987). *Altarity*. Chicago: University of Chicago Press.

Walsh, Sylvia I., (1987). "On 'Feminine' and 'Masculine' Forms of Despair," *International Kierkegaard Commentary: The Sickness unto Death*, Vol. 19, ed. Robert L. Perkins. Macon: Mercer University Press, 121–34.

Walsh, Sylvia I., (1988). "Forming the Heart: The Role of Love in Kierkegaard's Thought," in *The Grammar of the Heart*, ed. Richard H. Bell. New York: Harper & Row, 234–56.

14

GODLY AND UNGODLY WOMEN: GENDER AND SEXUAL POLITICS IN KIERKEGAARD AND AMERICAN FUNDAMENTALISM

In this essay I shall use the category of gender as a lens through which to compare the affinity or lack thereof between Kierkegaard and American fundamentalism with regard to the political agendas implied or advocated by their respective views vis-à-vis the role of women in church and society. Although Kierkegaard belonged to another continent and cultural tradition, many of the same or similar social changes were taking place in Denmark during his lifetime as in America.[1] Moreover, just as the centrality of gender has been well-documented in the literature of the fundamentalist movement in America,[2] so feminist interpreters of Kier-

---

[1] On political, economic, and social trends in Denmark in Kierkegaard's time, see Bruce H. Kirmmse, *Kierkegaard in Golden Age Denmark* (Bloomington: Indiana University Press, 1990), 40–76; and John W. Elrod, *Kierkegaard and Christendom* (Princeton: Princeton University Press, 1981), 3–46. Chief among these trends were the rise of an urban intellectual and commercial bourgeois class and the beginnings of capitalism, Danish liberalism, peasant reforms, and a peaceful revolution from a conservative absolute monarchy to a constitutional monarchy in 1848, with freedom of assembly, speech, and press, and suffrage for male householders. There was also a budding women's emancipation movement in Denmark and other Scandinavian countries that coincided with the rise of women's suffrage movements in England and America. On the Danish and other Scandinavian feminist movements see Julia Watkin, "Serious Jest? Kierkegaard as Young Polemicist in 'Defense' of Women," in *International Kierkegaard Commentary: 'Early Polemical Writings,'* Vol. 1, ed. Robert L. Perkins (Macon: Mercer University Press, 1999), 7–25; and my article, "When 'That Single Individual' is a Woman" in the present collection.

[2] On the centrality of gender in American fundamentalism, see Betty A. DeBerg, *Ungodly Women: Gender and the First Wave of American Fundamentalism*

kegaard have shown that gender was an important category and consideration in his authorship as well.[3] Thus Kierkegaard makes an apt subject for comparison and contrast to the American fundamentalist movement.

Two recent analyses of first and second wave fundamentalism in America provide the point of departure for this effort: Betty A. DeBerg's *Ungodly Women: Gender and the First Wave of American Fundamentalism* and Margaret Lamberts Bendroth's *Fundamentalism and Gender: 1875 to the Present*.[4] DeBerg's book is a seminal and well-documented account of the rise and growth of American "popular" or grassroots fundamentalism in reaction to changes in gender ideology and behavior between 1880 and 1930 in this country. Her account details the disruption of traditional gender roles by the forces of industrialization and urbanization, the reconfiguration and solidification of those roles in middle-class Victorian society, the later challenge to and demise of that reconfiguration brought

---

(Macon: Mercer University Press, 2000); Margaret Lamberts Bendroth, *Fundamentalism and Gender: 1875 to the Present* (New Haven: Yale University Press, 1993); Brenda E. Brasher, *Godly Women: Fundamentalism & Female Power* (Rutgers, 1998); and Carl L. Kell and L. Raymond Camp, *In the Name of the Father: The Rhetoric of the Southern Baptist Convention* (Southern Illinois, 1999). References to DeBerg and Bendroth in this essay will be placed in parentheses in the text.

[3] For a range of feminist interpretations of Kierkegaard, see *Feminist Interpretations of Søren Kierkegaard*, ed. Céline Léon and Sylvia Walsh (University Park, PA: The Pennsylvania State University Press, 1997).

[4] As defined by Bendroth, American fundamentalism is "a coalition of conservative, predominantly Calvinist, Protestants that emerged from within a broader, more ecumenical evangelical culture in the late nineteenth century" (3–4). DeBerg more specifically locates its roots in dispensational premillennialism, the Keswick Holiness Movement, and late nineteenth century revivalism (8–12). Differentiating itself from pentecostal and holiness groups, the fundamentalist movement "began as a northern, urban phenomenon, socially rooted in the lower middle classes" (Bendroth, 3–4). Although closely related on gender ideology as well as theology, the fundamentalist movement is also distinct from the neo-evangelical movement that arose in this country in the mid-1940s (Bendroth, 105). According to Bendroth, five "fundamental" tenets are typically affirmed by the movement: the virgin birth of Christ, substitutionary atonement for sin, the bodily resurrection of Christ, miracles, and biblical inerrancy (4). Most fundamentalists are dispensational pre-millennialists and oppose the theory of evolution and modernism or liberalism.

about by the emergence of the "New Woman," epitomized by "the flapper" of the late 1910s and 1920s, and the attempt of popular fundamentalists to counteract this deconstruction by reclaiming the Victorian gender ideology in their rhetoric and social policies. DeBerg identifies five areas of fundamentalist reaction and reclamation: 1) defense of the notion of separate spheres for women and men; 2) divinization of the home as the locus of religious meaning and the foundation of the Christian church; 3) reclaiming the church for men in reaction to the "feminization of religion" and the relegation of it to the female domain in late Victorian society; 4) the manifesting of an anti-amusement mentality in the rejection of theatre, dance, movies, and inappropriate styles of female dress associated with such forms of entertainment; and 5) reliance on the tenets of dispensational pre-millennialism and biblical inerrancy to justify and sanctify the Victorian gender ideology. American fundamentalists did not always speak with one voice on these issues, but there was large scale agreement among them.

Since second wave fundamentalism embraced many of the same concerns and goals as its progenitor,[5] these five areas of reaction and reclamation will serve as the basis for comparison and contrast between American fundamentalism and Kierkegaard. I shall begin with a brief description of these factors in the gender ideology of American fundamentalism and then turn to a consideration of comparable and disparate viewpoints in the writings of Kierkegaard. Needless to say, the sheer quantity of Kierkegaard's writings necessitates the exercise of a good deal of selectivity and economy in making reference to his works. For the most part I shall focus on works published under his own name rather than those of his pseudonyms, although there is enough continuity of viewpoint on the issue of woman and gender in the authorship to war-

---

[5] On second wave fundamentalism, see Bendroth, chapters 4 and 5, which examine the tightening of restrictions on women's vocations in evangelism, missionary work, and Bible teaching; the renewed emphasis on the Christian family; woman's vocation as wife and mother in the home; and the need for an "ordered hierarchy" in conformity with the order of creation. See also Brasher on some of the differences between first and second wave fundamentalism, including appropriation of contemporary media, political activism, an emphasis on the teaching of creationism in public schools, greater employment of women in jobs outside the home, and more flexibility in matters of appearance on the part of the later fundamentalist movement (23–24, 128, 136, 179–80).

rant the making of at least some generalizations that obtain across the board in the esthetic, ethical, and religious spheres.

I. The Gender Ideology of American Fundamentalism

1. *Separate spheres for women and men.* According to DeBerg, one of "the most distinguishing marks" of the late Victorian period was "a rigid delineation of genders" through the assignment of separate characters and spheres for women and men (DeBerg, 17). With the rise of industrialization and urbanization, men found their identity and vocation primarily in the public sphere, working in factories and businesses, while women were restricted to the private realm of the home and the vocation of motherhood. However, the closing decades of the nineteenth century saw a movement by significant numbers of women into the public sphere, at first in domestic service but increasingly in business and professions such as nursing and teaching as the opportunity for higher education opened up to them. This movement gave rise to what historians have called the "New Woman," who was usually college educated, married late, had fewer children, and generally worked in business or a profession (DeBerg, 27). Along with the rise of women's rights, temperance, and missionary movements, this phenomenon led to an unraveling of the Victorian gender ideology by the end of the century, giving rise to a reaction by the emerging American fundamentalist movement, which strongly reaffirmed the Victorian separate spheres ideology in their rhetoric and practices. Glorifying motherhood, self-sacrifice, and submission for women, they reasserted patriarchal authority in the family and overwhelmingly opposed women's suffrage and higher education for women, which in their view would destroy true womanhood and offend God (DeBerg, 51–52, 56).

2. *Divinization of the home.* The second area of fundamentalist reaction and reclamation was directed toward "the supposed corruption and decline of the family" (DeBerg, 67). The economic, educational, and other social changes noted above brought about changes in family patterns as well, leading fundamentalists not only to reaffirm patriarchal marriage but also to assert the priority of the family over the church as the locus of religious meaning and worship (DeBerg, 62). The Christian home constituted "a church within a church" in which the husband acted as "the priest of the household," while the wife oversaw the religious edu-

cation of their children (DeBerg, 60, 64–65). One of the domestic evils fundamentalists sought to curb and counteract by imposing religious sanctions on offenders was divorce, which was "decried as the 'deadliest foe to the home,' and a 'monster of iniquity' that 'threatens to destroy the American home'" (DeBerg, 68).[6] They also opposed birth control and abortion, which in their view undermined "the holy estate of motherhood" (DeBerg, 112).

3. *Rejection of the feminization of religion.* Not only did fundamentalist men attempt to reclaim the public realm by restricting women to the domestic realm and glorifying the patriarchal family as the foundation of church and society, they also sought to reclaim authority and leadership in the church, which in late Victorian society had been relegated to the domestic realm and largely left to women to do its work. One of the ways this was accomplished was to require women to be silent in church and other assemblies. Another was to oppose the ordination of women, although women's lay leadership and participation continued to be tolerated simply because they were sorely needed (DeBerg, 83).[7] A third way was to associate women who sought equality and leadership positions in the church with the "ungodly women" of the women's rights movement and sectarian religious movements in which they played important roles (DeBerg, 84).[8] In addition to these attempts to diminish women's influ-

---

[6] According to DeBerg, "divorce was permissible only on the grounds of adultery, and remarriage of the adulterer was prohibited" (70). Interestingly, however, in Brasher's study of second wave fundamentalist churches, the conditions justifying divorce cited by female members she interviewed were physical abuse and drug or alcohol abuse, not adultery (152). Moreover, divorce was often a motivating factor in women's conversions to fundamentalism (56, 109).

[7] See Brasher for an account of how second wave fundamentalist women managed to acquire *power* in the church, even though they lacked *authority*, through the formation of women's ministry programs in which, among other activities, they could teach but not preach (27, 58–90)

[8] The latter included not only the women's temperance movement but also sectarian religious groups such as theosophy, spiritualism, Christian Science, and Pentecostalism. One commentator quoted by DeBerg notes that "nearly all the leaders of these 'isms' are women" who "with their public teaching and leadership are disobeying the Word of God. If they were to take the place which Nature and the Word of God assigns to them, some of these movements would come to an end" (85).

ence and power in the church, fundamentalist ministers sought to replace what were regarded as effeminate and thus godless Christian symbols with "manly" ones, thereby associating Christianity, Christ, and the ideal Christian life with masculinity, virility, strength, athleticism, militancy, and heroism.

4. *Anti-amusement mentality.* Fundamentalists also sought to redress what they saw as a widespread corruption of morality among youth, particularly young women, fostered by such pastimes as theatre, dancing, cards, gambling, contemporary fiction, and motion pictures. Of particular concern to them was the improper dress some of these activities promoted in women, encouraging them to don men's clothes or else skimpy women's attire such as tight skirts. The paradigm of the New Woman and the primary target of the fundamentalist attack was the flapper of the 1920s, who was excoriated for her "immodest dress, improper dancing, frequenting immoral plays, and indulging in smoking, gambling, swearing, and joyriding," and was described as "a coarse, daring, vulgar young woman of questionable morals" who "cared nothing about modesty, or propriety, or virtue, or righteousness, or God" (DeBerg, 107).

5. *Reliance on pre-millennialism and biblical inerrancy.* The gender ideology of American fundamentalists was justified and sanctified theologically and biblically on the basis of two distinguishing tenets of the movement: (1) *dispensational pre-millennialism* or the belief that a millennium of peace and blessing will be established with the second coming of Christ, thereby doing away with the corruption and apostasy of the present age; and (2) *biblical inerrancy* or a belief in the divine origin and verbal accuracy of the Bible. The former provided the historical perspective for viewing the social changes in the late Victorian age as evidence of social decay and as a sign of the "end times" or "approaching apocalypse" (DeBerg, 123–24). The latter provided scriptural authority for the fundamentalist attempt to root its gender ideology in the created order and / or the Fall and in the eternal and unchanging social norms revealed in the Bible.[9]

[9] The Princeton biblical inerrancy movement, founded by Calvinist theologians, rooted the subordination of women in the created order as a result of Eve being formed from Adam's rib, while dispensational pre-millennialists traced it to the Fall as part of the curse placed upon Eve for original sin. See Bendroth, 34–36, 44–45.

II. Gender in Kierkegaard's Authorship

Coming into manhood at the beginning of the Victorian age, Kierkegaard shared the Victorian ideology of separate spheres for women and men. Nowhere is this more apparent in his authorship than in Part Two of *Upbuilding Discourses in Various Spirits*, where he distinguishes between "woman's work," which consists in staying at home, keeping house, and being chiefly occupied with self-adornment, and "man's work," which involves going out into the world and earning a living (UDVS, 163–64, 171, 197; FSE, 48). [10] But this division of labor, even though based on what were believed to be natural differences between the sexes,[11] does not appear to be rigid in his thought inasmuch as he recognized legitimate public professions for women, such as writing and acting (TA; C). Like American fundamentalists, however, Kierkegaard and his pseudonyms consistently opposed the emancipation of women, regarding it variously as a male plot to corrupt and exploit women (EO, 2: 22, 53, 311–12) and as "an invention of the devil" (JP, 4: 4992).[12] Although Kierkegaard just as consistently affirmed the spiritual equality of man and woman (EUD, 142–43; TDIO, 90; TA, 88–89; WL, 68, 138; CD, 51, 99–100; WA, 165–66), in his view that is not equivalent to social equality or equal rights, nor is the latter something Christianity has "required or desired" to establish in the temporal realm (WL, 136, 139). Rather, "[t]he man is to be the woman's master and she subservient to

[10] For a closer look at, and critique of, the gender associations in this text, see my essay, "If the Lily Could Speak" in the present collection.

[11] Women and the feminine are associated naturally with passivity, weakness, dependence, sympathy, self-giving, self-sacrifice, devotion, modesty, humility, submissiveness, coyness, cunning, imagination, and immediacy in Kierkegaard's writings, while men and the masculine are active, strong, self-assertive, competitive, independent, prideful, willful and reflective or intellectual in nature. But Kierkegaard does recognize that the social environment in which one lives plays an important role in the formation of character. On natural and environmental factors that contribute to shaping the life and destiny of women, see my essay, "Issues that Divide: Interpreting Kierkegaard on Woman and Gender" in the present collection.

[12] On Kierkegaard's views on the emancipation of woman, especially in his very first publication, a satirical newspaper article titled "Another Defense of Woman's Great Abilities," see also Watkin, "Serious Jest? Kierkegaard as Young Polemicist in 'Defense' of Women."

him" (WL, 138). Yet Kierkegaard suggests that true equality "can be victorious and be preserved in any externality whatever" in the individual who is willing to fight "the principalities and powers" of the world in order to "free himself for equality before God, whether this battle is more a war of aggression against the differences that want to encumber him with worldly favoritism or a defensive war against the differences that want to make him anxious in worldly perdition" (EUD, 143).[13] Moreover, the pseudonym Judge William, who like Kierkegaard is adamantly against female emancipation, views marriage oriented in the religious as emancipating both man and woman from a patriarchal mentality inasmuch as by referring marriage to God, man is freed from a false pride that leads him to try to conquer and assert superiority over woman, and woman is freed from a false humility that causes her to surrender and submit herself to him as if she were nothing (SLW, 124; cf. EO, 2: 57, 61). The judge also envisions a new prototype for marriage, imagining his wife as standing upright by her husband's side rather than kneeling before him in adoration and submission (SLW, 168). Yet Judge William continues to think that the wife will love her husband so much that she will always want him to be dominant (SLW, 144). In advocating the Christian command to love others as neighbors, however, Kierkegaard maintains in *Works of Love* that the husband is to love his wife (and vice versa) fundamentally as he loves others, that is, as a neighbor or human being like and equal to himself (WL, 141–42). Thus, while the status quo of patriarchy remains in place externally for Kierkegaard, the inward transformation of conscience brought about by Christianity has outward consequences in marital relations that should at least temper, if not outright negate, its expression in the external realm.[14]

Although Kierkegaard did not divinize the Christian home over the church as in American fundamentalism, he did think it was woman's "crucial quality" and universal responsibility to make a house a home and within the home to be "the image of the hearer and reader of the Word" by creating and indirectly teaching the silence that is needed "if God's

[13] On Kierkegaard's view of social and spiritual equality as these relate to women, see my essay, "When 'That Single Individual' Is a Woman" in the present collection.

[14] See, for example, my essay on "Desire and Love in Kierkegaard's *Either/Or*" in the present collection.

Word is to gain a little power over people" (FSE, 47–49). He also thought it "fitting" that women should be silent in the congregation as they were admonished to do in 1 Cor. 14: 34. Yet, in his view silence "does not consist simply in the absence of speaking" but rather is "the fundamental tone" that lies at the base of the eternal art of making a house into a home (FSE, 46, 49–50).[15] Thus it is incumbent upon woman to take time every day "to collect" herself "in the impression of the divine," especially since men are far too busy in the noisy world, with the consequence that holy silence will never enter the home if the woman does not see to it (FSE, 50).

This suggests that woman has an important role to play in Kierkegaard's understanding of religion, and indeed she does, but it is a rather ambiguous role, as Kierkegaard is not altogether consistent on this matter. In an upbuilding discourse of 1850 he presents "the woman who was a sinner" in Luke 7: 37 as a teacher and prototype of piety and even defines piety or godliness itself as being "fundamentally womanliness" (WA, 149).[16] While man is credited with having more earnestness in thought or reflection, woman possesses more earnestness with respect to "feeling, passion, decision" and is more able to concentrate on the one thing needful, namely proper sorrow over sin (WA, 150). This association of womanliness or femininity with godliness may also be seen in *The Sickness unto Death*, where in spite of the fact that Anti-Climacus, the

---

[15] See also WA where Kierkegaard says: "Even if 'the woman should keep silence in the congregation' and to that extent not teach—well, being silent before God does indeed belong essentially to true godliness and therefore you may be able to learn that from the woman" (149). For contrasting critical discussions of Kierkegaard's views on woman and silence, see Wanda Warren Berry, "The Silent Woman in Kierkegaard's Later Religious Writings," *Feminist Interpretations of Søren Kierkegaard*, 287–306; and Louise Carroll Keeley, "Silence, Domesticity, and Joy: The Spiritual Life of Women in Kierkegaard's *For Self-Examination* in *International Kierkegaard Commentary: 'For Self-Examination' and 'Judge For Yourself!,'* Vol. 21, ed. Robert L. Perkins (Macon: Mercer University Press, 2002), 223–57.

[16] On the female sinner in Kierkegaard's authorship, see Mark Lloyd Taylor, "Practice in Authority: The Apostolic Women in Søren Kierkegaard's Writings," in *Anthropology and Authority: Essays on Søren Kierkegaard*, ed. Paul Houe, Gordon D. Marino, and Sven Hakon Rossel (Amsterdam: Rodopi, 2000), 85–98. See also my essay on the woman who was a sinner in the present collection.

Christian pseudonymous author of this text, regards femininity or devotedness as constituting a "lower synthesis" than does masculinity, which alone falls within the qualification of spirit inasmuch as it possesses more consciousness of self and despair (SUD, 67), the self is defined in a feminine manner as devotion to God, which holds true equally for man and woman, although Anti-Climacus points out that "it is probably true that in most cases the woman actually relates to God only through the man" (SUD, 50n).[17] In a journal entry of 1854, however, Kierkegaard suggests that the truly religious consists in "an eminently masculine intellectuality joined to a feminine submissiveness," thus incorporating both the masculine and the feminine in his understanding of the religious (JP, 4: 5006). Yet in another entry from that same year he concludes that New Testament Christianity "has such prodigious aims that, strictly speaking, it cannot be a religion for women, at most secondhand" (JP, 4: 5007).

Perhaps the rationale for this shift or ambivalence in his viewpoint can be found in *Practice in Christianity*, where Kierkegaard in the voice of Anti-Climacus associates the natural person and woman with "all the weaker, softer elements in a person" that make them want to coddle themselves, lead an easy life, and enjoy it in coziness and comfort (PC, 117). Indeed, in his later religious writings and journals Christendom itself is seen as having so compromised the sublimity of Christianity that it had become a religion for women and children:

> What has really happened in Christianity, then, is that this sublimity, which is the essentially Christian position, this sublimity which no man has reached…this sublimity Christendom has so flatly and heartily jabbered down into the vulgar gossip which is characteristic of the ordinary human mentality, that this sublimity has even become too light and easy for the kind of creatures dressed up to look like and whom we nowadays call men, and it is turned over to women and children, for whom religion really is intended, after all (JP, 4: 5007).

Like the early fundamentalists, then, Kierkegaard objected to the "feminization of religion," or more specifically Christianity, that had taken place in his time, but for a somewhat different reason, inasmuch as for

[17] For a more extensive discussion of gender categories and issues in SUD, see my essay, "On 'Feminine' and 'Masculine' Despair" in the present collection.

him it was because Christendom had replaced the essential rigor of Christianity with an effeminate leniency that required no effort or striving (PC, 227). Yet he still maintained that ultimately Christianity and Christ are "love and leniency itself," thus essentially feminine in character (PC, 196).

As Kierkegaard began to focus more specifically on Christianity in his later religious writings, he issued a small esthetic work, *The Crisis and a Crisis in the Life of an Actress* (written in 1847) as evidence that he was not an esthetic author who had morphed into a religious author but was from the beginning a religious author who remained "esthetically productive" at the end (PV, 31). Expressing appreciation of two prominent actresses of the time, this little esthetic work also shows that he did not share the anti-amusement mentality of fundamentalism. An earlier, highly complimentary literary review of a novella by a prominent female writer of the time testifies to the same with regard to contemporary fiction (TA). Kierkegaard frequented the theatre, especially in his youth, and more than once used the metaphor of dancing to characterize the religious in his writings.[18] Thus he was not opposed to esthetic entertainment and enjoyment *per se*. But he was highly critical of the esthetic as a way of life, inasmuch as it was egoistic, hedonistic, amoral, ironic, deceptive, and manipulative, among other qualities antithetical to an ethical and religious orientation toward existence. The paradigm of the esthetic for him, however, was not the emancipated woman, even though he was opposed to her, but rather the reflective male seducer who preys on women and makes an art out of it.[19]

---

[18] See Chapter 5, "Dancing Lightly in the Sphere of the Religious," in my book, *Living Poetically: Kierkegaard's Existential Aesthetics* (University Park, PA: The Pennsylvania State University Press, 1994), 127–65, for a discussion of the metaphor of dancing in Kierkegaard's early authorship.

[19] Julia Watkin points out in "Serious Jest? Kierkegaard as Young Polemicist in 'Defense' of Women" that in the newspaper article by a fellow theology student, Peter Engel Lind, which provoked Kierkegaard's own journalistic debut in a satirical-ironic piece on women's emancipation, Lind makes an allusion to the trousers worn by the French writer Baronne Dudevant (1804–76), better known under her pseudonym as George Sand, who was a forerunner of women's liberation (and the American flapper) inasmuch as she wore men's dress, assumed their lifestyle, and advocated as well as practiced free love (11–12). Kierkegaard does not comment on Sand's trousers in his article, but he does poke

Although Kierkegaard was highly critical of the present age for its estheticism, lack of passion, social leveling, envy, chatter, superficiality, abstraction, anonymity and other characteristics which indicated to him that it was in a state of decline and degeneracy, he did not adopt a theory of pre-millennialism to explain or rectify the situation (TA, 94). Rather, in his view, the age will be saved by a reaffirmation of the principle of individuality, which will happen only by single individuals making "the inspired leap of religiousness" by themselves—even women, with the result that "God's infinite love will not become a second-hand relationship for them" (TA, 87–89, 92, 106, 108–109).[20]

While Kierkegaard believed in the authority of the Bible and found sanction for much of his own gender ideology in it, just as American fundamentalists did, he did not adopt a position of biblical inerrancy to substantiate that authority. Rather, for him "[a]ll human speech, even the divine speech of Holy Scripture, about the spiritual is essentially metaphorical...speech" (WL, 209). Thus, as he sees it, God's Word is a mirror in which one is to observe oneself, not the mirror, and which, like a love letter from one's beloved, does not require a translator or higher criticism in order to be read and understood (FSE, 25–51).[21] Knowing how to distinguish between a scholarly or objective way of reading the Bible and the personal, intimate way in which it is meant to be read, the earnest reader understands that it is *to* and *about* oneself that the Word is addressed and that, like any wish expressed by the beloved in a love let-

---

fun at the Saint-Simonist movement, which promoted social equality for both sexes.

[20] For an insightful interpretation of the "prophetic-apocalyptic" vision and its social implications in the closing pages of *Two Ages*, see Michael Plekon, "Towards Apocalypse: Kierkegaard's *Two Ages* in Golden Age Denmark," in *International Kierkegaard Commentary: Two Ages: The Present Age and the Age of Revolution, A Literary Review*, Vol. 14, ed. Robert L. Perkins (Macon: Mercer University Press, 1984), 19–52.

[21] On the nature and authority of the Bible in Kierkegaard's authorship, especially the metaphor of the mirror and the analogy of the love letter in *For Self-Examination*, see John H. Whitaker, "Whence the Authority of God's Word?" 259–85; Julia Watkin, "The Letter from the Lover: Kierkegaard on the Bible and Belief," 287–313; and Martin Andic, "The Mirror," 335–62 in *International Kierkegaard Commentary: For Self-Examination' and Judge for Yourself!*, Vol. 21, ed. Robert L. Perkins (Macon: Mercer University Press, 2002).

ter, one is to comply at once with the wishes or commands expressed in this divine love letter. Like the fundamentalist tenet of biblical inerrancy, however, such a biblical hermeneutic presents problems for female readers of the Word, as it naively serves to legitimate and perpetuate a gender ideology that is oppressive rather than liberating for women, even if, as in the case of Kierkegaard at least, deeper religious meaning may be found in the silence and domesticity seemingly commanded for them by the biblical text.[22]

III. Conclusions

The foregoing comparison and contrast of the gender ideologies of Kierkegaard and American fundamentalism has revealed some significant differences between them, suggesting that Kierkegaard's perspective is not fundamentally congenial with that of American fundamentalists even though they share the same (Victorian) gender ideology in certain respects. Moreover, inasmuch as the gender ideology defended by American fundamentalism is not unique to that movement but is one that is shared, at least in part, not only by Kierkegaard but by other religious traditions and cultures as well, even the points of agreement that have been noted between them do not necessarily make him a fundamentalist. On the contrary, while Kierkegaard was definitely a man of his time with regard to his views on women and gender, often manifesting great am-

[22] For a critique of Kierkegaard's biblical hermeneutic from a feminist perspective, see Berry, "The Silent Woman in Kierkegaard's Later Religious Writings," 295–97, in *Feminist Interpretations of Søren Kierkegaard*. See also Timothy Houston Polk, *The Biblical Kierkegaard: Reading by the Rule of Faith* (Macon: Mercer University Press, 1997), who rejects identification of Kierkegaard's biblical hermeneutic with a "hermeneutics of either suspicion or naïveté," seeing it instead as being rooted in the ancient church's rule of faith, in which Christian love is the governing principle of interpretation of scripture (1–2). However, while recognizing patriarchal conditioning and shortcomings in the Bible and being sensitive to the problem of oppression, Polk does not show how this principle negates or relativizes many of the problematic passages in the biblical text relating to women which Kierkegaard seemingly takes and affirms at face value. For an appreciation of the deeper religious significance and liberatory effects of silence and domesticity, see Berry, 297, 299–305, and Keeley, "Silence, Domesticity, and Joy: The Spiritual Life of Women in Kierkegaard's *For Self-Examination*," 223–57.

bivalence and contradictory stances on the subject quite apart from those of his pseudonyms, we have seen that the thrust of Kierkegaard's authorship is toward a rejection of the kind of patriarchal domination and religious exclusion of women embraced by the American fundamentalist movement. Moreover, although American fundamentalism has been thought by some scholars to be nonpolitical or concerned only with personal ethics, examination of its gender ideology of separate spheres and female subordination reveals that it is "thoroughly political," constituting a "political agenda with far-reaching consequences for the distribution of wealth, electoral politics, social policy, the labor movement, health care delivery, public education, and economic growth" (Brasher, 149). In like manner, it is evident that there is a sexual politics in Kierkegaard's authorship as well, inasmuch as his views on women and gender have concrete social, political, and economic implications for the lives of both women and men and for the possibility of mutually upbuilding relationships between them. Kierkegaard envisioned the religious as a cure for social ills but perhaps unwittingly contributed to the perpetuation of some of those ailments by failing to subject his own cultural upbringing and prejudices concerning gender to the same radical critique and polemic as were brought against estheticism and Christendom in his writings. From a feminist standpoint, that is probably the single most regrettable shortcoming of his authorship, which otherwise has much to teach us about what it means to be godly women (and men) in an ungodly and unloving world.

15

KIERKEGAARD'S EROTIC HERMENEUTICS AS A PROTO-FEMINIST ALTERNATIVE TO HEGELIAN, NIETZSCHEAN, AND DERRIDEAN-DECONSTRUCTIVE HERMENEUTICS*

If one wishes to examine Kierkegaard's hermeneutics, the best place to begin is with *The Concept of Irony*, where Kierkegaard sets forth what I have described elsewhere as an "erotic hermeneutics."[1] It is my thesis that this method of interpretation, while not fully qualifying as a non-patriarchal hermeneutics that would satisfy a feminist mentality, nevertheless is preferable to a Derridean deconstructionist hermeneutics of suspicion, which has its basis in a Nietzschean will to power that is every bit as violent and imperialistic, if not more so, than the Hegelian hermeneutics countered by Kierkegaard in *The Concept of Irony* and elsewhere.[2] Thus, if we wish to do justice to Kierkegaard as an interpreter and writer, we would do well to examine the hermeneutics sketched and employed in this early work.

Kierkegaard immediately signals his opposition to Hegelian hermeneutics in the opening paragraph of *The Concept of Irony*:

> If there is anything that must be praised in modern philosophical endeavor in its magnificent manifestation, it is certainly in the power of genius with which it seizes and holds on to the

---

* Reprinted by permission from *Søren Kierkegaard and the Word(s): Essays on Hermeneutics and Communication,* ed. Poul Houe and Gordon H. Marino (Copenhagen: C. A. Reitzel, 2003), 71–80.

[1] See my essay, "Ironic Love: An Amorist Interpretation of Socratic Eros" in the present collection.

[2] On the intimate relation between Nietzsche and the French postmodernists, especially Derrida, see Alan D. Schrift, *Nietzsche and the Question of Interpretation: Between Hermeneutics and Deconstruction* (New York: Routledge, 1990), 77–119.

> phenomenon. Now if it is fitting for the phenomenon, which as such is always *foeminini generis* [of the feminine gender], to surrender to the stronger on account of its feminine nature, then in all fairness one can also demand of the philosophical knight a deferential propriety and a profound enthusiasm, in place of which one sometimes hears too much the jingling of spurs and the voice of the master. The observer ought to be an amorist; he must not be indifferent to any feature, any factor. But on the other hand he ought to have a sense of his own predominance—but should use it only to help the phenomenon obtain its full disclosure. Therefore, even if the observer does bring the concept along with him, it is still of great importance that the phenomenon remain inviolate and that the concept be seen as coming into existence [*tilblivende*] through the phenomenon. (CI, 9)

This passage captures in a nutshell both Kierkegaard's critique of Hegelian hermeneutics, which is the "modern philosophical endeavor" alluded to in the passage, and the essence of Kierkegaard's own erotic hermeneutics being proposed there as an alternative to it. Hypothetically identifying the "phenomenon" or historical subject of interpretation as being feminine in gender and the corresponding interpreter or "observer" as a masculine "philosophical knight," Kierkegaard suggests that the interpreter ought to be an "amorist" (*Erotiker*) or passionate lover who is deferential toward and attentive to every feature of the phenomenon. This "proper" erotic relation between the interpreter and phenomenon is contrasted to the domineering relation that obtains between them in modern philosophy, where one hears too much of "the jingling of spurs" and "the voice of the master" on the part of the interpreter (CI, 9). In other words, Kierkegaard objects to the patriarchal character of Hegelian hermeneutics, which in his view violates the phenomenon by imperialistically imposing its interpretation on the phenomenon rather than lovingly assisting it to emerge from the phenomenon.

Construing the interpreter, the phenomenon, and the relation between them in terms of gender categories and heterosexual relations clearly enables Kierkegaard to differentiate his conception of hermeneutics from that of Hegel. From a feminist standpoint, however, it does not go far enough in repudiating patriarchal hermeneutics inasmuch as the masculine interpreter is still recognized as being "superior" to the feminine phenomenon even if he does not lord it over her in a domineering fashion. Admittedly, Kierkegaard maintains that the interpreter should use his "predominance" over the phenomenon "only to help the phenomenon obtain its full disclosure," and the phenomenon is recognized as having "rights" that keep it from being "intimidated" by the superiority of philosophy (CI, 9). Moreover, later in the text Kierkegaard describes the relation between the phenomenon and the concept or explanation of it arrived at by the interpreter as being reciprocal in character: "it [every conclusion] has felt itself drawn to what it was supposed to explain and what it is supposed to explain is drawn to it" (CI, 155). Thus, while Kierkegaard does not fully transcend a patriarchal understanding of the relation of the interpreter to the phenomenon, he does considerably temper it in the direction of a reciprocity that recognizes the independence, rights, and self-disclosure of the phenomenon vis-à-vis the interpreter. Moreover, insofar as the amorist interpreter can be said to embrace the role of the feminine in his concern to function as a Socratic midwife who assists in the self-disclosure of the phenomenon, Kierkegaard's erotic hermeneutics can be seen as offering not merely a modification of patriarchal hermeneutics but a radical re-visioning of hermeneutics in its conception of the erotic and the feminine as constituting the very essence of interpretation.[3]

My concern here, however, is not to debate this issue but rather to show how Kierkegaard's erotic hermeneutics, flawed though it may be, constitutes an advance not only over the imperialistic, patriarchal hermeneutics of Hegel but also—indeed, even more so—over that of Nietzsche and the Derridean deconstructive hermeneutics of suspicion spawned by him. We have already seen that, at the very outset of *The Concept of Irony,*

---

[3] See Walsh, "Ironic Love," in the present collection. Whether this radical re-visioning would qualify as a feminist hermeneutics remains controversial and ambiguous, since many feminists regard the traditional concept of the feminine as a patriarchal construct that needs to be rejected and /or reconceived, while others object to Socratic midwifery as another instance of male appropriation of the feminine for purposes of gaining or retaining power over women. See, for example, Simone de Beauvoir, *The Second Sex,* tr, H. M. Parshley (New York: Vintage Books, 1989), and the essays by Page deBois, Nancy Tuana, and William Cowling in *Feminist Interpretations of Plato*, ed. Nancy Tuana (University Park: The Pennsylvania State University Press, 1994).

Kierkegaard proposes a method or way of getting beyond an imperialistic, patriarchal hermeneutic of oppression and violence toward the phenomenon. He then proceeds to spell out and employ this method in interpreting the historical sources on the phenomenological existence of Socrates, of whom he seeks to formulate a "reliable and authentic view" on the basis of a determination of the possibility, actuality, and necessity of obtaining such a view (CI, 9). Briefly stated, his procedure is to establish first of all the *possibility* of an authentic view of Socrates through an examination of the accounts of Xenophon, Plato, and Aristophanes in a manner that accentuates and explains the discrepancies between them.[4] As an amorist interpreter himself, Kierkegaard attempts to mediate between these conflicting accounts by projecting the possibility of arriving at a "final view" of Socrates that is not merely an *interpretation*, or a view "in the ordinary sense" such as the classical accounts, but a *reproduction* or *reconstruction* of the phenomenon by means of "a view in the stricter sense of the word" (CI, 155). This latter sort of view involves the double or reciprocal task of explaining the misunderstandings of the phenomenon through an explanation of the phenomenon and, vice versa, explaining the phenomenon through an explanation of the misunderstandings (CI, 155n). As Kierkegaard sees it, the "unknown quantity" that explains the historical phenomenon Socrates and the classical misinterpretations of him is *irony,* understood not merely as a rhetorical device but as an existential standpoint characterized by absolute infinite negativity (CI, 154).

It is important to note that, for Kierkegaard, a final view is something that comes into existence or emerges *from* the phenomenon rather than precedes it as in "the now widespread and in so many ways meritorious scholarly method" (of Hegel) (CI, 156). Thus, with respect to a final view of Socrates, he says: "If I had posed the final view first of all and in each particular portion had assigned each of these three considerations its place, then I would easily have lost the element of contemplation, which is always important but here doubly so, because by no other way, not by immediate observation, can I gain the phenomenon" (CI,

[4]Briefly, Kierkegaard determines that Xenophon interprets Socrates purely historically as an "apostle of finitude;" Plato idealizes him as a tragic figure striving for an ideal infinity; and Aristophanes provides a corrective or counterpoint to Plato by viewing Socrates ideally as a comic figure (CI, 126–28, 154, 155n).

156). Insofar as the interpreter has a final view in mind from the beginning, it is present and hovers over the exploration only as a *possibility* that must be established by the historical data it is supposed to explain. Consequently, the second step in Kierkegaard's procedure is to attain the *actualization* of this final view or explanation of Socrates through an examination of some historical facts that reveal "the actual, not the apparent, pinnacle of irony" in him (CI, 197).[5] Kierkegaard completes his formulation of a final view of Socrates as an ironist by demonstrating the *necessity* of this view for discerning Socrates' significance in the development of world history or world spirit. In Kierkegaard's view, Socrates acquired world-historical significance and validity as a turning point in world history by destroying classicism with his irony, thereby opening up the possibility for new developments of the world spirit to appear, e.g. the principle of subjectivity (CI, 198, 211–12). While the destruction of classicism reveals the "violent" character of Socratic irony, it is important to note that for Kierkegaard irony in both its Socratic and Romantic forms needs to be "mastered" or curtailed in such a way as to limit, finitize, and circumscribe the personal life (CI, 326). The destructive possibility of irony is thereby tempered and it comes to acquire its "true validity" and "proper meaning" as a "serving spirit" in the life of the individual (CI, 325–26).[6]

From this brief overview of Kierkegaard's erotic hermeneutics, let us now turn to the perspectival hermeneutics of Nietzsche, which receives perhaps its clearest expression in *On the Genealogy of Morals*, where he says: "There is *only* a perspective seeing, *only* a perspective 'knowing,' and the *more* affects we allow to speak about one thing, the *more* eyes, different eyes, we can use to observe one thing, the more complete will our

[5] These consist of two (presumably) uncontested facts: 1) that Socrates possessed a daimon which made him stand in a negative relation to the state, and 2) that he was accused and condemned to die for not accepting the gods of the state and for seducing the youths, thereby undermining the religious as well as familial establishments of the Athenian state (CI, 160, 168, 185).

[6] On the indirectly positive role of mastered or controlled irony as a "serving spirit" in the life of the individual, see my article "Ironic Love" in this collection and my book, *Living Poetically: Kierkegaard's Existential Aesthetics* (University Park: The Pennsylvania State University Press, 1994), 60–61.

'concept' of this thing, our 'objectivity,' be."[7] Lest one should think that this objectivity is disinterested or that it will lead to some final view such as Kierkegaard has in mind, Nietzsche makes it clear that:

> whatever exists, having somehow come into being, is again and again reinterpreted to new ends, taken over, transformed, and redirected by some power superior to it; all events in the organic world are a subduing, a *becoming master*, and all subduing and becoming master involves a fresh interpretation, an adaptation through which any previous 'meaning' and 'purpose' are necessarily obscured or even obliterated (GM, 77).

This passage expresses in a nutshell what Nietzsche means by "the will to power," the central concept of his philosophy, as it pertains to hermeneutics.[8] According to Alexander Nehamas, for Nietzsche "the will to power is manifested in the ability to make one's own view of the world and one's own values the very world and values in which and by which others live."[9] Thus Nietzsche's writings constitute an attempt to exert his will to power to shape and establish his own perspective or subjective interpretation of the world, just as Socrates and Plato, in Nietzsche's opinion, sought to project and impose their wills to power on others through their teaching and writing. However, as Nehamas points out, Nietzsche differentiates himself from Socrates and Plato in that he recognizes that his view is simply *a* view, not an "accurate description of the real world which forces its own acceptance and makes an unconditional claim on everyone's assent" such as Socrates and Plato dogmatically and self-deceptively proclaim of their views.[10] In Nietzsche's opinion, Nehamas claims, they lack "the courage of the conscience that...admits that the view being projected is nothing more than a reading onto the world

[7]Friedrich Nietzsche, *On the Genealogy of Morals and Ecco Homo*, tr. Walter Kaufman and R. J. Hollingsdale (New York: Random House Vintage Books, 1969), 119, hereafter referred to in parentheses in the text with the siglum GM followed by page number.

[8] See also *The Will to Power*, tr. Walter Kaufmann and R. J. Hollingsdale and ed. Walter Kaufman (New York: Random House, 1967), entry nos. 616, 720, 954, 957, 958, 962.

[9] Alexander Nehamas, *Nietzsche: Life as Literature* (Cambridge and London: Harvard University Press, 1985), 32.

[10] Ibid.

of the conditions under which its own author can thrive, and which need not be the right condition for anyone else."[11]

In response to Nietzsche and Nehamas, it could be argued that Nietzsche is equally dogmatic, self-deceived, and universalist in his claim that life and interpretation are nothing but the will to power (cf. GM, 79). More importantly for our purposes, however, it should be noted that these subjective musings of Nietzsche involve potentially violent consequences not only for the interpretation of a phenomenon or text but also for the lives of others, upon whom the author's conditions are to be imposed for the sake of his—but not necessarily their—personal thriving. In nostalgically advocating an overturn of the slave morality of the masses and the reinstitution of the values of the aristocracy or conqueror races, Nietzsche does not hesitate to characterize the latter as "beasts of prey" who engage in sporadic acts of violence to exert their power and strength over others (GM, 40–41). "To demand of strength that it should *not* express itself as strength, that it should *not* be a desire to overcome, a desire to throw down, a desire to become master, a thirst for enemies and resistances and triumphs, is just as absurd as to demand of weakness that it should express itself as strength," he says (GM, 45). Consequently, the sovereign individual who is able to liberate himself from the morality of custom and become his own master is aware that "this mastery over himself also gives him mastery over circumstances, over nature, and overall more short-willed and unreliable creatures" (GM, 59–60).

As these passages clearly demonstrate, Nietzsche's hermeneutics, based on the will to power, is imperialistic and violent to the core, both in terms of its reinterpretation of phenomena and texts and in terms of the social implications of that reinterpretation. But may we say the same of its twentieth-century progeny, deconstructive hermeneutics? At first blush it might seem not, for according to the strategy of "double reading" advocated by the master of deconstruction, Jacques Derrida, the interpreter, like Kierkegaard's amorist interpreter, begins with an engagement with the text and pays close attention to it.[12] But unlike the amorist in-

---

[11] Ibid., 34.

[12] Indeed, Derrida likens his own approach to that of Kierkegaard, citing him as "a great example of some paradoxical way of contesting religious discourse in the name of a faith that cannot be simply mastered or domesticated or

terpreter, whose stance toward the phenomenon or text is one of deference, the close examination of the text by the deconstructionist critic is carried out with a suspicious eye for the purpose of spotting and disclosing a rupture, gap, crack, or blind spot in the text that destabilizes its accepted meaning, opening up the possibility of an alternative interpretation that subverts and displaces the dominant, traditional, or authoritative one from within by means of a double gesture, double science, or double writing. This double reading takes the form of a *supplément*, which both adds to previous interpretations and substitutes itself for them.[13] Like Nietzsche's violent hermeneutics, therefore, deconstruction seeks to displace and replace other interpretations with its own, not simply offer it as one among many, equally possible or valid accounts. It searches for an ambiguous place (*Khôra*) in the text and arbitrarily makes that the decisive basis for an alternative "transgressive" interpretation that contradicts or goes against what the text or author wants to say and mean, emphasizing instead those elements that are omitted, excluded, forgotten, marginalized, dismissed, scorned, slighted, taken lightly, or waved off by the text and / or traditional interpretations of it.[14] Thus deconstruction does not allow the text to reveal itself, as in Kierkegaard's erotic hermeneutics, but seeks to impose a different meaning upon the text on the basis of a subversive reading that brings an opposing interpretation to the fore and elevates it to a position of privilege. Moreover, this interpretation is motivated by an overarching desire to displace logocentrism, which in the deconstructive critic's opinion has dominated hermeneutics ever since Plato. [15] Consequently, deconstruction is not grounded in the text itself but in a preconceived agenda that governs the interpretation of every text.

---

taught or logically understood, a faith that is paradoxical," and refers to Kierkegaard frequently in his roundtable conversation at Villanova University (*Deconstruction in a Nutshell: A Conversation with Jacques Derrida*, ed. John D. Caputo (New York: Fordham University Press, 1997) 21–22.

[13] On the concept of supplement see Jacques Derrida, *Of Grammatology*, tr. Gayatri Chakravorty Spivak (Baltimore and London: The Johns Hopkins University Press, 1997), 141–64.

[14] *Deconstruction in a Nutshell*, 79.

[15] See, for example, *Of Grammatology*, where Derrida admits that his intention in the interpretation of Rousseau is "to identify a decisive articulation of the logocentric epoch" (162).

Derrida and his hermeneutical disciples, e.g. John Caputo, insist that deconstruction is not negative but affirmative, that it is not out to destroy texts but only to loosen them up and make them "flexible, internally amenable, and revisable" so as to improve upon them by developing possibilities that are potentially inscribed in them, and that this revisionary process is undertaken and carried out in the name of that which is indeconstructible, namely justice.[16] Certainly there is an affirmative aspect in deconstruction, although by its own principles anything that is affirmed ultimately cannot stand since it always falls short of justice, which never is. Whatever is affirmed in deconstruction consequently stands on shaky ground, without any firm or stable foundation, and is no more adequate to the text or phenomenon than the one(s) it seeks to overturn and replace. In fact, it may be deemed to be less adequate, since an interpretation based on what a text explicitly or implicitly excludes or denies by definition cannot be regarded as an adequate statement of what that text affirms and thus cannot constitute the meaning of the text, although it may very well be justified as a critique of the text and its meaning. In that event, what is called for is the writing of a new text that sees things differently or otherwise, not a revisionary interpretation of an old one to make it say something it (or the author) does not say or mean to affirm. Unlike Kierkegaard's erotic hermeneutics, deconstructive interpretation intends to be productive, not merely reproductive, of the text's meaning, but in its overweening desire to affirm new possibilities in and through interpretation, this productive impulse in deconstruction is not only misplaced but does violence to the text in question.[17]

This is particularly true with respect to the practice of deconstruction by some feminists, who have been attracted to Derridean deconstructive hermeneutics because it seems to offer a method by which they

---

[16] *Deconstruction in a Nutshell*, 5, 9–10, 16, 53, 79, 128–29, 130–32.

[17] On the productive, as opposed to reproductive, nature of deconstructive hermeneutics, see *Of Grammatology*, 158 and *Deconstruction in a Nutshell*, 82. On the violence implicit in deconstruction see the essay on "Violence and Metaphysics" in Jacques Derrida, *Writing and Difference*, tr. Alan Bass (Chicago: University of Chicago Press, 1978), where Derrida accuses logocentrism of violence against the other yet apparently condones the parricide of Parmenides and Plato by Levinas in his break with tradition in the affirmation of pluralism and the solitude of the other over against unity and attempts to encompass the other through concepts (89, 95,104, 107).

can open up the traditional philosophical, theological, and biblical canons to the inclusion of women's thought, concerns, and values.[18] Situated on the margins of the dominant, patriarchal symbolic order, in which they have been excluded from positions of power and authority, they are sensitive to Levinas' claim that history is "always the history of the victors, never the victims," and that deconstructive hermeneutics is "history read from the standpoint of the victims of that history."[19] But they would do well to consider the words of Audre Lorde, who reminds us that "the master's tools will never dismantle the master's house."[20] If we truly want to move beyond a patriarchal, imperialistic symbolic order and mode of interpretation, the way to do so, I would suggest, is not by adopting an equally imperialistic methodology, whether it be Hegelian, Nietzschean, or Derridean in design. Rather, if truth is a woman, as Nietzsche suggests, then she must be allowed to disclose herself in the text to the interpreter who, like Kierkegaard's attentive philosophic knight, is an amorist, not an intellectual rapist, nor a beast of prey, nor a subversive revolutionary at heart.

---

[18] For a collection of feminist essays that largely endorse Derridean deconstruction and seek to construe feminist deconstruction on the basis of it, see *Feminist Interpretations of Jacques Derrida*, ed. Nancy J. Holland (University Park: The Pennsylvania State University Press, 1997).

[19] Quoted in Simon Critchley, *The Ethics of Deconstruction: Derrida and Levinas* (Edinburgh: Edinburgh University Press, 1992), 30.

[20] Audre Lorde, "The Master's Tools will never Dismantle the Master's House," in *This Bridge Called My Back: Writings by Radical Women of Color*, ed. Cherrîe Moraga and Gloria Anzaldúa (New York: Kitchen Table Press, 1981), 98. For a critique of both Nietzsche and Derrida from a feminist perspective, see Kelly Oliver, *Womanizing Nietzsche: Philosophy's Relation to the 'Feminine'* (New York: Routledge, 1995).